BOLINGBROKE
AND HARLEY

BOLINGBROKE and HARLEY

BY

Sheila Biddle

LONDON   GEORGE ALLEN & UNWIN LTD
Ruskin House   Museum Street

CONTENTS

Acknowledgments

A GREAT MANY INDIVIDUALS and institutions have contributed in one way or another to the writing of this book. For permission to make use of manuscripts in their possession, I should like to thank the Marquess of Bath, the Earl of Dartmouth, the Marquess of Downshire, Mr. Christopher Harley, the Duke of Marlborough, and the Duke of Portland. To Miss A. Green, the Berkshire County Archivist, and to the staffs of the Bodleian Library, the British Museum, the Cambridge University Library, the Herefordshire and Hertfordshire Record Offices, the Nottingham University Library, and the Staffordshire Record Office further thanks are due for help provided along the way.

From the beginning of this undertaking Peter Gay and Robert K. Webb were the wisest of mentors and the most helpful of critics: my debt to them is difficult to convey. James L. Clifford's comments and suggestions were invaluable, his encouragement still more so. Shirley Lerman prepared the manuscript with care and skill and extraordinary patience. Finally, a Chamberlain fellowship from Columbia University enabled me to finish the research for the book and revise the manuscript for publication. While the book has benefited from all these varied forms of assistance, responsibility for it as it now stands rests, of course, entirely with me.

BOLINGBROKE
AND HARLEY

Abbreviations Used in the Footnotes

Add. MSS	Additional Manuscripts
BM	British Museum
HMC	Historical Manuscripts Commission
R.O.	Record Office

A Note on Dates

Until the middle of the eighteenth century, England continued to use the Julian Calendar, which was, by the beginning of the century, eleven days behind the Gregorian Calendar in general use on the Continent. In addition, under the Julian Calendar the new year began on 25 March rather than 1 January. All dates given here are Old Style unless indicated N.S., New Style, though in references where both dates are given in the original (e.g., 12/23 September 1710) I have retained the writer's usage. However, in every case I have corrected the year to begin 1 January.

Prologue

ON the last day of May 1714 Jonathan Swift left London for the country, "upon finding it impossible after two years endeavor to reconcile My Lord Treasurer [Robert Harley, Earl of Oxford], and My Lord Bolingbroke: from the quarrel between which two great men all our misfortunes proceeded."[1] Removed from the contentious scenes of recent months, he pondered the circumstances that had led to his retirement: how it was that two men of birth and talent, "who . . . had long lived under the strictest Bonds of Friendship," and who were in addition "supported by a vast Majority of the landed Interest, and the Inferiour Clergy almost to a Man," had brought the present administration "very near the Brink of Ruin, together with the Cause of the Church and Monarchy committed to their Charge."[2] Later he wrote that when he first knew the ministers, "in the Infancy of their Power," he "could not forbear taking notice of the great Affection they bore to each other . . . so that notwithstanding the old Maxim which pronounceth Court Friendships to be of no long Duration, I was confident their's would last as long as their Lives. But it seems, the Inventor of that Maxim happened to be a little wiser than I, who lived to see this Friendship first

1 Jonathan Swift, "Some free Thoughts upon the present State of Affairs," *Political Tracts, 1713–1719*, ed. by Herbert Davis and Irvin Ehrenpreis (Oxford: Basil Blackwell, 1964), p. 76. Hereafter cited as Swift, "Some free Thoughts."
2 *Ibid.*, p. 82.

degenerate into Indifferency and Suspicion, and thence corrupt into the greatest Animosity and Hatred, contrary to all Appearances, and much to the Discredit of me and my Sagacity."[3] Swift wished to inquire "by what Degrees, and from what Causes those Dissentions grew":[4] this is also the purpose of the present essay.

Swift's name figures largely in this account as observer and commentator, historian and pamphleteer. A word to explain his ubiquitous presence would seem to be in order. Swift arrived in England at the beginning of September 1710 on business for the Church of Ireland, just after the change of ministers that brought Harley to power. He met both Harley and Henry St. John, later Viscount Bolingbroke, shortly thereafter and was immediately set to work writing for the government.[5] He was employed by the ministers over the next three and a half years as apologist and propagandist for government policy. And while they benefited from the services of his acrid pen, they enjoyed the pleasures of his society as well. Swift dined frequently, at times daily, with Harley and St. John; from February 1711 he was one of the select group—"lord keeper [Harcourt], secretary St. John, . . . and sometimes lord Rivers"[6]—who dined with Harley every Saturday. He saw them constantly on business matters; he traveled back and forth with them to Windsor. He listened and observed. And he recorded—in his letters, particularly those that compose the *Journal to Stella*, and in a number of political tracts recounting the events of Harley's ministry.

Swift wrote in the Preface to *The History of the Four Last*

---

[3] Jonathan Swift, "An Enquiry into the Behaviour of the Queen's Last Ministry," *Political Tracts, 1713–1719*, ed. by Herbert Davis and Irvin Ehrenpreis (Oxford: Basil Blackwell, 1964), p. 144. Hereafter cited as Swift, "An Enquiry."

[4] *Ibid.*, pp. 144–5.

[5] He took over the weekly *Examiner*, which he continued to write until June 1711. See Herbert Davis's introduction to Jonathan Swift, *The EXAMINER and Other Pieces Written in 1710–11*, ed. by Herbert Davis (Oxford: Basil Blackwell, 1957).

[6] Jonathan Swift, *Journal to Stella*, ed. by Harold Williams (Oxford: The Clarendon Press, 1963), I, 205.

Years of the Queen that he had been "daily conversant with the persons then in power; never absent in times of business or conversation, until a few weeks before her Majesty's death; and a witness of almost every step they made in the course of their administration."[7] But while Swift was in daily converse with the ministers, he was never fully in their confidence, and certainly not to the extent that he supposed. He was indeed a witness to events, but more often than he knew he was ignorant of the motives and policies that lay behind them. So that Swift's account is frequently inaccurate and, of necessity, incomplete. But in his role as witness he is invaluable. He reported the truth as he saw it, and generally in some detail. He was an astute judge of character, remarkable both for his honesty and his insight. And however much he was or was not privy to the secret springs of policy, much of the time he was, quite simply, there.

Robert Harley was born in 1661 and first entered Parliament under Whig auspices in 1689. His political talents were soon recognized. In 1701 he was chosen Speaker of the House of Commons and he served Queen Anne as Secretary of State from 1704 to 1708, when he was dismissed. Returning to office as Chancellor of the Exchequer in 1710, and aligned now with the moderate Tories, he was raised to the peerage in May 1711 and at the same time promoted Lord Treasurer. He remained in this post until his dismissal in July 1714, shortly before the Queen's death. During these four years he headed the ministry; they were also the years of his increasingly bitter rivalry with Bolingbroke. Impeached in 1715 by the Whiggish House of Commons elected on the accession of George I on charges of "high treason and other crimes and misdemeanours" stemming largely from his part in negotiating the Treaty of Utrecht, he was acquitted by the Lords but committed to the Tower pend-

---

[7] Jonathan Swift, *The History of the Four Last Years of the Queen*, ed. by Herbert Davis (Oxford: Basil Blackwell, 1964), p. xxxiii. Hereafter cited as Swift, *History*. See also pp. 181-3 for Davis's evaluation of Swift's claim.

ing the examination of further accusations.[8] He remained there for nearly two years, until in May 1717 he petitioned the Lords to bring his case to trial. The proceedings collapsed in a wrangle between Lords and Commons over parliamentary privilege, and Oxford was released; but he was forbidden the Court and he did not again play a significant role in political affairs. He died in 1724.

Henry St. John, raised to the peerage as Viscount Bolingbroke in 1712, was seventeen years younger than Harley, and Tory in his politics. Elected to Parliament in 1701, his association with Harley dates from about this time. He took office with Harley in 1704 as Secretary-at-War, resigning when he was dismissed in 1708; and he reentered the ministry with Harley in 1710 as Secretary of State. Harley's dismissal in 1714 was to have been his triumph, but the Queen's death interposed. Faced with impeachment proceedings, he went to France where for a short time he served the Pretender. In his absence he was tried and convicted of high treason; and while he eventually secured his pardon and recovered his forfeited property, he was not permitted to regain his peerage. Barred from his seat in the House of Lords, he was unable to resume an active political career. He lived out the rest of his life in England and in France until his death in 1751.

The quarrel between Bolingbroke and Harley, which smoldered through all of Harley's ministry and erupted violently in the last year of Queen Anne's reign, was rooted in profound differences of political attitude and personal style. Bolingbroke viewed politics in terms of party. His goal was to establish a Tory ministry secure enough to maintain itself in power at least to the end of the present reign, and he hoped, on into the next; and he thought that this could only be done by an outright commitment to Tory government. Whigs should be excluded from office, their places filled by loyal Tories. Harley,

---

[8] W. Cobbett, *Parliamentary History of England* (London, 1806–20), VII, 67. Hereafter cited as *Parliamentary History*.

nominally a Tory, and equally anxious to acquire power, was above all a moderate, committed to a scheme of nonparty government which emphasized the independence of the Crown and sought to protect it from the pressures of party. In Harley's view, no party should be strong enough to dictate policy to the Crown; and to prevent this he wished to employ those moderate men of both parties who had demonstrated their loyalty to the Queen. Neither approach was unprincipled, but the two were antithetical: Harley wished to avoid as the greatest of evils the party government Bolingbroke proposed.

In the early years of the eighteenth century politics were overwhelmingly the politics of party.[9] The struggle for power, and for place and favor, was carried on within the frame of party rivalry; and while the great questions of the day divided Whig from Tory, in the absence of great questions party itself was an issue. But substantial issues were not lacking. In 1701 Parliament had, by the Act of Settlement, established the succession to the English throne in the Protestant House of Hanover, a measure prompted by the death in 1700 of Princess Anne's only surviving child. Anne would succeed William; but Parliament wished to ensure that on her death the crown would go to the nearest Protestant heir, the dowager Electress Sophia of Hanover, and to her heirs in turn. The Act was passed by a Tory House of Commons but among large numbers of Tories support for Hanover was—and continued to be—minimal. In addition, the war against France, resumed in 1702 after five years' respite, occasioned differences on policy and strategy. Louis XIV's acceptance of the Spanish throne on behalf of his grandson, Philip of Anjou, posed again the threat

[9] For politics in the early eighteenth century and the central role of party, see especially G. S. Holmes, *British Politics in the Age of Anne* (London: Macmillan, 1967); J. H. Plumb, *The Growth of Political Stability in England, 1675–1725* (London: Macmillan, 1967), especially chap. 5; Keith Feiling, *A History of the Tory Party, 1640–1714* (Oxford, 1924), Part III; and G. S. Holmes, ed. *Britain after the Glorious Revolution, 1689–1714* (London. Macmillan, 1969).

of French hegemony in Europe, and England, in alliance with the Austrian Emperor and the Dutch, moved to prevent the union of the two crowns and to partition the Spanish inheritance. The allies' recognition, in 1703, of the Archduke Charles of Austria's claim to the crown of Spain became a further source of conflict, particularly after 1710 when the new ministry embarked on the peace negotiations that culminated in the Treaty of Utrecht. These events and the issues surrounding them colored the politics of Anne's reign. Tory resentment of the "moneyed interest," concentrated in the Bank of England and the great trading companies and generally associated with the Whigs, lent an edge to party warfare. And the disputes relating to the position of the Established Church and the status of Dissent were never far from the center of debate.

Whigs were likely to resist attempts to reduce the toleration afforded to Dissenters, to support wholeheartedly the war against France, and the succession in the House of Hanover. Tories preferred to fight the war at sea rather than on land, and, after 1708, they were increasingly anxious for peace; they approved all those measures that would strengthen the Established Church and reduce the power of Dissenters; and though it is difficult to track the shifting Jacobite currents within the party, a number of Tories openly espoused the cause of the exiled Stuarts and a great many more were sympathetic to the restoration of James, the Old Pretender. But apart from these divisions, the loyal Tory who wrote that he had met in Tunbridge Wells "a pretty many Whigs whose inseparable qualities, malice and hypocrisy, were very apparent,"[10] was expressing sentiments typical of honest Tory gentlemen. And the Whigs would have repaid him in kind. The correspondence of the time makes abundantly clear the passion with which most men held to their party allegiance.

Contemporaries distinguished between High and Low Tories, as well as between Whig and Tory, and they were

---

[10] A. Carleton to [?], 10 October 1711, HMC, *Portland MSS*, V, 98–9.

quite clear about what they meant. Moderates, as distinct from
"hot" men, High Churchmen, "High flyers," or "rigids," were
prepared to accept the toleration accorded to Dissenters; they
did not necessarily wish to forbid the practice of occasional
conformity, by which Dissenters received the sacrament of the
Church of England to qualify for public office, thus fulfilling
the requirement of the Test Act, and then returned to their
own religious services. When the Tories were in office, the
moderates did not insist that the former Whig ministers be
brought to account for their crimes, often simply the crime of
being Whigs. And they were "zealous for the supporting Her
Majesty's Title and the *Hanover* Succession, and do sincerely
approve the Revolution-Principles, and abhor the Slavish Doctrine of Unlimited Passive Obedience."[11] High Tories tended
to think the moderates no better than Whigs. "A very great
Majority of the Kingdom appear perfectly hearty and unanimous," Swift wrote,

that the Church of England should be preserved entire in all Her
Rights, Powers and Priviledges; All Doctrines relating to Government discouraged which She condemns; . . . Her open Enemies
(among whom I include at least Dissenters of all Denominations)
not trusted with the smallest Degree of Civil or Military Power;
and Her secret Adversaries under the Names of Whigs, Low-
Church, Republicans, Moderation-Men, and the like, receive no
Marks of Favour from the Crown.[12]

This was the High Tory position, and in the last four years of
Anne's reign at least, it represented the views of the great
majority of Tories. Harley's moderate scheme clearly could
not satisfy them. Bolingbroke was their champion, and he
shared their belief that Harley's policy barred the entrance to a
safe Tory world.

  In these circumstances the political conflict between Harley
and Bolingbroke was inevitable, but the course it took was

---

[11] [Simon Clement], *FAULTS on both SIDES* (London, 1710), pp. 47-8.
[12] Swift, "Some free Thoughts," p. 88.

determined by the nature of the combatants. The stakes were high—control of the ministry and, from Bolingbroke's point of view at least, the fate of the Tory party—but the extraordinary passion which informed the conflict stemmed from the collision of two utterly dissimilar personalities. They could not meet even in combat, for they practiced different styles of warfare. One has the sense that political or personal differences alone would have been sufficient to divide them. But how then account for their earlier association, the years between 1704 and 1708 when they served together in the Godolphin–Marlborough ministry? There was then at least the appearance of solidarity, for Bolingbroke (then still St. John) resigned when Harley was dismissed. And there is the point which so troubled Swift: "the great Affection they bore to each other" in the early days of the ministry. These are the questions around which the inquiry turns. But no satisfactory answers can be supplied without some knowledge of the characters of the two great men.

CHAPTER I

Robert Harley,

EARL OF OXFORD

UDITOR Edward Harley, brother to Robert Harley first Earl of Oxford and of Mortimer,[1] chose to begin his memoir of the Harley family "with adoration of the divine goodness that we sprung from such excellent parents, who from our infancy instructed and initiated us in all the principles of sincere piety and virtue."[2] The Auditor's language could have been his brother's, and it is significant: for the emphasis on divine will and the principles of piety and virtue characterized Robert Harley's public and private attitudes throughout his life. Of these excellent parents, the father, Sir Edward Harley, was a gentleman of Herefordshire. Member of Parliament for the county at the outbreak of the Civil War, he fought on the side of Parliament but was subsequently impeached for openly opposing Cromwell. At the Restoration he was appointed Governor of Dunkirk by Charles II; but

---

[1] Robert Harley was elevated to the peerage as Earl of Oxford and of Mortimer in May 1711, but in this discussion of his character, which ranges over his whole career, I refer to him throughout as Robert Harley.

[2] Edward Harley, Auditor of the Exchequer, "Memoirs of the Harley Family, especially of Robert Harley, first Earl of Oxford," HMC, *Portland MSS*, V, 641. The Auditor's "Memoirs" are printed as an appendix to Vol. V. Edward Harley was an Auditor of the Imprest, an official of the Exchequer whose function was to audit the accounts of various kinds of indirect taxes.

under James II, "foreseeing the King would atempt to set up Popery, he declined all manner of public employments, and neither he nor any of his family ever took any oath to that king."[3] Accordingly he welcomed the Revolution, and with his son Robert privately raised a troop of horse to support William.

Sir Edward was member for Hereford in the Convention Parliament, but in William's first Parliament he opposed "the insufferable avarice and insolence of the Dutch Ministers [which] quickly appeared, and met with all the support that the obsequious flattery and baseness of both parties could contribute"; and he opposed the Court's measures "for running the nation into a war with France."[4] When the King dissolved this first unruly Parliament, the Court party succeeded in preventing Sir Edward's reelection; but shortly thereafter the newly chosen member died, and Sir Edward was returned in his place. In this Parliament he continued to follow an independent line, opposing the Court on questions of taxation and on the suspension of the Habeas Corpus Act. "This," said the Auditor, "drew upon him and his family the implacable rage of the Lord Wharton, Lord Somers, and the other Whigs of their party, who had in many instances deserted, what they called Revolution principles."[5]

Sir Edward's father, an earlier Robert Harley, was a zealous Puritan who in 1644-5 chaired the House of Commons committee charged with destroying "idolatrous relics"—pictures, stained glass, statuary, vestments, plate—in churches and chapels throughout the country.[6] Sir Edward himself, though he conformed to the Established Church, was sympathetic to Dissent.

[3] *Ibid.*, V, 642-3.
[4] *Ibid.*, V, 644-5; and note, p. 645.
[5] *Ibid.*, V, 645.
[6] *Ibid.*, III, v-vi, 132-4. For Sir Robert Harley's iconoclastic activities, and for the early history of the Harley family, see A. McInnes, *Robert Harley, Puritan Politician* (London: Victor Gollancz Ltd., 1970), pp. 19-25.

Though he was a favourer of such as dissented from the Church for conscience' sake, and though sometimes he went to hear Mr. Baxter [the Presbyterian minister] and others in London, yet he constantly attended the Church, having by the grace of God, and a constant reading of the Scriptures attained to a very Christian temper, and therefore never engaged in the narrow principles with which the several parties in the Church had embroiled themselves and the nation.[7]

He had opposed the Test Acts and all acts against Dissenters, but he rejected equally James II's Declarations of Indulgence as devices to reestablish Popery. This being the greater evil, he urged the Dissenters to ignore them. Still, on the single occasion when he was defeated for reelection to Parliament, the cry of enemy to the Church was raised against him.[8]

The religious element in Sir Edward's character was strong, and strongly Presbyterian. He was devout and strict in the practice of his religion, and he held his family to the same standard. "Your order is duly observed," his son wrote from the country, "in going constantly every morning to prayers by six o'clock."[9] But for all his Presbyterian sternness, Sir Edward's temper, according to the Auditor, "was naturally very passionate, though mixed with the greatest tenderness and humanity. His passion he kept under a strict restraint, and had in a manner totally subdued, but his generosity and tender compassion to all objects of charity continued to his last."[10] And Robert Harley, long after his father's death, writing to his granddaughter on "the birthday of my father and your great grandfather," commended his "courage and firmness," his "sweetness, gentleness, and piety."[11]

[7] Edward Harley, "Memoirs," HMC, *Portland MSS*, V, 643.

[8] *Ibid.*, V, 645.

[9] Edward Harley to his father, 14 March 1693, HMC, *Portland MSS*, III, 514.

[10] Edward Harley, "Memoirs," HMC, *Portland MSS*, V, 641.

[11] Oxford to his granddaughter, Lady Margaret Harley, 21 October 1/23, HMC, *Bath MSS*, I, 250.

The Auditor remembered his mother as

a person of most exemplary piety and absolutely free from all those passions with which the female sex do so commonly disturb themselves and others. She had religion with a most discerning judgment without the least affectation, and took all fitting occasions from our youth to instruct us in principles of religion, virtue and honour, which she did in so tender a manner that I well remember that her discourses on these subjects made a very deep impression.[12]

Even without the Auditor's direct acknowledgment, the correspondence of the Harley family provides sufficient proof that the instruction of both parents made a deep impression on their children. The strongly religious outlook, the concern with piety and honor and virtue that pervades these letters, testify to the enduring influence of lessons learned early and well. Toward the end of his life, writing to his sister on the occasion of his son's birthday, Robert Harley thanked God, as he had many times before, for "the intrepid Virtue & Constancy of so many Relations; I am proud in the right place when I speak upon this Subject; & when the Revelation of all things is, I doubt not but our Dearest Father will receive joy that neither his Example or Instructions were lost upon you his Children."[13]

Robert Harley appears to have been his father's son in many ways. As a young man of twenty he attended for a year or two the Huguenot Monsieur Foubert's Academy in London, an establishment for the teaching of "riding, fencing, dancing, handling arms, and mathematics."[14] Thirty years later, when he was elevated to the peerage and made Lord Treasurer of England, one of his old classmates recalled him as a student at M. Foubert's.

[12] Edward Harley, "Memoirs," HMC, *Portland MSS*, V, 645.

[13] Oxford to Mrs. Abigail Harley, 2 June 1719, Herefordshire R.O., Harley Papers, C64. These papers are photographic copies of originals at Brampton Bryan Hall, Herefordshire.

[14] Sir Edward Harley to Lady Harley, 6 July 1680, HMC, *Portland MSS*, III, 366. Foubert was a Huguenot refugee.

I remember he was always sober, virtuous, and good, and if I may without vanity say I was less "rakelly" than some others there, I have oft since thought that induced him to show me a goodness and civility, which on many occasions he then expressed towards me, and as young as he was at that time he appeared to have a very solid judgment, and was very studious, yet he always showed abundance of good nature and affability.[15]

The portrait of the young man sketched here remains a remarkably good likeness of the Earl of Oxford, Lord Treasurer, and the Queen's first minister; and as Harley moved into public life, the qualities he praised in his father—courage and firmness, sweetness, gentleness, and piety—were equally praised in him. According to Swift, "he is Firm and Steady in his Resolutions" and "Fear, Avarice, Cruelty, and Pride are wholly strangers to his Nature."[16] Lady Orkney, in her "Character" of Harley, said that "he adores God. . . . Lives without Fear, and will dye with true Honor."[17] And the Auditor's words about his father are echoed by Swift's comment on Harley's passionate nature:

[15] Earl of Inchiquin to his Cousin Lundie, 27 July 1711, *ibid.*, V, 64.

[16] Swift, *History*, pp. 73-4.

[17] "Lady Orkney's Character of Oxford," printed as an appendix to *The Correspondence of Jonathan Swift*, ed. by Harold Williams (Oxford: The Clarendon Press, 1963-5), V, 224. Lady Orkney, daughter of Sir Edward Villiers, had been the mistress of William III. Swift attached the following comment to her "Character":

> The Lady who drew the above character . . . is a person of as much good naturall Sense and Judgment as I have ever known, and hath received all the Improvments that Courts and Conversations of Princes and other great Persons could give her. Her Advice hath many years been asked and followed in the most important Affairs of State. . . . But her great Misfortune was that in her Education she fell short even of that little share of Reading which belongs to her sex. So that she has neither Orthography, Grammar, nor choice of proper Words, which last never fails her in Conversation, and in Subjects she is conversant with. . . . I think Ladyes thus qualifyed should never hold a Pen but upon Occasions of perfect Necessity, or when they do, they should employ some other Hand to correct and putt into English.

All references to Swift's *Correspondence* are to the edition cited here, unless otherwise indicated. Hereafter cited as *Swift Correspondence*.

He abounded in good Nature and good Humour, although Subject to Passion, as I have heard it affirmed by others, and owned by himself; which however he kept under the Strictest Government, till towards the End of his Ministry, when he began to grow sowred, and to suspect his Friends, and perhaps thought it not worth his pains to manage any longer.[18]

Harley shared as well the Puritan emphasis of his father's religion: his life was governed by his belief in an unalterable divine providence that guided human affairs, and a powerful sense of submission to the designs through which providence revealed itself.[19] Now it is true that in an age when sickness and death occupied a prominent, if not preeminent place in the concerns of most people, submission in the sense of accepting the realities of a precarious existence was obviously necessary, or living from one day to the next would have been unbearable. Expressions of acquiescence in the decrees of providence filled the correspondence of the time and represented a common response to the uncomfortable immediacy of death. But Sir Edward Harley went beyond these conventional phrases when he preached submission to God's will and the need to prepare for God's call. Whole sections of his letters were miniature sermons, full of scriptural references and thanks to

[18] Swift, "An Enquiry," p. 135.

[19] McInnes, in his *Robert Harley, Puritan Politician*, emphasizes Harley's Puritan background as a formative influence on his political personality, arguing that "Harley's political outlook was in large measure a secularisation of his spiritual inheritance" (pp. 189–90). While one might not wish to follow McInnes all the way to his conclusion, the thesis carries conviction. At the same time it raises a further, perhaps unanswerable, question: this is, why the Puritan influence remained so strong in the second generation of a family where formal Dissent had been rejected in favor of conformity. In spite of Harley's early Puritan indoctrination in both school and home, there was no objective reason for him—or his brothers and sisters—to cleave so strongly to the Puritan heritage: great numbers of Presbyterians who chose to conform drifted rather quickly away from the old faith. The interesting point is that Harley reembraced it. The Puritan emphasis on divine providence and submission to the will of God evidently accorded with Harley's own needs; it reenforced and sanctioned existing tendencies in his personality, the result at least in part of early family relationships and experiences.

God for his grace and mercy in adversity as well as in good fortune. Mr. Marston died on Wednesday last, he informed his son, "overwhelmed with encumbrances upon his Estate leaving instruction to all honest men to beware of grasping at more then they can Embrace. The hinges of tru Wisdome are Distrust of Creatures, and Trust in ye Creator both these are fixed upon Humility wch is ye basis of Faith."[20] When he was ill, he hoped that the Lord would "please to spare his poor worm";[21] on another occasion when he had not been well, he wrote that "it pleased God . . . to visit mee with a very sore distemper. . . . Every diseas and pain is a derivation from Sin, and a degree of death; therefore should be improved to mortifie ye one and prepare for ye other."[22] On the death of a member of the family he allowed himself freer rein.

It hath pleased God to take your Uncle Robert Stephens. . . . I beseech God Sanctifie this breach and in mercy spare us that we may be allway discharging the parts of faithful Servants, remembring wee must give account for Every moment of time, and Every mercy wee Enjoy, And how soon that Cal may be not any one knowing therefor betimes Learn to answer ye End of Life To glorifie God in all you doe, for be assured there is not any thing wil at last prove so bitter as Time spent in Vanity.[23]

The endless succession of births, sicknesses, deaths went on, accompanied by the praise of God and submission to his will.

Robert Harley's own letters are in the same vein, and like his father's, they go far beyond the common rhetoric of divine providence and human mortality. In 1691, when he was thirty years old and the head of his own family, he answered a letter from his father, received the night before, which evidently

[20] Sir Edward Harley to Robert Harley, 21 September 1680, BM, Portland Loan, 29/140.
[21] Sir Edward Harley to Robert Harley, 19 March 1700, HMC, *Portland MSS*, III, 619.
[22] Sir Edward Harley to Robert Harley, 6 August 1677, BM, Portland Loan, 29/140.
[23] Sir Edward Harley to Robert Harley, 6 November 1675, *ibid*.

took him to task for frequenting public houses excessively. He denied the charge, but the manner in which he did so is instructive.

In the first place I desire to look up to Heaven, without the permission of which neither a hair falls to the ground nor a cubit taken from our reputation, and I doe most humbly and syncerely bend my knees to the Father of mercies imploring his mercie and grace, that this rebuke may bring forth in my soul a joyful harvest of humble, strict walking, with al circumspect holyness, in faith and obedience. . . . It is possible from many shots of the like nature, I could easily guess the bow whence this poisoned arrow was shot; but I desire to look higher that it may be admonition to more heavenly mindedness and humility, for which I humbly beg the concurrence of your prayers, and that you wil please to permit me to interpret this holy jelosie of yours over me an additional mark of your most tender affection to him who with al humility and obedience beseeches your blessing.[24]

In this instance Harley was all obedience and submission, and equally so to his human and heavenly fathers, between whom there appears to be some confusion. On other occasions his passion broke through that strict government which kept it in check. When his first wife died in November 1691, he wrote a letter to his father that is remarkable enough to be quoted at length. It begins as a meditation upon the Christian's duty to accept the afflicting strokes God has laid upon him.

I confess and acknowledge the Lord afflicts less than our iniquities have deserved, and the yeares of comfort I enjoyed with that deare one were beyond anything of merit, only from fre grace. Yet this is a bitter cup. Let it not O my God be given in wrath, let not thy tender mercies fail for evermore. O lay not more on this wretch than thou will enable him to bear. Thine arrows stick fast in me and my hand presseth me sore; there is no soundness in my flesh because of thine anger, neither rest in my bones because of my sin. Lord al my desire is before thee and my groning is not hid from

[24] Robert Harley to Sir Edward Harley, 13 June 1691, HMC, *Portland MSS*, III, 467–8.

thee. Wil the Lord cast off for ever and wil he be favorable no more? Hath God forgotten to be gracious? Is his mercy clean gon for ever more? Hath he in his anger shut up his tender mercies? But I wil remember the yeares of the right hand of the Most High. I wil meditate of all thy workes and talk of thy doings. The Lords way is in the sea, his path in the great waters. Thy footsteps are not known. Oh let me come into thy sanctuary then shal I understand these things; in this time of fear and troble I wil trust in thee, yea tho thou slayest me wil I trust in thee. Leave not my soul desolate, do not thou forsake me; in the midst of the fires I wil prays thee. Just are thou in all thou hast done unto me. Blessed be the name of the Lord.

This, Sir, is a heart searching grief, a wound in the most sensible part, nay it is an amputation of oneself. . . . Many lasting considerations occurs to embitter this dispensation and the dark side of the province is very gloomy. The affliction is grievous. I humbly beg prayers that it may bring forth in my soul the quieting fruits of righteousness. I desire to look up into the hand that gives the stroke that only can heal and make up this irreparable loss, as to the world, with abundant graces of his spirit. . . . I dare not, I would not wish her back again, for I doubt not her holy soul is in the fruition of the joy of her Lord, with whom she walked upon earth. . . . She is gone to the city of the living God, to an innumerable company of angels, to the general church of the firstborne, to God, the judge of all, and to the spirits of just men made perfect, and to Jesus the mediator of the new covenant, and to the blood of sprinkling, to which happy state and place may the same blood and mercies in our appointed time bring us. . . . I beg only God will not forsake me but sanctifies his hand to me and humble me under it, and if it be his blessed wil to spare those little babes, if it be his wil, for I desire to resigne al I have, if he thinks fit to take away root and branch, I lay my mouth in the dust for it is his doing.[25]

Harley added as a postscript: "I desire greif and sorrow may excuse this disjoynted letter." Here indeed is the man of strong

<hr>

[25] Robert Harley to Sir Edward Harley, 5 December 1691, *ibid.,* pp. 483–4.

passions struggling to control them, trying to reconcile himself to overwhelming loss. The context of the struggle is wholly religious, its rhetoric the language of Scripture. But the accents are those of Geneva rather than the Church of England: the years of comfort he enjoyed were "beyond anything of merit, only from fre grace"; he desired "to resigne al I have, if he thinks fit to take away root and branch, I lay my mouth in the dust for it is his doing." And although from the depths of his grief Harley dared to ask if God in his anger had turned away, his rebellion, if such it can be called, was momentary. He subdued his despair, forced himself, almost brutally, to submit. "In the midst of the fires I wil prays thee. . . . Blessed be the name of the Lord."

For Robert Harley as for his father, God ruled the body politic as surely as simple mortality: the hand of God was immanent in the conduct of human affairs. "I gave an account of God's mercy to the public at the end of the session," he wrote to his father in 1700. "Everyone discovers more and more the danger and the wonderfulness of the rescue. So many minute things were ordered by the hand of God to come between us and ruin." The following month he had further news: "It pleases God that the Attorney General cannot yet be prevailed with, and I see little hopes now of it. I pray God direct this poor nation."[26] A decade later, in the autumn of 1710, shortly after his return to power as the Queen's first minister, he observed of his new situation: "we are in the hands of God & good is every word of his: let integrity & uprightness preserve me; and his goodness support me."[27]

The attitudes reflected here—the religious outlook with its marked Presbyterian emphasis on virtue and submission to providence—persisted throughout Harley's life. His capacity for submitting to the will of God waxed if anything stronger as the

[26] Robert Harley to Sir Edward Harley, 13 April, 9 May 1700, HMC, *Portland MSS*, III, 618, 619.
[27] Harley to [his sister-in-law or his brother?], 10 October 1710, Herefordshire R.O., Harley Papers, C64.

years went by. "I have oft proposed yr Lp to my self as an example of ye greatest submission to providence & most entire acquiessence under all events yt ever I knew,"[28] wrote the Bishop of Chester in 1717; and most observers would have agreed with him. Yet it is significant that where the misfortunes of others were concerned, Harley relaxed the severe moral stance from which he viewed the vicissitudes of his own life. The emphasis and tone of a pair of letters he wrote to near relations who had lost a son are strikingly different from the characteristic Harley response to untimely death. To the father he said:

I do suggest to you that the taking part in your Greif is a real alleviation thereof, because the respect others shew for your Son, ought to administer Comfort to his Mother and you, that you had One so deserving, who paid his Debt to Nature with applause, though with regret of all who knew him; accept I beseech you these few Lines dropt over his Grave, and remember that the virtues of the Dead are not to depress the value of the living.[29]

And to the mother:

It is unreasonable to desswade you from being trobled. . . . But on the other hand your Greif is not to be indulged beyond reason; remember what you owe to your self, and what you owe to your other Children.[30]

Here is no stern admonition to submit to God's will and praise his infinite mercy, but compassionate, eminently sensible counsel which has about it a very modern ring. So does the advice he dispatched to his brother the Auditor when his wife was extremely ill.

I must now entreat you on yr own account, I know yr spirit is willinger than yr Constitution will bear, & the tenderness of yr nature will have greater influence on yr health than you think for;

---

[28] Francis Gastrell, Bishop of Chester, to Oxford, 10 January 1717, BM, Portland Loan, 29/137.
[29] Oxford to S. Winnington, 20 September 1718, *ibid.*, 29/160.
[30] Oxford to Mrs. Salwey Winnington, 20 September 1718, *ibid.*

therefore beleive One who loves you beyond any in the world, & have a care of yr Self; you owe it to my sister, you owe it to yr family, & to the Public, & do not let her recovery be accompanied with yr sickness.[31]

Years later, he could not forbear telling this same brother that he was "to blame, greatly, in one respect—that is Neglect of your Health permit me Dearest Brother to tell you that there is a Duty owing to that Body wch is to be raisd again: that neglecting the Body is a fault, as well as Luxury: you owe it in obedience to Gods Command to take care of your Health, to be fitter to serve him— . . . forgive this overflowing of my concerne."[32]

About his own health and his private affairs Harley seems to have been highly imprudent. From his youth to the series of illnesses that beset him at the end of his life there is no break in the pleas from family and friends that he take more care of himself. In 1689, when he was still in his twenties, he received this anxious communication from his wife:

It is an extream great troble to me to hear my Dear is not well, I am afraid you do not take care of your Self: you may express as great love to me as you will but I shall not think that you love me with out you take care of your Self. when you take care of your Self I take it as a great love and kindness to me.[33]

And from his father-in-law the following year:

I rejoyce you are better than you were, I earnestly beg & beg againe you will take more Care of your Selfe, doe not so much

31 Robert Harley to Auditor Harley, 28 September 1706, Herefordshire R.O., Harley Papers, C64. The letter is endorsed "28 Sept 1708" by the Auditor's son but it is almost certainly misdated.

32 Oxford to Auditor Harley, 11 December 1719, ibid. Harley and his brother exchanged such reproaches the length of their lives. The Auditor was as deeply imbued with Presbyterian piety as his elder brother and, apparently, as careless of his health. See especially Abigail Harley, the Auditor's daughter, to her uncle, Oxford, 29 August 1722, wishing he could prevail with her father to take more care of himself. BM, Portland Loan, 29/69.

33 Elizabeth Harley to Robert Harley, 16 October 1689, ibid., 29/143.

depend upon your youth & Strength but be blouded before you
See So much nead of itt, the Publicke & your Familey as well as I
doe backe this request, that you should love your Selfe.[34]

After a serious illness in 1695 his friend Sir Christopher Musgrave blessed God for Harley's recovery and went on to
observe that "country aire & some exercise certainely is absolutely necessary, yr studious Sedentary Life I am conffident is
very prejudiciall to you. Ffor ye sake of yr ffriends have
greater regard to yr health."[35] On into the next decade (and
the new century) the refrain was the same. "By the discourse I
had with you just now at Kensington," wrote Godolphin in
1706, "I am sorry to be forced to put you in mind that you
never take any tolerable care of your own health."[36] "Lord
treasurer is still out of order. . . ." Swift reported in 1711.
"He is often subject to a sore throat, and some time or other it
will kill him, unless he takes more care than he is apt to do."[37]
The chorus of reproaches continued through Harley's retirement after his release from the Tower, though he had not then
the press of public affairs as an excuse for his negligence. In the
last years of his life when he was by all accounts, including his
own, extremely ill, he steadfastly refused to come up to town
where the best doctors and medicines were available. "As I
have a very tender concern for your welfare," a friend wrote
to him in August 1721, "I must ye more press yr Lordship to
be brought up to Town as soon as you are able to bear ye
jorney that you may not be lost in ye Country for want of
proper help. Dr Mead sayes he cannot give proper advice
unless you will come to Town & is in great Pain for you if yr
Lordship should stay another Winter in ye Country." The
roads were now good, and Harley could come by horse litter if
he was not able to bear a coach.[38] But two months later

---

[34] Thomas Foley to Robert Harley, 2(9) September 1690, *ibid.*, 29/136.
[35] Sir Christopher Musgrave to Robert Harley, 11 July 1695, *ibid.*, 29/151.
[36] Godolphin to Robert Harley, May 1706, HMC, *Bath MSS*, I, 81.
[37] Swift, *Journal to Stella*, II, 386.
[38] Charles Caesar to Oxford, 26 August 1721, BM, Portland Loan, 29/129.

Harley's son was still trying to persuade him to make the journey. He was sure his father had "not wanted being put in mind of coming to London," he wrote to his aunt in October, "for I have not wrote to him in many months but that every letter had something in it relating to his coming up. . . . if those about him cannot prevail I am sure I must dispair. I do dread the consequences of these delays."[39] But Harley was equally unmoved by the pleas of family and friends, and by the eminent Dr. Mead's quite reasonable wish to see his patient. He did not see London until the following summer, three years from the time he had left it. One can view his resistance to the entreaties of his correspondents as sheer perverseness: there is, to be sure, a kind of massive obstinacy about his refusal to be moved—and to move. But it is an obstinacy born of passivity, another manifestation of his acquiescence in the dictates of providence: if matters of sickness and health, of life and death are in the hands of God, what profits it man to concern himself with them? Once again it must be pointed out that Harley operated on a double standard: where the afflictions of others were concerned, he spared no worry and no pains; his indifference extended only to himself.

Harley's neglect of his health was paralleled by neglect of his private affairs. Rare among office-holders of his day, he seems to have made no money out of public office but on the contrary to have left it poorer than when he came in. Swift said of him that "he cannot be more careless of other Mens Fortunes than he is of his own"[40] and that "his Liberality and Contempt of Money were such, that he almost ruined his Estate while he was in Employment."[41] Dr. Stratford, canon of Christ Church and a long-time friend of the Harley family, advised Harley's son that being a statesman "was a dangerous Trade, but if it is your fate to follow it, I hope you will make

[39] Lord Harley to his aunt Abigail Harley, 26 October 1721, *ibid.*, 29/66.
[40] Swift, *History*, p. 180.
[41] Swift, "An Enquiry," p. 136.

more advantage of it to yourself than your father has done."[42] When in 1713 Harley negotiated the marriage of his son to Henrietta Cavendish-Holles, daughter of the late Duke of Newcastle and heir to one of the greatest fortunes in England, his friends congratulated him openly and without embarrassment for putting his family's financial affairs on a solid footing. But when he was dismissed from office in 1714 he was in extremely tight circumstances. Although he had provided for his son, he had not improved his own situation. This was in part a question of principle. In an age when the line between bribery and the legitimate perquisites of office was extremely fine, he seems to have taken an unusually rigid position on the matter of fees for services rendered. In 1707, when he was Secretary of State, he wrote an uncompromisingly stern letter to an individual who had asked his help in securing a place.

I must tell you very plainly I resent your going about to offer me mony, and much more your continuing to insinuate it in your last letter even after I had told you so plainly before I would hear nothing of it; I told you before that you did not know me when you went that way to work; . . . I now repeat again to you that until you are cured of thinking to Bribe me, I shall never think my Self capable to serve you; when you stood upon yr Father's merit, I did what I could to serve you, and till you turn from thinking mony can prevail with me, you must find some other friend; when you return to your Father's merit, you shall find me.[43]

Dartmouth described Harley's ministry as "four years cessation from plunder," adding that "no man had more affectionate zeal for the interest of his country, or less for his own."[44] Dart-

[42] Dr. Stratford to Edward Harley, 10 July 1710, IIMC, *Portland MSS*, VII, 3. Dr. Stratford had been Robert Harley's chaplain until he was appointed canon of Christ Church in 1703; and he supervised Harley's son's studies when he went up to Oxford in 1707.

[43] Robert Harley to W. Brenand, 28 June 1707, BM, Portland Loan, 29/127.

[44] Gilbert Burnet, *History of His Own Time* (2nd edn. enlarged, Oxford, 1833), VI, 50, Dartmouth's note.

mouth was a friend and political supporter, but even Harley's bitterest enemies never accused him of corruption.

Harley was by nature unassuming, self-effacing, apparently without pretension. Pride and vanity were the worst sins in his canon, the antitheses of virtue and piety, and he never tired of saying so. In a letter to his son beginning his studies at Christ Church, Oxford, Harley admonished him to use his time well and then continued:

I hope your mind is so well seasoned with virtue & piety that any examples of vice will appear to you but as so many Rocks where others have been Shipwrecked, and consequently require your care to avoid them.

As to your General Conversation, remember that truth is the most necessary quality, & affability & humanity the best ornament of a Gentleman; for want of manners is always want of sense, and Pride & Vanity are the most depreciating things in any ones behavior; & commonly appear first in affectation & quickly proceed to further excesses, wch al proceeds from the desire to be thought singular wch is a very wretched thing in every thing else, but to be singular & eminent in goodness & virtue & learning.[45]

Some years later, when he was confined in the Tower, he wrote of the benefits of a well-instructed mind in regulating and ordering the passions, "and when the effects of that shine forth in the course of ones life it adds a Lustre to ye most beautiful Person, & prevents from running into those odious *faults* Pride and affectation."[46] Harley strove to guide his own life by these principles, alternately exasperating and inspiring his contemporaries.

His inclination to excessive modesty was itself something of an affectation. In 1700 he was for a long time in regular correspondence with Henry Guy, a former secretary to the Treasury, on matters relating to changes in the ministry, and from August at least they exchanged letters every few days, usually

45 Robert Harley to his son, 1707, *ibid.*, 29/143.
46 Oxford to [?], August 1715, *ibid.*, 29/12.

in cipher. Yet toward the end of September, Guy had to write: "I most earnestly beg of you to leave off the formality of excusing what you write to me: it is time to quit that between you and I at this time of day."[47] Harley's friend Henry Boyle was more amused than annoyed by these repeated self-deprecatory apologies: "Your making excuses for your very entertaining letters has a great deal of the country fashion in it. I have been at two or three great treats and very handsom ones since I came down, but all the while one is feasting the good people of the house never fail to ask pardon for putting us in danger of being starved."[48]

But there were more positive aspects of Harley's unpretentiousness. During the time when he was Secretary of State, a cousin recently returned from a visit to London reported to his sister: "In good manners I should have mentioned your brother the Secretary in the first place, whose greatness doth not make him forget his old acquaintance and relations, being still the same cousin Robin Harley; he was so kind soon to find me out and invited me to dinner."[49] And in May 1711, on the eve of Harley's promotions, Swift wrote: "So to-morrow or next day I suppose he will be declared earl of Oxford, and have the staff. This man has grown by persecutions, turnings out, and stabbing. What waiting, and crowding, and bowing, will be at his levee? yet, if human nature be capable of so much constancy, I should believe he will be the same man still, bating the necessary forms of grandeur he must keep up."[50] Swift later described Harley as "the only Instance that ever fell within my Memory or Observation, of a Person passing from a private

[47] Henry Guy to Robert Harley, 24 September 1700, HMC, *Portland MSS*, III, 629.

[48] Henry Boyle to Robert Harley, 14 September 1696, *ibid.*, p. 578.

[49] Lady Pye to her cousin Abigail Harley, 8 October 1705, *ibid.*, IV, 257. The Harley family abounded in Abigails. His sister, the lady addressed in this letter, was Abigail, as was his second daughter, Lady Dupplin, afterwards Countess of Kinnoull; also his brother Edward's wife and their daughter.

[50] Swift, *Journal to Stella*, I, 274-5.

Life through the severall Stages of Greatness, without any
perceivable Impression upon his Temper or Behaviour."[51]
Lady Orkney observed him to be "proud onely by disregard-
ing his own Greatness. . . . He hates being commended, but
must know he deserves it, reflecting his Superiority cannot last
without Humility, ever suspecting he may err."[52] Thus
Harley when he was Earl of Oxford, Lord Treasurer, and the
Queen's first minister.[53]

One of the charges most often leveled against Harley by
friends and enemies alike was his steady procrastination in
dealing with both public and private business. Dr. Arbuthnot
believed the law of inertia was the "Law of Nature to which
the Dragon [Harley] is most subject."[54] And an exasperated
correspondent wrote in 1712: "If I had that sloth in my temper
that you have, I would on purpose keep a man to pull me by
the sleeve to remember me of things that I was to do."[55] But
Harley's behavior was not merely a matter of indolence. His
schoolmate at M. Foubert's Academy remembered him as
"very studious"; Sir Christopher Musgrave advised country air
and exercise as antidotes to his "studious Sedentary Life." And
a friend's request that he attend a parliamentary committee on
a particular day began: "Though I have oft desir'd you,
without effect, not to prejudice yr health by Sitting up too
Late in yr Study, Let me prevail with you, pray, at Least for
One Night, to dispense with it."[56] There is ample evidence

---

[51] Swift, "An Enquiry," p. 135.

[52] "Lady Orkney's Character," *Swift Correspondence*, V, 224.

[53] Curiously, in the light of all the evidence to the contrary, Dartmouth
remarked that Harley's "greatest fault was vanity." Perhaps he was referring
to Harley's unshakable belief in his own rectitude, which certainly is a kind
of vanity. Burnet, *History*, VI, 50, Dartmouth's note.

[54] Arbuthnot to Swift, 11 December 1718, *Swift Correspondence*, II, 305.
Swift called Harley the Dragon, "by Contraryes, and for he was the mildest,
wisest and best Minister that ever served a Prince." Erasmus Lewis to Swift,
17 July 1714, *ibid.*, pp. 67–8, Swift's note.

[55] Sir Scipio Hill to Oxford, [?] February 1712, HMC, *Portland MSS*,
V, 141–2.

[56] Auditor Newport to Robert Harley, 11 January 1699, BM, Portland
Loan, 29/301.

that Harley continued these habits when he was appointed to public office. "I cant tell you wither I shall see Herefordshire this sumer or not," his daughter Abigail wrote from London when he was Secretary of State.

For my part I can't see how my Ffather can be spared certainly this place is twice as fatigueing as Speaker tuesday & Ffriday & nights ye earlyst that he comes home is one a clock & very often 'tis 2 or 3 in ye morning & every day 'tis allmost 4 a clock before he can get home from his ofice to diner but thank God all this agrees with my Ffather he looks as well or better yn when you were in town & grows mighty fat I believe his takeing ye 2 or 3 days every week at Windsor is a great advantage to him.[57]

Harley could, then, work extremely hard, and generally he did. Prince Eugene, visiting England in January 1712, described him as "an indefatigable man of business," the Whig Bishop Burnet, hardly a sympathetic witness, as "a man of great industry and application."[58] And when Swift complained of the long dinners and late nights spent in the company of the ministers, he never accused them of idleness, but marveled rather that in spite of the hours spent dining and drinking, they found time to attend to public affairs as well.[59]

Yet Harley's correspondence in the years after 1710 is full of increasingly desperate letters from solicitors for place and favor, election managers asking for directions and assistance, envoys abroad seeking further instructions, all complaining that Harley agreed, Harley promised, and the thing has not been done; or that nothing has been heard from him. Sir David Hamilton, the Queen's physician, denounced Harley for "promising, & not performing." The Treasurer was deaf to the "Cry of ye Poor for wt is owing ym," said Hamilton, thinking

[57] Abigail Harley to her aunt Abigail Harley, 15 July 1709, *ibid.*, 29/68. This letter appears to be misdated. Robert Harley was out of office in July 1709, but the reference to him is unmistakable. The letter was most probably written in July 1704 during his first summer as Secretary of State. It could not be later than 1707 as he was dismissed in February 1708.

[58] Prince Eugene's "Characters," HMC, *Portland MSS*, V, 156; Burnet, *History*, IV, 197.

[59] Swift, *Journal to Stella, passim.*

chiefly of himself, to whom three years' salary was past-due.[60] Thomas Roper, Earl of Sussex, began in June 1711 trying to collect two years' arrears of salary. The last in the series of his letters is dated May 30, 1714: though Harley had promised, nothing had been done.[61] And the continued ill success of Lord Pagett's efforts to procure a title from the Queen at length produced an angry accusation: "Since the Queen as yor Ldp has oft told mee, consented to grant wt I desir'd soe long agoe, nothing but yor forgetfullness of, and unkindness to mee can prevent confirming the favor."[62]

Now it must be said that solicitors for place and favor made the lot of a minister, particularly a first minister, a distinctly unhappy one. There was no respite, ever, from the stream of petitioners asking for places and pensions, payment of arrears of pensions and salaries, and quite often for outright charity. No pretext for an address of congratulations or condolence was allowed to pass unexploited: the petitioner would give what he considered due attention to the occasion at hand and then take up the real purpose of his letter. "Since I have presum'd to write You," ran a letter ostensibly written to congratulate Harley on the birth of a grandson, "Give me Leave to remind you of the affair I mentioned before."[63] A month later the mother of this child, Harley's elder daughter, died, and among the messages of condolence were these two rather startling amalgams of decorous grief and unembarrassed self-interest. The first writer went quickly to the point without so much as a new sentence. "We have had too late an Instance of Mortality, nor can you receive so great a Loss, and I not bear a Part therein; But my Lord you are too wise not to submit to God Almighty's Will, and as the Glass spends, and I have your Lordship's Honour you will take Care of me. . . ."[64] And on

[60] Hertfordshire R.O., Panshanger MSS, Sir David Hamilton's Diary, f. 58.
[61] Thomas Roper, 4th Lord Dacre, Earl of Sussex to Oxford, BM, Portland Loan, 29/155.
[62] Lord Pagett to Oxford, 22 February 1714, *ibid.*, 29/153.
[63] Richard Hampden to Oxford, 10 November 1713, *ibid.*, 29/138.
[64] Philip Bertie to Oxford, 10 December 1713, *ibid.*, 29/126.

to his request. The second writer, presumably out of a sense of propriety, moved to a new paragraph before he broached his own affair. He had come to town to pay his respects to Harley, he said,

> wch ye Lordship's great loss unhappyly prevented me. I condole with ye Ldsp from ye bottom of my heart, but a particular sorrow cannot appear where ye greif is so generall; & 'tis renewing of greif to mention it.
>
> If you will give me leave therefore I will, pass from ye tenderness to ye generosity, & tell you how you may for ever oblidg one who would be proud to serve you. Mr. Web is either dieing or dead; & if so, I beg ye Government of ye Isle of Wight.[65]

Given the constant barrage of such importunings, the permanent imbalance between places and seekers, and the fact that the cries of the hungry are always louder than the contented murmurings of the satisfied, every minister was criticized to some extent for delaying on places and pensions: the indignant letters of dissatisfied men do not in themselves constitute an indictment. But that Harley was excessively slow in dealing with these matters was the unanimous opinion of his contemporaries, even those who greatly admired him and attempted to justify or at least explain his habitual delaying. In Lady Orkney's view, "he appears to be dilatory not from want of the satisfaction to serve all, but to search out those with the fewest Faults."[66] Swift, commenting on his "Love of Procrastination (wherein doubtless Nature hath her Share)," observed that "this is an Imputation laid upon many other great Ministers; who, like men under too heavy a Load, let fall that which is of the least consequence, and go back to fetch it when their Shoulders are free. For, Time is often gained as well as lost by Delay; which at worst is a Fault on the securer side."[67] Swift shifted much of the blame on to the Queen, who, he said, hurried more slowly even than Harley. How true this was

---

[65] Lord North and Grey to Oxford, 1 December 1713, *ibid.*, 29/308.
[66] "Lady Orkney's Character," *Swift Correspondence*, V, 224.
[67] Swift, *History*, p. 75.

remains to be seen; but if Harley did move slowly, if once he was at the head of affairs he was increasingly reluctant to act, the first question is why, the second is how and to what extent this reluctance affected his conduct of affairs. The second question is central to this inquiry; some possible answers to the first may be considered here.

The evidence suggests that Harley's chronic procrastination stemmed from an unwillingness to assert his power and authority in a direct and open way. It was not that he spurned power: Burnet described him accurately enough as a man "much turned to politics, and of a restless ambition."[68] In Swift's opinion, "his Love of Power is no greater than what is common to Men of his Superiour Capacities." But Swift went on to observe: "Neither did any Man ever appear to value it less after he had obtained it, or exert it with more Moderation."[69] Harley appears to have valued his power more and to have exerted it more forcefully in the earlier stages of his political career, when he was Speaker of the House of Commons and then Secretary of State; and when he was out of office maneuvering to get back in. He functioned most effectively behind the scenes, at the back stairs, and in circumstances where he was not singly, visibly, and undeniably responsible for decisions made and action taken. In the arts of management and negotiation he seems to have had no peer. He made his political reputation as a parliamentary manager—he "knew forms and the records of parliament so well, that he was capable both of lengthening out and of perplexing debates," Burnet remarked rather sourly;[70] and when in 1708 his scheme to restructure the Godolphin–Marlborough government failed, observers marveled at how nearly he had succeeded. Furthermore, while in the early years of Anne's reign, his influence was considerable and recognized to be so—"The Duke, the Treasurer and yourself are called the Triumvirate, and reck-

68 Burnet, *History*, IV, 197.
69 Swift, "An Enquiry," p. 135.
70 Burnet, *History*, IV, 197.

oned the spring of all public affairs," a correspondent reported to Harley in 1704, a few months after he joined the ministry as Secretary of State[71]—Godolphin and Marlborough were the nominal heads of the ministry and as such directly responsible for its actions. But when, as first minister, Harley himself was called upon to make public commitments and openly to accept responsibility for his decisions, he was slow to act. He tended to move too late, too indecisively, and sometimes not to move at all. It was not that he had no principles or that he lacked strong views on public issues: on the contrary, he was remarkably consistent in his devotion to moderate political principles. The point is rather that in public affairs Harley was essentially passive: he chose not to take a clear-cut public position unless it was unavoidable. And the politics of moderation, emphasizing conciliation and the avoidance of divisive action, afforded some justification for his stance.

Harley's passiveness and his habitual posture of defense were reflected in an inclination toward secrecy and concealment which observers tended to equate with cunning and deceit. Burnet wrote of "the cunning of a man, who has not hitherto shewed any token of a great genius, and is only eminent in the arts of deluding those that hearken to him."[72] Lord Cowper meant Harley when he spoke of those who "carry on things, by Trick & Contradiction & Shuffle"; so did the Earl of Jersey when he blamed the sourness of his blood on some who "think that no government can be carried on without a trick."[73] And it was Cowper who described Harley's dinner of reconciliation with the Whigs in January 1706, when the Secretary

took a Glass, & drank to Love & Friendship & everlasting Union, & wish'd he had more Tockay to drink it in (we had drank two

---

[71] Stanley West to [Robert Harley], 29 August 1704, HMC, *Portland MSS*, IV, 118.

[72] Burnet, *History*, VI, 144.

[73] Hertfordshire R.O., Panshanger MSS, Sir David Hamilton's Diary, f. 18; Jersey to Dartmouth, 6 October [1710], Staffordshire R.O., Dartmouth MSS, D. 1778, I, ii, 169.

Bottles, good, but thick). I replied, his white Lisbon was best to drink it in, being very Clear. I suppose he apprehended it (as I observ'd most of the Company did) to relate to that humour of his, which was, never to deal clearly or openly, but always with Reserve, if not Dissimulation, or rather Simulation; & to love Tricks even where not necessary, but from an inward Satisfaction he took in applauding his own Cunning. If any Man was ever born under a Necessity of being a Knave, he was.[74]

Sir David Hamilton told Harley "People sd he wd learn ye Q——to Equivocate," and afterwards reported the conversation to the Queen, "as also wth how much good nature he [Harley] recd. it. I hop'd he was not wt ye world thought him to be, but sincere, To wch she sd she hopd so."[75]

Swift shared the Queen's faith in her minister. "His [Harley's] Detractours who charge him with Cunning, are but ill-acquainted with his Character," Swift wrote; "I know no Man to whom that mean Talent could be with less Justice applyed."[76] Yet Swift did not deny Harley's secretiveness.

However, it must be allowed, that an Obstinate Love of Secrecy in this Minister seems at distance to have some Resemblance of Cunning; For, He *is* not only very retentive of Secrets, but *appears* to be so too; which I number among his Defects. He hath been blamed by his Friends for refusing to discover his Intentions, even in those points where the Wisest Man may have need of Advice and Assistance; and Some have censured him upon that account, as if he were jealous of Power: But, he hath been heard to answer, That he seldom did otherwise without Cause to repent. However, so undistinguished a Caution cannot in my Opinion be justifyed, by which the Owner loseth many Advantages; and whereof all Men, who deserve to be confided in, may with some reason complain.[77]

---

[74] *The Private Diary of William, First Earl Cowper, Lord Chancellor of England*, ed. by E. C. Hawtrey (Eton, 1833), p. 33. Hereafter cited as Cowper, *Diary*.

[75] Hertfordshire R.O., Panshanger MSS, Sir David Hamilton's Diary, f. 20.

[76] Swift, *History*, p. 74.

[77] Swift, "An Enquiry," p. 137.

That Harley refused to confide in his colleagues was indeed
a constant complaint, and it merged with the further reproach
that on that account administration suffered. Unwilling to
delegate authority, he was left to do everything himself. In
1711 his friend Dr. Hickes congratulated him on his recovery
from a recent illness and beseeched him "for your healths sake
to consider Exod. XVIII. I believe you are not stronger or
more Athletick, than Moses, though I wish you were."[78] The
biblical text recounts the advice given Moses by his father-in-
law that he appoint able men as rulers to judge the people lest
he wear himself out by judging all himself. This was Bolingbroke's theme as well when he wrote in 1713:

> You are forced to execute more than you should, and cannot
> therefore supervise. You are pulling at the beam when you should
> be in the box whipping and reining in, as the journey you have to
> go or the ways you pass through require.
>   . . . Consider who you have left to employ; assign them their
> parts; trust them as far as it is necessary for the execution each of
> his part; let the forms of business be regularly carried on in Cabi-
> net, and the secret of it in your own closet.[70]

Bolingbroke's advice may have been sound, but there was in
fact good reason for the Treasurer's reluctance to trust his
colleagues, particularly in the latter part of his ministry. Defoe
wrote of this same period that, while the Treasurer's enemies
represented him "as acting with such a Reserve in all the
publick Administration, that not the Queen Her self, much less
the rest of the Ministry, were acquainted with any thing till
they saw it done; . . . *the sum of all this was,* That as the
Success of all his Management was, in a great measure, owing
to his being Master of his own Measures, . . . he saw great
Reason not to put his Schemes in some hands, who were
mighty importunate to be trusted."[80]

---

[78] Dr. George Hickes to Oxford, 8 November 1711, BM, Portland Loan,
29/146.
[79] Bolingbroke to Oxford, 27 July 1713, HMC, *Portland MSS*, V, 311.
[80] [Daniel Defoe], *The Secret History of the White-Staff* (2nd edn.,
London, 1714), pp. 40-1.

Yet when Harley did choose to confide in or at least consult his colleagues, they complained that they could not understand him. Summoned to a meeting with the Treasurer at St. James's, Cowper remembered that "he [Harley] had written down Heads on a Paper, yet spake, as always, very dark & confusedly, interlaceing all he said with broken hints of Discoveries he had made. . . ."[81] The Duchess of Marlborough, with characteristic vitriol, asserted that "he had long accustomed himself so much to dissemble his real intentions & to use the ambiguous & obscure way of speaking that he could hardly ever be understood when he really designed it or be believed when he never so much desired it."[82] And Pope, writing long after Harley's death and, one suspects, much influenced by many years' close friendship with Bolingbroke, recalled the Treasurer as "huddled in his thoughts, and obscure in his manner of delivering them." He "talked of business in so confused a manner that you did not know what he was about."[83] Yet for all Harley's supposed obscurity, he was regularly consulted on the style as well as the content of the Queen's speeches in the early years of the reign—"I have drawn a line under such expressions where I am doubtful either of the expressions themselves, or that they are not proper in the paragraph where at present they are inserted," Godolphin wrote in 1702, enclosing a draft of the speech from the throne[84] —and he could scarcely have served so long and so effectively as Speaker had he really found it difficult to make himself understood. One is left with the sense that the obfuscations of Harley's language, like his refusal to trust his opinions to proven friends, is another manifestation of his reluctance to commit himself openly. He could be clear enough advising

81 Cowper, *Diary*, p. 54.

82 Blenheim MSS, G, I, 9, quoted by David Green, *Sarah Duchess of Marlborough* (New York: Charles Scribner's Sons, 1967), p. 117.

83 Joseph Spence, *Observations, Anecdotes, and Characters of Books and Men Collected from Conversation*, ed. by James M. Osbourn (Oxford: The Clarendon Press, 1966), I, 96.

84 Godolphin to Harley, 16 September 1702, HMC, *Portland MSS*, IV, 47.

Godolphin on the Queen's speech; he was supremely skillful in managing the House of Commons. But when he had to defend his own policies publicly, he tended to retreat into obscurity. Abidingly suspicious of his ministerial associates, he avoided confiding in them as long as he could; when forced by circumstance to discover his intentions, consciously or unconsciously he veiled them in confusion. There was perhaps some truth in Bolingbroke's accusation that "when you had a Mind not to be understood, your L——p could be effectually unintelligible, without putting your self to much Trouble."[85]

Not unexpectedly, Harley's unwillingness to commit himself openly extended to the written as well as the spoken word: beyond the limits of his family, he was a hopelessly poor correspondent. "I am very sensible," Swift wrote from Ireland in 1722, complaining of Harley's neglect of him, "that next to receiving thanks and compliments there is nothing you more hate than writing letters."[86] And after Harley's death Swift observed to his son that "I never knew any person more hardly drawn to write letters of no consequence than my late lord your father."[87] It is significant that part of Swift's complaint related to his efforts to secure Harley's cooperation in supplying materials for a history of his ministry. Harley had agreed to the project; furthermore he knew that Swift was a sympathetic observer and would attempt to vindicate his administration. Even so, he would never commit himself to a definite plan for proceeding with the work. At his death he still had not complied with Swift's request.

Harley's dilatory tactics in an enterprise that he favored and that would ultimately have been to his advantage raise a further point, and this is his refusal to defend himself when under attack. Swift found this attitude odd and distressing.

---

[85] [Bolingbroke], *Considerations upon the Secret History of the White Staff* (5th edn., London [1714]), p. 7.

[86] Swift to Oxford, 11 October 1722, HMC, *Portland MSS*, V, 632.

[87] Swift to the 2nd Earl of Oxford, 27 November 1724, HMC, *Bath MSS*, I, 250–1.

There is One Thing peculiar in his Temper, which I altogether disapprove, and do not remember to have heard or met with in any other Man's character: I mean an Easiness and Indifference under any Imputation, although he be ever so Innocent; and, although the strongest Probabilities and Appearances are against him. So that I have known him often suspected by his nearest Friends for some Months in Points of the highest Importance, to a degree that they were ready to break with him, and only undeceived by Time or Accident.[88]

Defoe wrote of 1714, when Harley's political life was on the line, that "it was now high Time for the *White-Staff* to be in earnest to himself; his own Preservation, a thing he had not always listen'd much to, call'd upon him" to act against his enemies. But when the Treasurer did act, laying before the Queen the designs forming against him, Defoe conceded that he had not "altogether the success in prevailing upon her belief of the latent particulars, as was usual to him in things less concerning himself."[89] Reluctant to act on his own behalf, inept at pleading his own cause, Harley preferred to stand on his innocence, sure in the knowledge that he was right. "I am not Idle heer in preparing what I could not do in London," he wrote from the country in 1715, when he was drafting his defense for the forthcoming impeachment proceedings, "but I intirely & wholy rely upon the Goodness of God, I have done nothing but what became an honest man & a true Lover of his Country & I depend upon his Providence who is the God of Peace that integrity & uprightness shal preserve me."[90]

The double standard prevailed here as elsewhere: he was quick to defend the Queen and his colleagues—"dutifully advises his Soveraign," said Lady Orkney, "and if Things go amiss, he would rather have it thought his Mistake or any body's but hers"[91]—but he was not prepared to justify him-

---

[88] Swift, *History*, p. 74.
[89] [Defoe], *The Secret History of the White-Staff*, pp. 39, 48.
[90] Oxford to [Auditor Harley], 25 March 1715, Herefordshire R.O., Harley Papers, C64.
[91] "Lady Orkney's Character," *Swift Correspondence*, V, 224.

self, at least in personal terms, and he eschewed personal revenge. Lady Orkney's phrase is apt if ungrammatical: "Forgives, and unmindfull if his Enemy repents."[92] The point is underlined in a letter from Dr. Stratford written to Harley the year before his death. Stratford was congratulating him on his health and strength and prayed God to increase them to his Lordship.

I doubt not, but you might enjoy them in a greater measure, if your Lordship had but a small degree of that concern for your self, which your Friends and Servants have for you. We had an account from many hands of the indecent Joy upon Ld Cowpers Death. Methinks your Lordship might allow your Self one honest Piece of revenge in disappointing those, who rejoyced so at Ld Cowpers Death, of that which would be a much greater occasion of Joy to them.[93]

But Harley's Christian principles forbade revenge: "The most inveterate of my Enemys never charged me with being selfish, and they themselves are monuments of my being free from Revenge; I look upon forgiving enemys to be one of the Noblest and necessary Dutys of a Christian."[94] And these were not empty words. When his impeachment was pending, he wrote to Stratford:

I beleive you wil be told that some people hope, & others fear I should accuse them & tell what I know, I thought my conduct had convinc'd the world I am above such things.

Though I have been betraid; & insulted by libels under pretext as if I had wrote or encoragd or knowne of any of the writings pretendedly for me but in truth only to give a handle to Answers . . . yet wil not I returne the injury, but they shal find no body go further than my Self on reasonable grounds to vindicate the Queens administration; and our Constitution, without any regard to my Self.[95]

92 *Ibid.*
93 Dr. Stratford to Oxford, 28 November 1723, BM, Portland Loan, 29/158.
94 Harley to Dr. Williams, 5 August 1710 (copy), Herefordshire R.O., Harley Papers, C64.
95 Oxford to Dr. Stratford, 12 March 1715, *ibid.*, 29/171.

He did in fact draw up a reasoned vindication of the Queen's administration during his ministry but, following his own principles, he did not try to justify himself against attacks of a personal nature. And here he was at his best: on the defensive, standing on the record of his accomplishment. Several months earlier he had told his brother that, though he thought events "in all human probability" would justify the peace,

yet I foresee that the malice of those who have so often sought my life will, with the utmose rage, pursue my blood upon this account. That which is called common prudence might prompt me to avoid the storm that I see is falling upon me, but having thoroughly considered this matter, and not being conscious to myself of doing any one thing that is contrary to the interest of my country, I am come to an absolute conclusion to resign myself to the Providence of the Almighty, and not either by flight, or any other way to sully the honour of my Royal Mistress, though now in her grave, nor stain my own innocence even for an hour. . . . I am come, by the help of God, to an unalterable resolution of abiding the worst that can befal me.[96]

There is a comparable passage earlier in the Auditor's "Memoirs" describing Harley's behavior when, during his years as Secretary of State, a clerk in his office was taken up for spying, and attempts were made to implicate Harley himself.

During this whole transaction, I never observed the least discomposure in Mr. Harley; coming to him one morning, I met with Dr. Atterbury, the now Bishop of Rochester, upon the stairs. He took me aside, and said, "Your brother's head is upon the block, and yet he seems to have no concern about it, you should therefore persuade him to do something that may prevent the impending danger." This, I told my brother, who said, "I know nothing that I can do, but entirely to be resigned to, and confide in the Providence of God."[97]

Entirely resigned to the Providence of God, Harley was largely indifferent to his own safety, and his courage was

[96] Edward Harley, "Memoirs," HMC, *Portland MSS,* V, 663.
[97] *Ibid.,* p. 648.

legendary. "I think one thing very necessary," Dr. Stratford wrote in November 1712, "that my Lord Treasurer's friends should have a little care for him, since he has so little for himself. Every one is not of his Lordship's temper to live unconcerned in the midst of daggers, pistols, and subornations."[98] According to his granddaughter, the Duchess of Portland, he once received an anonymous letter that directed him to meet an unknown person in Lincoln's Inn Fields. When he got there, "it was *dark;* the man started up out of the grass *where he lay hid* (for in those times it was not paved); and said: 'Sir, now you are in my power;' 'Yes I am (said Mr. Harley), but I am not apprehensive of any thing, for I never injured any one,' *etc.,* *etc.*" The Duchess went on to relate that Harley had the man "a fortnight conceal'd in ye house, and not even ye servants knew of his being there; he learnt many things of this man relative to politics."[99] An apocryphal tale perhaps, but a true reflection of Harley's character. Long after Harley's death Pope remarked that "they were quite mistaken in his temper who thought of getting rid of him by advising him to make his escape from the Tower. He would have sat out the storm, let the danger be what it would. He was a steady man and had great firmness of soul, and would have died unconcernedly, or, perhaps like Sir Thomas More, with a jest in his mouth."[100] Harley's letters from the Tower during the period of his imprisonment confirm Pope's judgment. "Before I came into this place, I consider'd what it is to dye," he wrote in one of them, "& by Gods assistance, I wil never sacrifice my own Reputation, or the liberty of my Country to save a poor perishing Life." He had served the Protestant Succession well, "but if my Blood must be applyed to the root of that Succession, I hope

[98] Dr. Stratford to Lord Harley, 22 November 1712, HMC, *Portland MSS,* VII, 113.

[99] *The Autobiography and Correspondence of Mary Granville, Mrs. Delany,* ed. by the Rt. Hon. Lady Llanover (2nd series, London, 1862), III, 183.

[100] Spence, *Observations, Anecdotes, and Characters of Books and Men,* I, 97.

God wil Enable me to defend my self as an honest man, & to dye, as I have liv'd a true Lover of my Country."[101]

Lady Orkney perceived most acutely the element of resignation in Harley's character. "He never will tear up his own Bowells, from Despair," she wrote, "but will ever act and shew he expects a Blessing from a Superior Power for every wise Action."[102] But while he expected a blessing for every wise action, Harley also feared the disapproval of the Superior Power, which for him seems to have worn the face of the human father who watched over his young life with "holy jelosie," merged now into the figure of the heavenly father. Thus his passivity: whenever possible, it was safer to avoid action and with it the risk of incurring paternal wrath. In addition, for Harley assertion of his own authority may have appeared as a challenge to this human-divine father, and he had learned too well the lesson of submission to lay down such a challenge without fear of punishment. In any case, since the design of providence was unalterable, human action could operate only within its limitations. In the Presbyterian emphasis of his religion Harley's natural inclination found justification and safe refuge.

Harley's passivity and his deep sense of resignation lent him great strength when he was under attack: it was in the victim's role that he shone most brightly during his years in power. His reputation was never higher than after the attempt on his life in the spring of 1711, and his friends viewed his impeachment and imprisonment as perhaps the finest hours of his career—"He was a much greater Man, when the Ax was born before him," the Auditor wrote, "than when he carried the Lord high Treasurers Staff."[103] These events framed the years of his ministry. On both occasions he showed extraordinary courage

---

[101] Oxford to his brother, 13 February 1717, Longleat, Portland MSS, X, ff. 88–9.
[102] "Lady Orkney's Character," Swift Correspondence, V, 224.
[103] [Auditor Harley] to [one of his children], 7 May 1726, Herefordshire R.O., Harley Papers, C64.

in the face of danger: external events acted upon and against him, and he responded by standing his ground, facing his assailants without fear. In these two situations his fate really was in hands other than his own, and his response was appropriate. But more often this characteristic response was not appropriate. His tendency to be a willing victim, to accept unfavorable circumstances rather than try to alter them, undermined his ability to deal with political realities, particularly when some exercise of his power and authority was at issue. His natural intelligence and his extraordinary political skill were ultimately rendered ineffective by his refusal to act even when his own political future was at stake.

I I

Robert Harley had throughout his life a reputation for great learning and as a patron of learned men. "I believe there are few Examples to be produced in any Age," Swift wrote, "of a Person, who hath passed through so many Employments in the State, endowed with so great a Share both of Divine and Human Learning."[104] Swift's judgment was confirmed by Dr. George Hickes, an early student of Anglo-Saxon philology and culture and perhaps the greatest English scholar of the age. Congratulating Harley on his appointment as Secretary of State, Hickes wrote that his joy was somewhat tempered by the prospect of "losing the great benefit, and pleasure of your conversation, by wch I will ever own I have been more improved in all knowledge than by any other of the learned, wth whome I have conversed."[105] He added: "You will get credit, and honour among learned men by preferring of them, and as they have no expectations from any other persons, so I dare promise for them, you will always find them gratefull

[104] Swift, *History*, p. 75.
[105] Dr. George Hickes to Robert Harley, 20 May 1704, BM, Portland Loan, 29/146.

men, and never have occasion to repent of what you shall do for them." There is not much direct evidence of Harley's prodigious learning, but there is ample testimony for his role as a patron. Scholars wrote to ask his assistance for their projects, for permission to dedicate their works to him or to consult his library; and as Hickes had suggested, they were always grateful for his help. The learned men honored him, and with good reason, for besides accepting their fulsome dedications, he did find them places, subscribe to editions of their works, and otherwise provide for their support. He saw to it that Congreve kept his place when he was nearly blind with cataracts; Mrs. Manley, the political hack-writer he had once employed, asked for and received his charity; and his correspondence is filled with the testimonials of many more who benefited from his generosity.

Harley "was a great Favourer of Men of Witt and Learning," Swift observed, "particularly the former, whom he caressed without Distinction of Party, and could not endure to think that any of them should be his Enemies; and it was his good Fortune that none of them ever appeared to be so, at least if one may judge by the Libels and Pamphlets published against him."[106] That he enjoyed the society of learned men is clear; it is equally clear that they enjoyed his, and this is perhaps more surprising in view of his reticence and his fundamental seriousness and sobriety. Harley and Bolingbroke were both part of the literary circle which included Swift and Pope, Prior, Gay, and Arbuthnot. And though Harley was left out of the club known as "the Society" or "Brothers Club," in which many of them met to dine and converse, this seems to have been only because he was the Queen's first minister, and they feared the weight of his office would dampen the spirit of their gatherings.[107] But he spent a great deal of time with these

---

106 Swift, "An Enquiry," pp. 135–6.

107 Harley's son and one of his sons-in-law were members of the Society. In the same way, Lord Keeper Harcourt was excluded while his son was a member. Harley seems not to have been offended. He not only knew what

men; they were his devoted friends and remained so after his retirement. The letters in Swift's correspondence, and Pope's, to and from Harley and about him, leave no doubt whatever of the affection and esteem in which he was held by the literary men. In 1721 Pope wrote to Harley asking permission to dedicate an edition of Parnell's poems to him, and enclosing the dedicatory verses. Harley's reply is characteristic in its modesty, but beyond that it reveals something of his own feelings toward his literary friends.

I received your Packet, which could not but give me great Pleasure, to see you preserve an old Friend in your Memory: but it must needs be very agreable, to be remembred by those we highly value: but then how much Shame did it cost me, when I read your very fine Verses? Indeed my Mind reproached me, how far short I come of what your great Friendship & delicate Pen would partially describe me.

you ask my Consent to publish it: to what Streights does this reduce me? I look back indeed to those Evenings, I have usefully & pleasantly spent with Mr. Pope, Mr. Parnell, Dean Swift & the Doctor. [Arbuth.] etc. I should be glad the World knew you admitted me to your Friendship; and since your Affection is too hard for your Judgment, I am content to let the World know how well Mr. Pope can write upon a barren Subject.

I return you an exact Copy of the Verses, that I may keep the Original as a Testimony of the only Error you have been guilty of.[108]

The qualities that endeared Harley to these men were less visible in his public personality. Swift spoke of "the Goodness of his Humour, and agreeable Conversation in a private Capac-

---

transpired at the Society's meetings but also contributed to its support. Swift, *Journal to Stella, passim.* The Society did not meet after 1713, but Harley was a member of the much smaller Scriblerus Club started by Pope and Swift early in 1714. The other members were Arbuthnot, Parnell, and Gay. Bolingbroke, who was responsible for starting the Society, was not a member of the Scriblerus group.

[108] Oxford to Pope, 6 November 1721, BM, Add. MSS, 5834, f. 313.

ity,"[109] and Harley's correspondence, in the early years especially, at moments reveals him as a gay and charming
companion. Countless short notes from the Marquis of Halifax,
phrased in bantering, affectionate terms, concerned themselves
mostly with the pleasures of Harley's company and arrangements for their next meeting.

I would know, sir, whether after your morning sacrifice for the
public, you can allow yourself an idle part of a day so as to call
upon me at half an hour past one, and make a trip to Acton this
fine day, where we will eat a bunch of grapes to whet us for a
piece of mutton at eight of clock when we return. I would know
whether you would have a third, to be sure I want nobody when I
have Mr. Harley.[110]

Halifax was past sixty when he issued that invitation, but
Harley seems to have been as easy and as welcome among his
younger friends. "I am now going to meet with some grave
divines," wrote Henry Boyle from Cambridge, "and therefore
must not converse too long with an enemy of the church."[111]
And in 1709 George Granville assured him that "we constantly
remember you, I can't say in our prayers, for I fear we don't all
pray, but in our cups, for we all drink, and when our hearts are
most open, your image is most conspicuous."[112] Harley's
gaiety and wit, his capacity for pleasure, survived in later
years—Swift testified to this often enough—but the strain of
public life wore him down, particularly his last eighteen
months in office, when he no longer felt able to hold the
government together. Thus the image of Harley as first minister is predominantly somber: there is little in it of lightness or
charm, nothing, on the surface of things, to explain his welcome presence among the men of wit and learning.

[109] Swift, *History*, p. 75.
[110] Halifax to Mr. Harley, n.d., but among the letters of 1694, HMC,
Bath MSS, I, 51. See also HMC, *Portland MSS*, III, 544–7; and BM, Portland
Loan, 29/151.
[111] Henry Boyle to Robert Harley, 17 October 1695, HMC, *Portland
MSS*, III, 572.
[112] G. Granville to Robert Harley, 22 September 1709, *ibid.*, IV, 527.

The Harleian Library is, of course, the great monument to Harley's interest in scholarship and learning. Throughout his life, correspondents at home and abroad sent word of books and manuscripts, sometimes entire collections, worth his consideration, and supplied him as well with descriptions of new and notable buildings and recently discovered antiquities. A conscientious agent on one occasion informed him that some Latin and Spanish books had been found on a captured Spanish ship, some of which might be worthy of his library;[113] Alexander Cunningham, traveling in Europe as tutor to a young nobleman, reported regularly on the people he had met, the sights he had seen, and the purchases he had made for Harley. "Now having passed the Weser," he wrote from Berlin, "you will think I may come on politics, which I would certainly do, if I did not think antiquities, architecture, medals, and the beautiful variety of colours that are in butterflies and shells were more agreeable to you than anything I can possibly say in matters of state here."[114] But whether he described the excavations at Herculaneum or the virtuosi he encountered on his travels, the refrain was always the same: he had found rare editions of Pliny or Plautus or Homer. "The purchases I have made . . . ," he wrote from Venice, "are what England has not yet seen. No Caesar that Tonson can print is to be compared with three I have."[115]

By 1715, the year he was sent to the Tower, Harley had built a vast and valuable collection. Humfrey Wanley, his librarian—a pupil of Hickes, a great student of manuscripts, and a great Anglo-Saxon scholar in his own right—described its contents and attempted to value them in July of 1715, doubtless because Harley, uncertain of his own future, wanted an accurate reckoning of his affairs.

---

[113] John Chamberlayne to Oxford, 27 March 1712, *ibid.,* V, 155.

[114] Alexander Cunningham to Robert Harley, 16 August 1710, N.S., *ibid.,* IV, 567.

[115] Alexander Cunningham to Oxford, 13 March 1712, N.S., *ibid.,* V, 146-7. The account of the excavations at Herculaneum is in *ibid.,* IV, 672-3; and there are other letters from Cunningham scattered through *ibid.,* IV and V.

The Harleian Library consists of books, &c., printed and written. The printed part is numerous and contains books, papers, prints excellent for their age, edition, use, richness, or rarity. . . . The manuscript part (wherein I include the drawings and paintings . . .) consists of books, charters or deeds, and rolls . . . written in about twenty-six languages or dialects, and treating upon all sorts of learning and business.

Among the manuscripts, there were three thousand books, and the thirteen thousand charters and deeds "of all ages up to 900 years" comprised "the largest collection that is known to be anywhere. . . . The rolls are in number about one thousand, . . ." and "the collection of letters and papers of state, of princes, nobles, scholars, &c." was "much the best and most valuable of any now in England, excepting only that of Sir Robert Cotton."[116] Wanley calculated that Harley had spent something upwards of three thousand pounds to acquire his library, but this did not include gifts, of which there had been many.

Quite apart from his interests as a collector, Harley was committed to learning for its own sake, and he never tired of exhorting his youthful relations to study hard and well. He urged his son to make the best use of the short time he had at Christ Church, for "this is the proper & only opportunity for the studies now before you."[117] This is the same letter where he pronounced it "a very wretched thing" to be thought singular "in every thing else, but to be singular & eminent in goodness & virtue & learning." He saw knowledge, properly used, as a means to virtue. To a young friend he wrote:

I see your cheifest aime for attaining knowledg is only to make yourself better, . . . & not to make use of the knowledg you shal attain as Some People do of fine clothes to make an appearance to others. Every thing must keep its due place, outward Ornaments are to be usd for the pleasing of others: but the ornaments of a wel

---

116 *Ibid.*, V, 514-16. The Harleian and Cottonian libraries were the principal founding collections of the British Museum, established in 1753.
117 Robert Harley to his son, 1707, BM, Portland Loan, 29/143.

instructed mind, must have its effects inward, in ye regulating & wel ordering the affections & Passions.[118]

And he dispatched the following stern reprimand to his nephew and namesake, aged eleven, who must have been a very half-hearted scholar:

And will you be willing to have your school fellows hereafter say, there was Ro: Harley a boy of fine Parts but he came to nothing, by downright carelessness and Negligence? What makes a man differ from a Beast? A Wise man from a Fool? But that his Mind directs his Actions? And he that cannot bring himselfe to consider what he is a Doing: will never do any thing becoming a Gentleman or a Man. . . . In one Word, what the World calls Idiots is only a perpetual incogetancy & want of Thought.[119]

These admonitions are in many respects utterly conventional and familiar. The awful warning that young Robert's school fellows would hereafter say "there was a boy of fine Parts but he came to nothing," must have been a cliché even in 1717, though to the boy it may indeed have seemed awful, coming from his eminent uncle. But beyond these very ordinary sentiments, there is something much more stirring, and this is quite simply Harley's commitment to the cultivation of the mind as necessary to both the public and the private man. There is, furthermore, no question of his sincerity. He may have expressed himself in moral platitudes, but he believed them; and he passed on to his children and grandchildren his own convictions. Proposing to instruct his son in the practice of politics, he wrote:

for an English Gentm: or Nobleman whose fortune or Birth gives him a pretence or a right to sit in either House of one of ye *Lawmakers* wil make but a scurvy figure without a competency of that knowledg. & if a smal portion of that time our young master spends in Learning dog Language, or so much of ye several sorts of

[118] Oxford to [?], 11 August 1715, *ibid.*, 29/12.
[119] Oxford to his nephew, Robert Harley, 23 October 1717, *ibid.*, 29/166.

Games as may better fit him to be *meat* for the Birds of Prey who wil hover over his fortune, I say if he had furnishd his mind with more of ye knowledg of ye Laws & Constitutions of his Country, with what is the Duty of a good Patriot & a dutiful subject; we had not seen so many beasts of Burden in England; nor had so many owners of great fortunes & Titles been the tools [of] faction & listned so Easily to the trumpets of sedition.[120]

These views are echoed in a letter from one of Harley's daughters reporting that her eight-year-old nephew, Harley's grandson, was "a mighty fine Boy & indeed Learns very well considering how long he was kept idle. there must be some grains of allowance for such an ill habit & the diversions he meets with in the Country but I hope he will be brought to delight in his Book & that Westmr School will put Dogs & Horses out of his head wch already he begins to despise."[121] In his daughter's hope and in the little boy's inclination toward books and away from dogs and horses, Harley's influence must have played a major part.

Harley gave his family a deep respect for learning, but beyond this, his attachment to his family was one of the strongest influences in his life. He appears to have been devoted to his own father, and he was himself a most affectionate parent. His early letters, when his children were very young, reflect a concern and tenderness for them much beyond what seems then to have been the conventional, rather perfunctory interest of a father in his young progeny, or even his particular pride in a son and heir; and he showed the same affectionate concern for his grandchildren. Congratulating his son on the birth of his first child, Harley thanked God for "our Dearest Hearts safe delivery" and earnestly implored "the continuance of the same mercy in perfecting Dear Lady Henriettas re-

---

[120] A paper in Harley's hand entitled "Advice to a son," 27 August 170[9?], Nottingham University Library, Portland Collection, Pw2, Hy 839.

[121] Lady Dupplin to Mrs. Auditor Harley, 5 November 1721, BM, Portland Loan, 29/68.

covery, & in blessing the sweet Baby, wch I trust God wil long continue to you both, & that she may live to imitate her so excellent Mother. Pray give the Babe a Kiss from me, & I pray God give you much joy. . . . God bless you both & our dear Babe."[122] It should be noted that the occasion of this outpouring of joy and thanksgiving was the birth of a daughter, an event that was often a cause for condolence, particularly in the case of a first child. Harley's attitude was remarkably modern; and it was apparent to his friends. "You are the father of children and therefore can give grains of allowance to those who trouble their friends with news of this kind," wrote Francis Gwyn, announcing the birth of another son, "but if one should write such a letter to Harry Boyl or such rake hells, they would wonder what was the satisfaction a man could take in things of this sort."[123]

But the real proof of Harley's devotion to his children comes from the children themselves. His son described him as "the best and most affectionate of fathers,"[124] and his daughters agreed. They all wrote to him regularly with news of themselves and their families, and there is no mistaking the affection that fills those letters.[125] The relationship was equally close with his own brothers and sisters, though he was fondest perhaps of his unmarried sister, Abigail, to whom he wrote on her birthday in 1719: "It is a Peculiar happyness, my Dearest Sister, that I look back with pleasure at the time we have spent together thru our Childhood youth & grown Estate, every Stage of Life you have filld with endeared Affection, The only Strife that ever was between us was wch Should

---

[122] Oxford to Lord Harley, 19 February 1715, Longleat, Portland MSS, X, f. 78.

[123] Francis Gwyn to Robert Harley, 26 September 1693, HMC, *Portland MSS*, III, 543.

[124] Lord Harley to his aunt Abigail Harley, 20 March 1720, BM, Portland Loan, 29/66.

[125] See BM, Portland Loan, 29/145 and 29/146 for Robert Harley's correspondence with his son, his daughters, and his daughter-in-law.

Love each other best."[126] These expressions are characteristic of a correspondence that lasted the length of their lives.

As Harley loved his family deeply, he was deeply touched by family death. "My Lord Oxford will certainly be much concerned at your Aunt's death," Dr. Stratford wrote to Lord Harley. "If I understand him right such a domestic affliction will sit heavier upon him than an impeachment."[127] And the aunt who had died was not Harley's own sister but his brother's wife. When Harley's elder daughter, Lady Carmarthen, died in 1713, his old friend Sir Thomas Mansell wrote that the news "truly surpriz'd & greived my heart being sensible how near it has touch'd yours who are with so much reason tender of al yr Children."[128] "I pity his [Harley's] case with all my heart," Dr. Arbuthnot wrote to Swift on the same occasion, "for what ever other affliction he has been used to he is much a stranger to domestick calamitys I have a true sense of his present condition for which I know philosophy & religion are both too weak. . . . I know My lord has the sentiment of humanity & paternall affection very strong, and I should not love him so well if he had not."[129] And Lady Harley, offering her condolences, spoke of her sister-in-law as "so desireable a person to her whole family; particularly to your Lordship that is so affectionate a parent to all your children."[130]

Harley was extremely popular with all children, not just his own, and his young relations and friends seem to have enjoyed corresponding with him as much as he with them. He adored his granddaughter, Lady Margaret Harley, and her letters to him are clearly more than the stiff communications of a dutiful

[126] Oxford to his sister Abigail Harley, 20 December 1719, BM, Portland Loan, 29/67.
[127] Dr. Stratford to Lord Harley, 2 July 1721, HMC, *Portland MSS*, VII, 301.
[128] Sir Thomas Mansel to Oxford, 26 November 1713, BM, Portland Loan, 29/151.
[129] Arbuthnot to Swift, November 1713, *Swift Correspondence*, I, 409.
[130] Henrietta C. H. Harley to Oxford, November 1713, BM, Portland Loan, 29/145.

and obedient child. A niece, another Abigail Harley, played at being his servant, addressing him as "My Lord and Master" and signing herself "your most dutiful Maid." On one occasion she enclosed an amusing letter from her brother, "in hopes it may make your Lordship laugh."[131] And the following epistle, without date and written in a large and childish hand, was directed "For My Dear Godfather":

I dont care if King Georg and all his Councell knows it that I love you Dearley beg your Blessing and am

Your Dutyfull
God daughter
Ann Granville[132]

With his family and with children Harley was accessible in a way he never seems to have been with his friends and associates: within the safety of this close circle his habitual wariness gave way to trust. In the public view his commitment to his family placed him squarely on the side of those good old virtues so celebrated by the gentlemen of England. As a private man he was wholly reassuring, the personification of the most admirable, the least questionable values in English life. Politically this should have been an incalculable asset: in fact it was to a great extent countered by his less fortunate public postures and by an approach to politics that eventually alienated a great part of his constituency.

131 *Ibid.*, 29/139.
132 Ann Granville to Oxford, n.d., *ibid.*, 29/137.

CHAPTER II

Henry St. John,

VISCOUNT BOLINGBROKE

HERE are particular difficulties in writing about Bolingbroke[1] in the years before 1715 when he was active in politics. He held office twice, from 1704 to 1708 as Secretary-at-War when Robert Harley was Secretary of State; and again from 1710 to 1714 as Secretary of State in Harley's ministry. He was appointed Secretary-at-War when he was twenty-six years old and thus was only thirty-six when he left office for the last time. Yet he lived on for nearly forty years, barred from active participation in politics by the House of Commons' refusal to reverse all the penalties of his attainder, never entirely abandoning hope of the full pardon that would enable him to resume his seat in the House of Lords and his political career. The years of his exile in France, enforced until 1723 when the conviction of high treason was revoked, voluntary after 1735, were broken by ten years' residence in England when, with enormous energy and considerable success, he directed the opposition campaign against Walpole. But while he lived in France he wrote a great deal on politics, history, and philosophy; and he corresponded on these and other matters with his friends on the continent and in England. Many of his works were framed as letters to friends, and much of his

---

[1] Henry St. John was raised to the peerage as Viscount Bolingbroke in July 1712. He is commonly known by his title, and in this sketch, which ranges over his whole life, I refer to him throughout as Bolingbroke.

regular correspondence reads as if it were designed for a wider audience than the particular person addressed. But through all his writing, essays and letters alike, the theme of self-justification runs strong: one is always aware of Bolingbroke's need to set the record straight, to justify his past conduct and his present circumstances before the world and for posterity. This obsessive concern with his public reputation led him frequently to distort, sometimes to falsify,[2] the record of his years in office. What emerges from the body of his writings is Bolingbroke's view of Bolingbroke; and while this is no doubt exactly what he intended, it leaves later generations with the problem of extricating him from the likeness he drew of himself. The image he chose to project is, of course, a key to the man; and my intention here is not to ignore it, which is in any case impossible, but rather to use it as a means of investigating his character and conduct. The further question is why he felt so strong a need to justify himself.

There is a second problem in dealing with Bolingbroke, and this is the absence of any substantial body of personal papers for the period before 1715. Some letters to friends and political

---

[2] The obvious instance of outright prevarication is his flat denial that he was in touch with the Pretender before Queen Anne's death. The Stuart Papers published by the Historical Manuscripts Commission confirm that Bolingbroke was in correspondence with James, and he admits as much in the "Letter to Sir William Windham," which was written in 1716: "I cannot forget, nor you neither, what passed when a little before the death of the queen, letters were conveyed from the Chevalier to several persons, to myself among others." Much later, in his account "Of the State of Parties at the Accession of King George the First," he not only asserted "that there was no design on foot, during the last four years of queen Anne's reign," to bring in the Pretender; but also, in evasive phrases, claimed that he did not know, "or at least I knew it not with the same certainty, and in the same detail, that I have known it since," that "there were particular men, who corresponded indirectly, and directly too, with the Pretender, and with others for his service." *The Works of Lord Bolingbroke* (Philadelphia, 1841), I, 168; II, 430–1. Hereafter cited as Bolingbroke, *Works;* all references are to this edition unless otherwise indicated. The editor misspells Sir William Wyndham's name, "Wyndham" was the usual contemporary spelling, and the *Dictionary of National Biography* does not give the alternative form for this particular family of Wyndhams.

associates exist—H. T. Dickinson, his recent biographer, would appear to have tracked down virtually all of them.[3] But for Bolingbroke there is nothing to compare with the extensive Harley family correspondence, which affords an insight into Robert Harley's attitudes and actions over the course of a lifetime. The fuller correspondence of the years after 1715, especially after 1735, reveals Bolingbroke preoccupied with justifying himself. These letters are almost all characterized by some degree of affectation: they are self-conscious in attitude and phrasing, seldom free from an element of pose, though the pose may be that of the man of feeling letting his emotions run free. Even when he was writing to his oldest friends, he was conscious of the impression he wanted to create. The style raises a point immediately relevant to the idiosyncrasies of Bolingbroke's career. In his letters, in fact in all of his writing, the element of contrivance, of purposeful control casts doubts on his sincerity. Carried over into politics, it explains at least in part why men were not inclined to trust him; and his inability to inspire trust accounted for many of his difficulties in politics.

There is a striking exception to this general characterization of Bolingbroke's epistolary style, and this is the series of letters he wrote to his half-sister, Henrietta St. John. A child of his father's second marriage, she was twenty years younger than her illustrious elder brother. She loved and admired him through all his changing fortunes, and he repaid her loyalty with deep affection and unremitting concern for her well-being during the difficulties she encountered in her own life. His letters to her are affectionate and charming. Strikingly free of affectation, they afford a rare glimpse of Bolingbroke relaxed from his pose, for a moment less conscious of the role he had to play.[4] The tenderness and charm of the letters to Henrietta

[3] H. T. Dickinson, *Bolingbroke* (London: Constable, 1970).
[4] The correspondence of Bolingbroke and Henrietta St. John is in the British Museum, Add. MSS, 34196. Extracts of Bolingbroke's half are printed in the appendix to Walter Sichel, *Bolingbroke and His Times* (New York, 1902), II.

also marked whatever he wrote of his second wife, Madame de Villette. His attachment to her was probably the strongest of his life, and when he spoke of her his feelings were clear and undisguised. The quality of Bolingbroke's relationship with these two women seems to have been extremely rare for him. Presumably he felt totally sure of their loyal support: neither would question his motives or his actions, he would not be called upon to justify or explain. Less anxious about his public reputation, he had less need to maintain his public face.

I I

The St. John family traced its ancestry back to the days before the Conquest, and Bolingbroke was proud of his aristocratic birth. In the Civil War the family's allegiance was divided between Parliament and King, but two of its branches were reconciled when Bolingbroke's royalist grandfather, Walter St. John, married his cousin Joanna, daughter of Oliver St. John, who was Chief Justice of common pleas under Cromwell. Their son, Henry St. John, married Lady Mary Rich, daughter of the Earl of Warwick. Bolingbroke, the only child of this marriage, was born in 1678.[5] His mother died shortly thereafter and he probably grew up in the family house at Battersea, where he lived with his father and his paternal grandparents. His father was a notorious rake whom fortune rather outrageously favored through a long and boisterous life—he received an earldom from George I and survived in cantankerous good health until 1742—and Bolingbroke seems to have been brought up principally by his grandmother, a lady whose Presbyterian sympathies are said to have influenced his early education. There is, according to Dickinson, "precious little

[5] Dickinson, reviewing the meager evidence for Bolingbroke's early years and correcting the inaccuracies of earlier biographers, puts together a tentative account, which I follow here. (*Bolingbroke,* pp. 1-4.)

evidence" that he went either to Eton or to Christ Church, Oxford, as has often been claimed; it is equally possible that he attended a Dissenting Academy.[6] At any rate, when he had finished his formal education he traveled abroad, where he found time to observe the politics and customs of the continent as well as to savor its pleasures.[7] In 1700 he married Frances Winchcomb, the daughter of Sir Henry Winchcomb of Berkshire, a man of considerable fortune. She brought her husband a large settlement, including the estate of Bucklebury, near Reading, where they lived together with her sister. Beyond these few pieces of information, nothing is known of Bolingbroke's early years. It is not until after his marriage and his entrance into Parliament that a somewhat fuller view of him is possible.

In November 1711, just a year after he first met Henry St. John, Swift gave Stella a dazzling account of the young Secretary of State. St. John, he said, was "the greatest young man I ever knew; . . . His only fault is talking to his friends in way of complaint of too great a load of business, which looks a little like affectation; and he endeavours too much to mix the fine gentleman, and man of pleasure, with the man of business."[8] Several years later Swift described Bolingbroke as

fond of mixing Pleasure and Business, and of being esteemed excellent at both. . . . His Detractors charged him with some Degree of Affectation, and perhaps not altogether without Grounds, since it was hardly possible for a young Man with half the Business of the Nation upon him, and the Applause of the whole to escape some Tincture of that Infirmity.[9]

Lord Orrery began his character of Bolingbroke: "Lord B had early made himself Master of Books and Men: But in his first

---

[6] *Ibid.*, pp. 2–3.
[7] See Bolingbroke's letters to Sir William Trumbull in HMC, *Downshire MSS*, I, ii, 777, 783, 785, 790–4.
[8] Swift, *Journal to Stella*, II, 401.
[9] Swift, "An Enquiry," pp. 134–5.

Career of Life, being immersed at once in Business and Pleasure, he ran through a Variety of Scenes in a surprizing and eccentric Manner."[10] Bolingbroke's ability in business and his intellectual capacities were by all accounts superior, and his talents brought him public recognition at an early age. "I am thinking what a veneration we used to have for sir William Temple, because he might have been secretary of state at fifty," Swift wrote; "and here is a young fellow, hardly thirty in that employment."[11] In 1711 Marlborough thought that among the Queen's ministers "only the Secretary of State, St. John, applies himself to business and, as he has ability, he will master it. . . . In council he speaks to Her Majesty more boldly than anyone else."[12] According to Swift, the Secretary's mind "was adorned with the choicest Gifts that God hath yet thought fit to bestow upon the Children of Men; a strong Memory, a clear Judgment, a vast Range of Wit and Fancy, a thorow Comprehension, an invincible Eloquence, with a most agreeable Elocution. . . . He had been early bred to Business, was a most Artfull Negotiator, and perfectly understood foreign Affairs."[13] Lord Chesterfield observed that

notwithstanding the dissipation of his youth, and tumultuous agitation of his middle age, he has an infinite fund of various and almost

---

[10] [David Mallet], *Memoirs of the Life and Ministerial Conduct, with Some free Remarks on the Political Writings, of the Late Lord Visc. Bolingbroke* (London, 1752), pp. 345-6. This character of Bolingbroke, "drawn by an able and noble Pen, and which appeared about the Time he died, or, at least, a very little before it," was printed in the *Memoirs* but the able and noble pen was not identified. It was printed again in Mallet's edition of Bolingbroke's works, this time under Lord Orrery's name. *The Works of the late Right Honorable Henry St. John, Lord Viscount Bolingbroke*, published by David Mallet, Esq (London, 1777), I, lvii. Mallet, a writer of very mediocre talents, was Bolingbroke's literary executor and published the first edition of his works in 1754.

[11] Swift, *Journal to Stella*, I, 92.

[12] O. Klopp, *Der Fall des Hauses Stuart* (Vienna, 1887), XIV, 673. The Hanoverian Ambassador Robethon's report from The Hague to Bernstorff in Hanover, of a conversation with Marlborough, 21 March 1711, N.S.

[13] Swift, "An Enquiry," pp. 134-5.

universal knowledge, which, from the clearest and quickest conception, and happiest memory, that ever man was blessed with, he carries about him. It is his pocket-money, and he never has occasion to draw upon a book for any sum. . . . He engaged young, and distinguished himself in business; and his penetration was almost intuition.[14]

With all these gifts, Bolingbroke had also a great capacity for work. "But what I have often wondred at in a Man of his Temper," said Swift, "was his prodigious Application whenever he thought it necessary; For he would plod whole Days and Nights like the lowest Clerk in an Office."[15]

Of Bolingbroke's ability and application testaments abound; and the direct evidence from his letters and dispatches first as Secretary-at-War, then as Secretary of State, amply justifies his reputation. His correspondence with both subordinates and superiors, with England's representatives abroad, with her allies, and with France, reveals a sure grasp of the issues, a remarkable capacity for analysis, and an elegant yet forceful prose-style. There is no comparable direct evidence for Bolingbroke's much praised skill as a public speaker, for with the exception of a few inconsequential fragments, his parliamentary speeches have not been preserved. Swift termed him "the best orator in the house of commons,"[16] and later commented that "his Talent of Speaking in publick, for which he was so very much celebrated, I know nothing of except from the Information of Others; But understanding Men of both Parties have assured me, that in this Point, in their Memory and Judgment he was never equalled."[17] Chesterfield was one of those who remembered:

[14] "Lord Chesterfield's Character of Lord Bolingbroke," printed in Mallet's edition of Bolingbroke's *Works*, I, liii.

[15] Swift, "An Enquiry," p. 135. Dickinson comments that Bolingbroke was "sufficiently astute as a politician to know that work meant power" (*Bolingbroke*, p. 45).

[16] Swift, *Journal to Stella*, II, 401.

[17] Swift, "An Enquiry," p. 135.

I am old enough to have heard him speak in Parliament. And I remember, that, though prejudiced against him by party, I felt all the force and charms of his eloquence. Like Belial, in Milton,
"He made the worse appear the better cause."
All the internal and external advantages and talents of an orator are undoubtedly his; figure, voice, elocution, knowledge, and, above all, the purest and most florid diction, with the justest metaphors, and happiest images, had raised him to the post of Secretary at War, at four-and-twenty years old; an age at which others are hardly thought fit for the smallest employments.[18]

Bolingbroke's gifts as an orator together with his mastery of business made him a formidable figure in the House of Commons. Once Harley had gone to the upper House, there was no reason to quarrel with Swift's judgment that "the Secrty is much the greatest Commoner in Engld, . . . and if he lives & has his health, will I believe be one day at the Head of Affairs."[19]

"If he lives and has his health . . .": long life and health were precarious at best in the eighteenth century, but in the case of Bolingbroke, Swift's reservation had more than conventional significance. The existence Bolingbroke chose for himself was by definition strenuous, and to have survived it so well he must have numbered an uncommonly strong constitution among his natural endowments. By his own account, the man of business worked long and late. The press of affairs in the Secretaryship was great, and the burden of Bolingbroke's Northern Department—there were in the early eighteenth century two Secretaries of State, one for the Northern and one for the Southern Department—was much increased by his role in the management of the peace negotiations. In 1709, following the Union, a third Secretary was appointed to deal primarily with Scottish affairs, but the office remained vacant for two years after the death of the first incumbent, and its business reverted to the Northern Department. "The load was

---

[18] "Lord Chesterfield's Character," Bolingbroke, *Works,* ed. by Mallet, I, lv.

[19] Swift, *Journal to Stella,* II, 495.

before great enough for shoulders as weak as mine," Bolingbroke wrote following the Scottish Secretary's death, "it is
now not a little increased. If I stagger under it, I will, however,
hope not to sink."[20] Several months later he told the Earl of
Orrery: "To another it would be affectation, to you I may say
with the freedom of a friend, that I am half murdered with a
load of business, in comparison of which all that I ever went
through in my life is a trifle."[21]

The Secretary appears to have risen early and retired late.
Swift complained on more than one occasion that the Secretary
summoned him so early he had to go without shaving;[22] and
during the final crucial phase of the peace negotiations Bolingbroke himself made constant reference to the long hours he was
forced to keep. In a note accompanying a long dispatch to the
Duke of Shrewsbury, then serving as Ambassador Extraordinary to France, he apologized for not answering Shrewsbury's
private letters: "But it is so extremely late, and I am so thoroughly spent, that I must beg your Grace to excuse me, till the
next opportunity of writing."[23] His communications to Prior,
also in Paris on the business of the peace, frequently concluded
with the same refrain: he would have spoken to the Lord
Treasurer on Prior's behalf, "but I have been tied to my desk
till three in the morning, at which hour I am writing to you."[24]

[20] Bolingbroke to Whitworth, 12 July 1711, *Letters and Correspondence,
Public and Private, of the Right Honourable Henry St. John, Lord Visc.
Bolingbroke; during the time he was Secretary of State to Queen Anne,*
ed. by Gilbert Parke (London, 1798), I, 269. Hereafter cited as *Bolingbroke
Correspondence.* The Duke of Queensberry, the Scottish Secretary, died July
6, 1711. The Northern Department originally included the countries of
Northern Europe and Scotland, while the Southern Secretary theoretically
presided over Britain's relations with Southern Europe and the colonies. The
negotiations with France thus fell officially within the Southern Department.
The third Secretary was to handle Scottish affairs and relations with Russia
and the Baltic powers.
[21] Bolingbroke to Orrery, 25 September 1711, *ibid.,* I, 365.
[22] Swift, *Journal to Stella,* I, 155, 158.
[23] Bolingbroke to Shrewsbury, 17 February 1713, *Bolingbroke Correspondence,* III, 440.
[24] Bolingbroke to Prior, 3 March 1713, *ibid.,* p. 464.

Or: "Adieu; whether I have writ sense or not, you will know, I am sure I do not; the incessant labor of four or five days, at committees, at conferences, in dictating, in writing, has almost crazed, your faithful friend, Bolingbroke."[25]

Swift had said the Secretary was capable of prodigious application "whenever he thought it necessary," and throughout the Utrecht negotiations he apparently thought it necessary much of the time. If his talk of too much business looked like affectation, it was in part because he played the man of pleasure too well. This was in part a matter of principle. Bolingbroke is reported to have said on one occasion that "he was persuaded no one could ever distinguish himself, and make his way in life . . . unless he had been a rake, or at least had the seeds of a rake in him," a remark which the company present took to be a "compliment upon himself, as showing abilities and rakery were so conspicuously united in Lord Bolingbroke's own character."[26] According to Chesterfield, Bolingbroke's "youth was distinguished by all the tumult and storm of pleasures, in which he most licentiously triumphed, disdaining all decorum. His fine imagination has often been heated and exhausted with his body, in celebrating and deifying the prostitute of the night; and his convivial joys were pushed to all the extravagancy of frantic Bacchanals."[27] David Mallet, Bolingbroke's friend and later his literary executor, concurred in slightly less flamboyant prose. As a young man, Bolingbroke's character, he said, was "exposed thro' great Blemishes, that is, from Libertinism in a very high Degree. He was much addicted to Women, was apt to indulge himself in late Hours, with all those Excesses that usually attend them."[28] Swift observed that "he had indeed been too great and Crimi-

[25] Bolingbroke to Prior, 19 January 1713, *ibid.,* p. 306.

[26] G. Harris, *The Life of Lord Chancellor Hardwicke* (London, 1847), II, 182-3.

[27] "Lord Chesterfield's Character," Bolingbroke, *Works,* ed. by Mallet, I, liv.

[28] [Mallet], *Memoirs of the Life and Ministerial Conduct, . . . of the Late Lord Visc. Bolingbroke,* p. 33.

nall a Pursuer" of his pleasures,[29] and Goldsmith said he had "spoke to an old man, who assured me that he saw him and another of his companions run naked through the Park, in a fit of intoxication."[30] Of Bolingbroke's addiction to women there is no doubt. He wrote of whores and whoring to his friend Tom Coke,[31] but he bestowed his attentions on women of higher station as well. He dazzled the ladies of Paris when he went there on government business in 1712 and was rumored to have taken for his mistress Madame de Ferriol, and perhaps her sister Madame de Tencin as well. His eye for beauty and charm in women was celebrated. Prior, thanking him for assistance to a young relation, could "not imagine how you came to know that snudging boy, for his mother is very homely."[32]

Bolingbroke himself confirmed the general view. In 1723 he wrote to Swift: "I have been then infinitely more uniform and less dissipated, than when you knew me and cared for me; that Love which I used to scatter with some Profusion, among the whole Female Kind, has been these many Years devoted to One Object."[33] The One Object was Bolingbroke's second wife, the Marquise de Villette, whom he had lived with since the first years of his exile and married in 1722. This second marriage was a marriage of love and it prospered: Bolingbroke's devotion to the Marquise was complete. But the period of his domestic happiness fell entirely outside his years in office, and it followed a conspicuously unsuccessful first marriage. His first wife was by all accounts a handsome and intelligent woman, but his infidelities and neglect of her were notorious: among his friends as well as her own she soon became "poor Mrs. St.

29 Swift, "An Enquiry," p. 134.

30 Oliver Goldsmith, "The Life of Henry St. John, Lord Viscount Bolingbroke," *Collected Works of Oliver Goldsmith*, ed. by Arthur Friedman (Oxford: The Clarendon Press, 1966), III, 439.

31 Henry St. John to Thomas Coke, 16 October 1704 and 28 May 1705, HMC, *Cowper MSS*, III, 49, 61.

32 Prior to Bolingbroke, 13–24 July 1713, *Bolingbroke Correspondence*, IV, 199.

33 Bolingbroke to Swift, August 1723, *Swift Correspondence*, II, 460.

John." In 1711 Dr. Stratford spoke of visiting "a poor discon-
solate lady in Berkshire. I met nothing there but sorrow and
disorder."[34] The following year Lady Bolingbroke's uncle,
writing for his niece, thanked Thomas Coke for his letter and
hoped he and his lady would stop by Bucklebury on their way
from Bath: "And if you should all happen to join in a visit to
the melancholy lady of this mansion, it will be a mighty
aggravation of the favour both to her Ladyship and her unworthy scribe, but your most humble servant."[35]

Surprisingly perhaps, Lady Bolingbroke was devoted to her
husband, and she remained fiercely loyal to him after his flight
from England.[36] In the spring of 1716, after he had been dismissed from the Pretender's service, she answered a letter from
Swift, who had written to inquire about Bolingbroke: "Do not
forsake an old friend, nor believe reports which are scandalous
and false. . . . As to my temper, if it is possible, I am more
insipid and dull than ever, except in some places, and there I am
a little fury, especially if they mention my dear Lord without
respect, which sometimes happens."[37] Lady Bolingbroke's devotion very sensibly stopped short of money matters. Through
the King's favor, she recovered for herself the Bucklebury
estate, originally part of the inheritance she brought to Bolingbroke but forfeit as a consequence of his attainder. When she
died in 1718, she left Bucklebury and what little remained of
her private fortune to a nephew, bypassing her husband entirely. It is difficult to see why she should have reconveyed any
of her estate to Bolingbroke. Her inheritance had supported
him since their marriage, she knew he was openly living with

[34] Dr. Stratford to Lord Harley, 18 July 1711, HMC, *Portland MSS,*
VII, 39.

[35] Edward Hungerford to Thomas Coke, 27 September 1712, HMC,
Cowper MSS, III, 103–4.

[36] See especially Swift, *Journal to Stella,* I, 238–9; and Dr. Stratford to
Lord Harley, 4 September 1714, HMC, *Portland MSS,* VII, 203.

[37] Viscountess Bolingbroke to Swift, 5 May 1716, *Swift Correspondence,*
II, 199–200. See also Viscountess Bolingbroke to Swift, 4 August 1716, *ibid.,*
p. 212.

Madame de Villette in France, and his legal situation was extremely uncertain. The Act of Attainder and all its penalties still stood, and while they remained in force, he could not hold property in England. Yet Bolingbroke was outraged and denounced his wife in tones of injured innocence. In his view she was apparently expected to reward his years of neglect by endowing his marriage to her successor.[38]

So much for Bolingbroke's addiction to women. Mallet spoke also of "late Hours, with all those Excesses that usually attend them."[39] and Swift of the Secretary's "Intemperance in Wine."[40] With Bolingbroke as with Harley late nights were the rule rather than the exception, and Swift found it difficult to break away. Frequently he was asked to dine in order to do business, but the event usually turned out otherwise. On a typical day, Swift spent the morning with the Secretary,

and we were to dine at Mr. Harley's alone, about some business of importance; but there were two or three gentlemen there. Mr. secretary and I went together from his office to Mr. Harley's, and thought to have been very wise; but the deuce a bit, the company staid, and more came, and Harley went away at seven, and the secretary and I staid with the rest of the company till eleven; I would then have had him come away, but he was in for't; and though he swore he would come away at that flask, there I left him. I wonder at the civility of these people; when he saw I would

38 For the denunciation of his wife, see Bolingbroke to Mme. de Ferriol, 6 December 1718, Sichel, *Bolingbroke and His Times*, II, 485–6. According to Dr. Stratford, "Bolingbroke when he left England reconveyed all his wife's estate to her; she immediately conveyed it to Lord Stawell and Sir William Wyndham for the payment of his debts, etc., giving the inheritance to Packer's eldest son [her nephew]. All this was done for his benefit with his consent. By this settlement the Government could not come in upon that estate till the debts were answered." Dr. Stratford is not a friendly witness, but if his version of the will is correct, Bolingbroke's attitude was still more outrageous. Dr. Stratford to Lord Harley, 23 December 1725, HMC, *Portland MSS*, VII, 410–11. See also the letter of 14 December 1725, *ibid.*, p. 409.

39 [Mallet], *Memoirs of the Life and Ministerial Conduct, . . . of the Late Lord Visc. Bolingbroke*, p. 33.

40 Swift, "An Enquiry," p. 134.

drink no more, he would always pass the bottle by me, and yet I could not keep the toad from drinking himself, nor would he let me go neither, nor Masham, who was with us.[41]

On this occasion Swift commented that "the secretary was in a drinking humour," but he must have been in a drinking humor much of the time. Mrs. Delany remembered "Lord Boling-broke's person, that he was handsome, had a fine address, but he was a great drinker, and swore terribly. She remember'd his coming once to her uncle Sr John Stanley's at Northend, his being very drunk, and going to ye greenhouse, where he threw himself upon a couch; a message arrived to say he was *waited for* at ye Council; he rous'd himself, snatch'd up his green bag of paper, and flew to business." Mr. Bryant, one of the company who heard this tale, replied "that the people used to say no man ever was so *early* and so active as Lord B. when he was in *place.* Ye truth was that he used to sit up drinking all night, and not having been in bed, he used to put a wet napkin on his forehead and eyes to cool the heat and headache occasioned by his intemperance, and then he appear'd and attend'd to business with as much ease as if he lived ye most temperate life!"[42] On more than one occasion Swift found the Secretary "very ill with the gravel and pain in his back, by Burgundy and Champagne, added to the sitting up all night at business; I found him drinking tea while the rest were at Champagne, and was very glad of it. I have chid him so severely that I hardly knew whether he would take it well."[43] Swift dined with him the following day: "I would not let him drink one drop of Champagne or Burgundy without water, and in compliment I did so myself. He is much better, but when he is well he is like Stella, and will not be governed."[44]

Though Swift was greatly flattered to be included in such

[41] Swift, *Journal to Stella,* I, 169.
[42] *The Autobiography and Correspondence of Mary Granville, Mrs. Delany,* 2nd series, III, 168.
[43] Swift, *Journal to Stella,* I, 237.
[44] *Ibid.,* p. 238.

illustrious company, he viewed the regime followed by his ministerial companions with a mixture of exasperation and awe. Sometimes he was philosophical: "I was again busy with the Secrty: . . . we read over some Papers, and did a good deal of Business; and I dind with him, & we were to do more business after dinner. But after dinner is after dinner—An old saying and a true, Much drinking little thinking; We had company with us, and nothing could be done, & I am to go there again tomorrow."[45] More often his exasperation was apparent:

The Devil's in this secretary; when I went this morning he had people with him; but says he, We are to dine with Prior to-day; at two Prior sends word, he is otherwise engaged; then the secretary and I go and dine with brigadier Britton, sit till eight, grow merry, no business done; he is in haste to see lady Jersey, we part, and appoint no time to meet again. This is the fault of all the present ministers, teazing me to death for my assistance, laying the whole weight of their affairs upon it, yet slipping opportunities.[46]

Swift's resentment at being taken for granted, perhaps trifled with, is clear. But beyond that, his comments reflect a kind of uneasiness at what seemed to him a lack of urgency and seriousness in the ministers' conduct. "I cannot but think they have mighty difficulties upon them," he wrote to Stella; "yet I always find them as easy and disengaged as schoolboys on a holiday."[47] In this remark there is a note of admiration but of skepticism as well. The easy and disengaged manner made Swift somewhat uncomfortable, presumably because he found it inappropriate for ministers of state to behave like schoolboys on holiday. Swift spoke of Harley as well as Bolingbroke, but while Harley stayed up as late and drank as much as the Secretary, in every other respect his private life was blameless. But Bolingbroke, while he cannot have been more strenuous in his

45 *Ibid.*, II, 498–9.
46 *Ibid.*, p. 398.
47 *Ibid.*, I, 162–3. Cf. Pope on Oxford: "He used to send trifling verses from court to the Scriblerus Club almost every day, and would come and talk idly with them almost every night, even when his all was at stake." Spence, *Observations, Ancedotes, and Characters of Books and Men*, I, 95.

pursuit of women than any number of his friends, carried on his amorous activities so publicly that they could not be ignored and openly treated his wife badly enough to create something of a public scandal. Swift was a sophisticated observer, and hardly prudish, yet Bolingbroke's behavior offended his sense of propriety. He minded that instead of doing business, the Secretary grew merry and made haste to see Lady Jersey. And the same tone of resignation and disapproval—though perhaps disapproval is too strong a word—was evident when he wrote that "Lord Radnor and I were walking the Mall this evening; and Mr. secretary met us and took a turn or two, and then stole away, and we both believed it was to pick up some wench; and tomorrow he will be at the cabinet with the queen: so goes the world."[48]

The Secretary's habits did not please the Queen. When Bolingbroke went to the House of Lords, Swift thought it was the Queen who refused him the earldom he hoped for, "because to say the Truth, he was not much at that time in her good Graces; some Women about the Court, having infused an Opinion into her that he was not so regular in his Life as He ought to be."[49] Whether or not this view was correct, it is true that Bolingbroke never gained the Queen's confidence and equally that the Queen was deeply religious and much concerned with matters of morality. She must have been aware of Bolingbroke's reputation, and she can only have disapproved. Shortly before Oxford's resignation in 1714, Dr. Stratford, hearing that Bolingbroke had begged his wife's "pardon for all his ill usage and promised amendment for the future," wondered if he had been advised to do so "to answer objections in the world, and that somebody may with a better grace confide in him."[50] "Somebody" was, of course, the Queen.

Bolingbroke's attitude to religion cannot have helped his reputation. The nature of his religious beliefs, that he was a

---

[48] Swift, *Journal to Stella,* I, 339.
[49] Swift, "An Enquiry," p. 151.
[50] Dr. Stratford to Lord Harley, 1 July 1714, HMC, *Portland MSS,* VII, 193.

deist if he was anything at all and strongly anti-Christian, is not the issue here. Though some of his friends knew his views, the writings in which he expressed them were not published during his lifetime; and as they were all written after 1715, they could not even have circulated privately while he was in office.[51] The point is that, though politically aligned with the Church party, he did not trouble to observe the rudimentary forms of piety, except when the law required it. "I was early with the secretary to-day," Swift wrote, "but he was gone to his devotions, and to receive the sacrament; several rakes did the same; it was not for piety, but employments; according to the act of parliament."[52]

Bolingbroke's private conduct would scarcely have mattered had he not been Secretary of State or had he acted with reasonable discretion. But he consistently violated the standards of behavior commonly expected of a man in his station, and by not attempting to conceal his dissipations, he seemed to flaunt them. Count Gallas, the Imperial Ambassador, wrote that "he is given to the bottle and debauchery to the point of almost making a virtue out of his open affectation that public affairs are a bagatelle to him, and that his capacity is on so high a level that he has no need to give up his pleasures in the slightest degree for any cause."[53] And Dr. Stratford observed: "This post [Secretary of State] was the last remedy; since that cannot restrain him from extravagances at least, it would be foolish to think anything can ever alter him."[54] In the public

[51] For Bolingbroke's denunciation of the Scriptures and his contempt for the Judaeo-Christian tradition, see especially Books III and IV of "Letters on the Study and Use of History," the last section of "A Letter to Sir William Windham," on the issue of the Pretender's religion; the "Letters . . . to M. De Pouilly," and "Essays Addressed to Alexander Pope, Esq.," passim. Bolingbroke, Works.

[52] Swift, Journal to Stella, II, 420-1.

[53] Count Gallas's report, 17 July 1711, quoted in Winston S. Churchill, Marlborough: His Life and Times (New York: Scribner's, 1933-8), VI, 478.

[54] Dr. Stratford to Lord Harley, 12 April 1711, HMC, Portland MSS, VII, 29.

view, the man of pleasure overshadowed and undermined the man of business: ordinary Englishmen looked for more solidity and substance in a minister of state. This is the point Erasmus Lewis was making when, in the summer of 1714, he wrote Swift that Bolingbroke's "character is to bad to carry the great Ensigns."[55] Mallet observed of Bolingbroke's indulgences that "these were his Failings, his Genius and his Understanding were great."[56] But in the political sphere genius and understanding were not enough. More often than not, extraordinary ability created suspicion, unless it was anchored to more reassuring qualities, and there was little in Bolingbroke's character to reassure. In view of his political ambition, one wonders whether he was aware of the extent to which the notoriety of his indulgences affected his public standing. Speaker Onslow remarked that Bolingbroke was not thought "to know enough of the real temper and constitution of [his] own country."[57] As there was nothing random about the personality he chose to project, one can only conclude that in this instance he misjudged the temper of his countrymen. His private conduct offended against the forms of public life and cast doubts on his sincerity.

Of Bolingbroke's ambition there was no doubt, though his contemporaries viewed it in varying lights. Chesterfield, con-

<hr />

55 E. Lewis to Swift, 6 July 1714, *Swift Correspondence,* II, 53–4.

56 [Mallet], *Memoirs of the Life and Ministerial Conduct, . . . of the Late Lord Visc. Bolingbroke,* p. 33.

57 "Speaker Onslow's Remarks on Various Parts of Sir Robert Walpole's Conduct, and Anecdotes of the Principal Leaders of the Opposition," printed in William Coxe, *Memoirs of the Life and Administration of Sir Robert Walpole, Earl of Orford* (London, 1798), II, 567–8. Hereafter cited as Coxe, *Walpole.* Arthur Onslow was Speaker of the House of Commons from 1728 to 1761, and an old political enemy of Bolingbroke. He wrote on Bolingbroke and Carteret together, saying that "as I know not enough of them to be very particular in their characters, I shall only describe them as they were generally spoken of." His comments were written after Bolingbroke's death, but, taken as he offered them, they provide an interesting indication of the impression Bolingbroke made on some of his contemporaries, most of whom were probably his political opponents.

cluding his florid account of Bolingbroke's "frantic Bacchanals," went on to say that "those passions were interrupted but
by a stronger, Ambition. The former impaired both his constitution and his character, but the latter destroyed both his
fortune and his reputation."[58] Speaker Onslow echoed this
judgment, describing Bolingbroke as "of unbounded spirit and
ambition, impatient of restraint, contemning the notion of
equality with others in business, and even disdaining to be any
thing if not the first and highest in power. . . . the lord
Bolingbroke was of a temper to overturn kingdoms to make
way for himself and his talents to govern the world."[59] Swift
observed simply, and perhaps more justly, that the Secretary
"was not without Ambition, which I confess I have seldom
found among the wants of great Men."[60] And Bolingbroke
himself, many years after his retirement from office, admitted:
"I have been fond of power, and as they were necessary to
that, desirous, but not fond of Riches."[61] How much Bolingbroke was led astray by his ambition is debatable. Ambition in
and of itself need not destroy fortune or reputation; rather, the
contrary would seem to be true. But ambition can be served
well or ill, and the question is how well Bolingbroke served his
ambition.

To begin with, Bolingbroke never underestimated his own
abilities. Writing to Prior toward the end of the peace negotiations, he remarked that "there are those in the world who, I
believe, think me troublesome; but I have the satisfaction, in
my turn, of knowing them to be ignorant."[62] Years later
when, in "A Letter on the Spirit of Patriotism," he spoke of
"superior spirits, men who show even from their infancy,

[58] "Lord Chesterfield's Character," Bolingbroke, *Works*, ed. by Mallet,
I, liv.

[59] "Speaker Onslow's Remarks," Coxe, *Walpole*, II, 567–8.

[60] Swift, "An Enquiry," p. 145.

[61] Bolingbroke to his brother-in-law, Robert Knight, 12 June 1738, Sichel,
Bolingbroke and His Times, II, 555.

[62] Bolingbroke to Prior, 20 April 1713, *Bolingbroke Correspondence*, IV,
77–8.

though it be not always perceived by others, perhaps not always felt by themsleves, that they were born for something more, and better," he meant to include himself among their number.[63] Fully aware of his own talents, intolerant of obtuseness and incompetence in others, he seems at the same time to have recognized, and when possible rewarded, ability in those who served under him. "Those expressions, which you say you read with confusion, were used with sincerity," he assured Whitworth, the newly appointed ambassador at Vienna. "I serve with zeal myself, I see others endowed with great capacity; but I observe these two characters united in so few instances, that you must not wonder if I appear a little transported when I meet them together, as I do, without any compliment, very eminently in yourself."[64] With less able men Bolingbroke had little patience, and his tendency to circumvent or ignore them multiplied his enemies and made his friends uneasy.

Swift discoursed at some length on the "Inconveniencies and Misfortunes" of "Men of exalted Abilities, when they are called to publick Affairs." "I take the Infelicity of such extraordinary Men to have been caused by their Neglect of common Forms," he wrote. Ministers neglected the strict observance of "Time, Place, and Method" at their peril. "Nothing is more apt to expose Men to the Censure and Obloquy of their Colleagues and the Publick, than a Contempt or Neglect of these Circumstances, however attended with a superiour Genius, and an equall Desire of doing Good." In sum, "a small Infusion of the *Alderman* was necessary to those who are employed in publick Affairs."[65] But there was nothing of the alderman in Bolingbroke. Mallet admitted it "as generally acknowledged, that [he] availed himself very little of those

[63] Bolingbroke, *Works,* II, 353.

[64] Bolingbroke to Whitworth, 29 May 1711, *Bolingbroke Correspondence,* I, 227.

[65] Swift, "An Enquiry," pp. 138–9. On the same subject, see also Swift, "Some free Thoughts," pp. 77–80, 88.

Helps to Business that arise from Method";[66] and Speaker Onslow said he was "deemed bold if not rash" in the conduct of affairs.[67] Impatient with method and the common forms, the Secretary also complained of the burdens imposed by the workings of the parliamentary system. He looked longingly to France, where ministers could go about their business untroubled by the demands of an unruly Parliament and public. There, he observed to Prior, ministers

have no affairs but that of their proper departments, and they are accountable to but one master, who knows when they serve well, and who has power to support and to reward.

Had they as many cross-grained fellows to manage, as I have been treating with of late; had they twice the business out of their office, that they have in it; in a word, were they to serve without reward, and instead of being supported by the prerogative of the Crown, were they to form a strength to carry on the service of the public, I am apt to think, that they would have a better opinion of us, than the part we act in foreign affairs, does perhaps give them.[68]

Bolingbroke was called "Mercury," and movement and speed were his element. His impatience with the tortuous proceedings of parliamentary government was understandable; but the mistrust it engendered was reflected in Speaker Onslow's observation that Bolingbroke was "made rather for the splendor of great monarchies, than the sober counsels of a free state, whose liberty is its chief concern."[69] Dickinson speaks of Bolingbroke's "inability to manage men" as his major political failing: "He could offer a bold lead, but he could not ensure a large following."[70] Bolingbroke's sense of his own superior talents,

[66] [Mallet], *Memoirs of the Life and Ministerial Conduct, . . . of the Late Lord Visc. Bolingbroke*, p. 224.
[67] "Speaker Onslow's Remarks," Coxe, *Walpole*, II, 567-8.
[68] Bolingbroke to Prior, 16 February 1714, *Bolingbroke Correspondence*, IV, 475-6.
[69] "Speaker Onslow's Remarks," Coxe, *Walpole*, II, 568.
[70] Dickinson, *Bolingbroke*, p. 12. Cf. J. H. Plumb, *Sir Robert Walpole* (London: The Cresset Press, 1956-60), I, 130: "He lacked loyalty and could not arouse it in others."

his contempt for the forms of business and for incompetence in others figured largely in his inability to inspire the trust on which a loyal political following must rest.

Mercury is quick, but it is elusive and slippery as well, smooth-surfaced and difficult to penetrate. Bolingbroke admitted to being quick, but the other mercurial qualities he disclaimed, presenting himself on the contrary as by nature open and without guile. Thanking the British resident at Dresden for a letter of compliment on his appointment as Secretary of State, Bolingbroke offered to do him what service he could. "And," he added, "you may depend upon me, for I have brought all my country sincerity with me to court, and by the grace of God I will preserve it."[71] In May 1712, he apologized to the Earl of Peterborough for "the state of darkness and uncertainty, which you complain you have been left in.

It would be a real and great mortification to me, if I imagined your Lordship had entertained the least doubt of that friendship which I profess to have for you; my habits at Court have neither taught me to show what I do not feel, nor to hide what I do; and my love and my hate are so far from not appearing in my words and actions, that they generally sit in my face.[72]

And to Strafford, whose self-esteem was continually threatened by real or imagined slights, he wrote: "For God's sake my Lord, be persuaded that I have less cunning and more frankness."[73] Now even taking into account the demands of custom in the making of fine compliments, and of expediency in soothing the tempers of the Queen's servants, it is still difficult to accept Bolingbroke's claim to country sincerity. Though Swift said he was "of a Nature frank and open," and "but an ill-Dissembler,"[74] Swift was totally deceived at least once, on the

---

71 Bolingbroke to James Scott, 16 January 1711, *Bolingbroke Correspondence*, I, 73.

72 Bolingbroke to Peterborough, May 1712, *ibid.*, II, 302–4.

73 Bolingbroke to Strafford, 26 October 1711, *ibid.*, I, 441–4.

74 Swift, "An Enquiry," pp. 152, 145.

question of Bolingbroke's negotiations with the Pretender. Repeatedly he asserted that in his four years of close association with the ministers, he found no reason to suspect their absolute loyalty to Hanover,

and I cannot but think that if such an Affair had been in Agitation, I must have had either very bad Luck, or a very small Share of common Understanding, not to have discovered some Grounds at least for Suspicion. Because I never yet knew a Minister of State, or indeed any other Man so great a Master of Secrecy, as to be able among those he nearly converseth with, wholly to conceal his Opinions, however he may cover his Designs.[75]

But Bolingbroke, it appears, was just such a Master of Secrecy. He *was* less than open with Strafford in keeping him informed of the progress of the peace negotiations. And the state of darkness and uncertainty Peterborough complained of was real enough: the delay in finding him an employment stemmed from the ministry's desire to place him where he could not be troublesome. Bolingbroke was, when he chose to be, an excellent dissembler.

His mastery of the ready compliment was equally indisputable. In February 1713, he wrote the Duke of Shrewsbury: "I am less and less satisfied every day with the Duke d'Aumont [the French Ambassador]; all the Abbé Gaultier can do to set him right is done, but he is too conceited ever to mend."[76] The following autumn, on the eve of the Duke d'Aumont's return to France, his recall brought about in part if not entirely by Bolingbroke's dissatisfaction with him, Bolingbroke sent him a farewell letter. "From my stable—Among the hounds and horses, in the middle of the most perfect retreat, I wish for nothing to be completely happy but the conversation of the dear Duke d'Aumont, for it appears I shall not see you for a

[75] *Ibid.*, p. 165. See also "Some free Thoughts," pp. 90–1; and *Swift Correspondence, passim,* where he frequently expresses the same view.
[76] Bolingbroke to Shrewsbury, 17 February 1713, *Bolingbroke Correspondence,* III, 440.

long time, perhaps ever."[77] In this instance the occasion required a graceful compliment from the Secretary of State to the retiring French Ambassador. The same cannot be said of a number of letters Bolingbroke wrote to Harley long after Bolingbroke, by his own admission, had come to despise him. Bolingbroke held in special contempt Harley's efforts to improve the fortunes of his family,[78] yet on the marriage of Harley's son to the daughter of the late Duke of Newcastle, he was able to write:

The fortune, the honourable manner of obtaining it, and the consequences of this establishment, are all considerations which affect me with as great pleasure as I ever felt. This truth, you may, my Lord safely entertain, since whatever faults I may have I am on two sides free from blemish, and these are zeal for the Queen's service and friendship to your Lordship.[79]

Bolingbroke's friendship was at that point the last truth Harley could safely entertain, and both men knew it. The point here is neither to dispute the requirements of form and political expediency nor to censure Bolingbroke for being less than sincere: compliments more or less lavish were part of the practice of politics and diplomacy; so was a fair amount of skillful deception and dissembling. But while he framed elegant and extravagant compliments, when he engaged in expedient dissembling, he all the while insisted on his frankness and sincerity and, what is more, seems to have expected people to believe him. But his protestations did not ring true. They were taken for a pose, which in this case they were, and in the end cast doubts upon his integrity.

There was, however, some truth to Bolingbroke's claim

---

[77] Bolingbroke to the Duc d'Aumont, 21 October 1713, *ibid.,* IV, 332-3.

[78] This was a constant theme in Bolingbroke's later denunciations of Harley: "Whether this man ever had any determined view besides that of raising his family is, I believe, a problematical question in the world. My opinion is, that he never had any other." Bolingbroke, "A Letter to Sir William Windham," *Works,* I, 121.

[79] Bolingbroke to Oxford, 2 September 1713, HMC, *Portland MSS,* V, 326.

that "my love and my hate are so far from not appearing in my words and actions, that they generally sit in my face." He did not always succeed in controlling his resentments, particularly when his own interests were involved: "I am rash my Lord, I confess it," he wrote to Cowper in 1714, "apt to resent too soon, and to express my resentment too warmly."[80] His attempts to conceal his hostility to Harley deceived no one, least of all Harley. And on one occasion when he lost patience with Strafford, who complained that his interests had not been well served, Bolingbroke replied with some warmth: "I have used my best endeavours to serve your Lordship, ever since it was in my power, and these endeavours have not been unsuccessful. Had I been as intent on my own interest as I have been in promoting the good of the service, and of my friends, things had not been at present just in the posture that they are."[81] Two weeks later Bolingbroke apologized for this letter. "When I have a real friendship, as I have for you," he said by way of explanation, "my passions work, as they do in cases where I am personally affected; to this, therefore, be pleased to ascribe, and for this to excuse, any sentiments of mine delivered in terms which you may think too strong."[82] The comment is significant, for Bolingbroke by inference affirmed what was perhaps his greatest weakness, his inability to temper his passions with judgment in cases where he was personally affected. Clear-headed and reasonable he might be in composing diplomatic dispatches and in dealing with the routine business of his office. But when his own fortunes were at issue, his own interests engaged, he tended to lose both detachment and judgment: his flight from England in 1715, his service with the Pretender, his later acceptance of a pension from France to further the opposition campaign against Walpole were no less

[80] Bolingbroke to Cowper, 11 September 1714, Hertfordshire R.O., Panshanger MSS, D/EP, F56.
[81] Bolingbroke to Strafford, 23 September 1713, *Bolingbroke Correspondence*, IV, 298-9.
[82] Bolingbroke to Strafford, 8 October 1713, *ibid.*, IV, 318.

than disastrous. In these moments of extreme pressure he appears to have acted without regard for the long-range consequences of his actions. In 1709 he wrote to Orrery: "The Men of profound Wisdom form to themselves a Scheme of Life; & every Action is preceded by a Thought. We, who are of a more ordinary Size of Understanding, act by Chance at first, & by Habit afterwards."[83] Unfortunately in Bolingbroke's case, acting by chance at first led to habitual bad judgment.

Bolingbroke spoke a great deal of the virtues of friendship, which he esteemed second only to love of country, and in the years after 1715 he complained bitterly of those false friends who deserted him in his misfortune. "We meet with few friends," he wrote to Swift. "The greatest part of those who pass for such, are properly speaking nothing more than acquaintance. . . . the fire of my adversity has purg'd the mass of my acquaintance; and the separation made, I discover on one side, an handfull of friends, but on the other, a legion of Enemys, at least of strangers."[84] Through the rest of his life he saw the handful of friends diminish while the legion of enemies increased; but from first to last he felt he was not to blame. "It is true that I have not failed in friendship, to my knowledge, to any who have not failed to me," he told his sister, "and that so many have done so has been one of the greatest mortifications I have met in a life that has been full of them."[85] In his will, written the year before he died, he spoke of "the injustice and treachery of persons nearest to me; . . . the negligence of friends and . . . the infidelity of servants."[86] Characteristically, Bolingbroke never allowed the possibility that he might have given his friends cause to repudiate or at least reprove

[83] St. John to Orrery, 9 July 1709, Bodleian Library, MS Eng. Misc. e. 180.

[84] Bolingbroke to Swift, 17 March 1719, N.S., *Swift Correspondence,* II, 314.

[85] Bolingbroke to his half-sister, 10 August 1745, Sichel, *Bolingbroke and His Times,* II, 576-7.

[86] Bolingbroke, *Works,* I, 86.

him. Utterly convinced of the purity of his own motives, he was quick to resent those who doubted and thus, in his view, betrayed him. "From our enemies we expect evil treatment of every sort," he wrote in the "Letter to Sir William Windham," ". . . but when our friends abandon us, when they wound us, and when they take, to do this, an occasion where we stand the most in need of their support, and have the best title to it, the firmest minds find it hard to resist."[87] The reference here was to those Jacobite Tories who refused to understand the circumstances of his departure from James's service in 1716. But he resented equally the former friends who failed to understand why he had joined James in the first place. His resentments were strong, and the list was long, headed of course by Harley, the author of all his misfortunes, who later shared first place with the Whig minister, Robert Walpole. It included Bolingbroke's first wife, and also Prior, who was guilty of complying with the government's order to produce his papers for the secret committee of the Privy Council in the first months of George I's reign. Prior's examination before this committee supplied no evidence to support the government's case against the old ministers: any papers that might have seemed damaging had presumably been destroyed.[88] Yet Bolingbroke never seems to have resumed his friendship with Prior on its old familiar basis, and when Swift informed him of Prior's death, he used the occasion to denounce the Harley family.

I am sorry . . . that our old acquaintance Mat:, liv'd so poor as you represent him. I thought that a certain Lord whose marriage to a certain Heiress was the ultimate end of a certain administration, had put him above want. Prior might justly enough have address'd himself to his young Patron, as our friend Aristippus did

[87] *Ibid.,* I, 113.

[88] Prior's account of his appearance before this committee and his answer to the report submitted by the committee to the House of Commons are printed at the end of Matthew Prior, *The History of His Own Time,* edited and with a preface by J. Bancks (London, 1740), pp. 417–58.

to Dionysius. you have money, which I want: I have wit and knowledg, which you want.[89]

Few tears were shed for Prior: the warmth in that comment was provoked by resentment of the Harleys. To those who by his standards did not fail him, Bolingbroke was a loyal and generous friend, and he must have been a delightful companion. "It happens to very few Men in any Age or Country," said Swift, "to come into the World with so many Advantages of Nature and Fortune, as the late Secretary Bolingbroke."[90] Sir William Trumbull would come to town on no other business than to see his young friend and be obliged with his conversation, "wch is ever so agreable to me," whether on politics, the verses of Horace, or the Progress of Poetry.[91] Chesterfield judged that "if his conduct, in the former part of his life, had been equal to all his natural and acquired talents, he would most justly have merited the epithet of all-accomplished." He added that once Bolingbroke's violent passions had subsided, "the character of all-accomplished is more his due, than any man's I ever knew in my life."[92] Swift spoke of his "admirable conversation";[93] Chesterfield rhapsodized on the "flowing happiness" of his diction, and observed that "his manner of speaking in private conversation, is full as elegant as his writings."[94] He was equally eloquent in French, according to Voltaire, who met him in France and was greatly impressed by the variety of his talents. "I have found in this illustrious Englishman all the learning of his country and all the

[89] Bolingbroke to Swift, 1 January 1722, N.S., *Swift Correspondence,* II, 415.

[90] Swift, "An Enquiry," p. 134.

[91] Trumbull to St. John, 29 August 1702 (draft), Berkshire R.O., Downshire Papers, Trumbull Add. MSS 133/14.

[92] "Lord Chesterfield's Character," Bolingbroke, *Works,* ed. by Mallet, I, liii-iv.

[93] Swift, *Journal to Stella,* II, 401.

[94] "Lord Chesterfield's Character," Bolingbroke, *Works,* ed. by Mallet, I, liii-iv, lvi.

politeness of ours. I have never heard our language spoken with more energy and correctness. This man who has all his life been plunged in pleasure and in business has still been able to learn everything and to remember everything."[95] Like Harley, Bolingbroke was genuinely interested in learning, though he pursued it more than casually only in periods of forced retirement. The love of study and the desire of knowledge he had felt all his life, he later wrote, "and I am not quite a stranger to this industry and application. . . . But my genius, unlike the demon of Socrates, whispered so softly, that very often I Heard him not, in the hurry of those passions by which I was transported."[96] He believed in education as the path to virtue and he was much interested in the education of the young, which he felt was sadly lacking in his own day. "An excellent education is preferable to everything which the indulgence of Parents can do for their Children," he wrote in 1720. And he reflected on another occasion that when one considered the care lavished on the education of the great men of antiquity as compared with the education of youth in his own day, "it is astonishing that a single man grows up capable of being useful to his country."[97]

Bolingbroke's erudition, his intelligence and charm attracted him to the men of wit and learning. The devoted friend of Pope and Swift, he corresponded with both men to the end of their lives and, when he was in England, spent a great deal of time in Pope's company. (Swift returned to Ireland in 1714 and, but for two visits to England in 1726 and 1727, remained there.) His philosophical "Essays" addressed to Pope may have influenced the *Essay on Man;* he stayed by Pope through his

[95] Voltaire to Thieriot, 4 December 1722, N.S., *Voltaire's Correspondence,* ed. by Theodore Besterman (Genève: Institut et Musée Voltaire, 1953–65), I, 178.
[96] Bolingbroke, "Of the True Use of Retirement and Study," *Works,* II, 344–5.
[97] Bolingbroke to his father and his stepmother, 12 August 1720, Sichel, *Bolingbroke and His Times,* II, 492–3; Bolingbroke to Mme. de Ferriol, 18 May 1721, *ibid.,* 497.

final illness and, if Spence is to be believed, he wept at Pope's death.[98] In intellect and taste, the literary group received Bolingbroke as one of their own; but he was also their patron and, though not a rich man, generous in providing for their support. He was responsible for setting up the club known simply as "the Society," which had as one of its ends "the encouragement of letters." His account of this association, and what he proposed to accomplish by it, is worth quoting at some length. In June 1711, he wrote to Lord Orrery:

I must, before I send this letter, give your Lordship an account of a club which I am forming; and which, as light as the design may seem to be, I believe will prove of a real service. We shall begin to meet in a small number, and that will be composed of some who have wit and learning to recommend them; of others who, for their own situations, or from their relations, have power and influence, and of others who, from accidental reasons, may properly be taken in. . . . The improvement of friendship, and the encouragement of letters, are to be the two great ends of our society. A number of valuable people will be kept in the same mind, and others will be made converts to their opinions.[99]

The scheme is a good example of Bolingbroke's inventiveness and shrewdness. His Society was to serve a political as well as literary purpose, and the implication is clear that one of its salutary consequences would be the recruitment of able pens for the government side. Swift was already writing for the ministry when the Society was formed—the first of his *Examiners* appeared November 2, 1710—but Bolingbroke's approach reflects his appreciation of the importance of political propaganda, a sense he shared with Harley and that was remarkable among their contemporaries.

[98] Spence, *Observations, Anecdotes, and Characters of Books and Men,* I, 266–8. The quarrel over Pope's unauthorized publication of Bolingbroke's *Idea of a Patriot King* was a posthumous one: Bolingbroke did not discover the existence of Pope's secret edition until after Pope's death.

[99] Bolingbroke to Orrery, 12 June 1711, *Bolingbroke Correspondence,* I, 246–7. The final membership of the Society is printed in Swift, *Journal to Stella,* II, 505, n. 43.

Whether through the Society or independently, Bolingbroke seems to have put what money and influence he could at the service of his friends, but in the matter of employments, he complained increasingly that he could get nothing from Harley, and the complaint seems justified. His correspondence records the efforts he made to secure an adequate allowance for Prior when he was in Paris, and an adequate place for him on his return. It is extremely unlikely that Prior's disappointment on both counts can be laid to Bolingbroke. Again, Bolingbroke did what he could to secure for Swift the post of Royal Historiographer: he failed, but not for lack of trying.[100]

Bolingbroke was at his best with Swift: a most delightful companion, a loyal and devoted friend. Swift was flattered by the Secretary's familiarity and greatly enjoyed the high good humor that pervaded their friendship. The Secretary was a practical joker, Swift an exasperated but willing victim. On the way to Windsor, Swift recounted, "I made the secretary stop at Brentford, because we set out at two this afternoon, and fasting would not agree with me. I only designed to eat a bit of bread and butter, but he would light, and we ate roast beef like dragons. And he made me treat him and two more gentlemen; faith it cost me a guinea; I don't like such jesting, yet I was mightily pleased with it too."[101] But while the relationship was marked by high spirits, it was rooted in affection and mutual esteem. Though Swift deplored the manner in which Bolingbroke accomplished Harley's dismissal in 1714, he never wavered in his friendship for Bolingbroke; and Bolingbroke's affection for Swift never weakened, though he knew Swift's sympathies were with Harley. "I pass over that paragraph of yr letter which is a kind of an Elegy on a departed Minister," he wrote to Swift in 1724, "& I promise you solemnly neither to mention him, nor think of him more, till I come to do him

---

[100] Swift blamed Bolingbroke, at least initially, for his failure to get the appointment. But Bolingbroke's letter to Shrewsbury proposing Swift is in *Bolingbroke Correspondence*, IV, 420–1.

[101] Swift, *Journal to Stella*, I, 360–1.

justice in an History of the first twenty years of this Century, which I believe I shall write if I live three or four years longer."[102] Bolingbroke did not keep his solemn promise— nor, for that matter, did he ever write his history. Several years later, writing to Swift, he spoke of "your Hero Oxf--d," to which Swift replied: "It was you were my Hero, but the other ne'er was, yet if he were, it was your own fault, who taught me to love him."[103] It is remarkable in the circumstances that Bolingbroke's resentment of Oxford did not prevail over his affection for Swift, but their correspondence provides ample proof of continuing friendship. In 1721, when Swift had asked for his picture, Bolingbroke replied he was "as little given to beg correspondents as you are to beg pictures, but since I cannot live with you, I would fain hear from you."[104]

Bolingbroke's elegance and charm served him well when, in the summer of 1712, he went to Paris to advance the peace negotiations. As the Queen's minister and an emissary of peace, he was entitled to due recognition in official circles and at Court, but the reception given him apparently surpassed what was required.[105] Apart from everything else, his mission was a social triumph. He stayed at the Hotel de Croissy, which belonged to the mother of Torcy, the French foreign minister, and he seems to have charmed that family together with most of the rest of Paris. On his return to England, he left a dazzling trail behind him. Informing Bolingbroke of the appointment of a new ambassador to England, Torcy wrote: "I envy him only the pleasure of seeing you without delay, and of making up for the little time we had you here. I

---

[102] Bolingbroke to Swift, 12 September 1724, N.S., *Swift Correspondence,* III, 27.

[103] Bolingbroke to Swift, 27 September 1729, N.S.; Swift to Bolingbroke, 13 October 1729, *ibid.,* pp. 348, 353-4.

[104] Bolingbroke to Swift, 1 January 1722, N.S. *ibid.,* II, 415.

[105] *Bolingbroke Correspondence,* III, 1-23; 55, note. Abel Boyer, *The History of the Life & Reign of Queen Anne* (London, 1722), pp. 596-8. Hereafter cited as Boyer, *History.*

shall leave to him the care of telling you what pride the ladies you distinguished by your praises took in an approbation such as yours."[106] Prior had traveled to France with Bolingbroke, and he stayed to manage the British end of the negotiations in Paris. As Bolingbroke's friend, he succeeded to the particular esteem Bolingbroke enjoyed in the Torcy–Croissy circle, and he served as intermediary for the succession of compliments and favors that passed back and forth between London and Paris. In October 1713, Prior reported to Bolingbroke:

I am now upon the greatest piece of negociation that I ever had in my life, the distribution of your cargo [of honey-water, sack, and eau de Barbade]: upon which the Noailles and the Croissys are in an uproar, but having wherewithal to appease them, I begin the great work this afternoon, and shall give you a full account of my actions by the next: both at Fontainebleau and Croissy, we have all remembered *le cher Henri* in the friendliest manner imaginable.[107]

In the autumn of 1713 William Bromley replaced Dartmouth as the other Secretary of State, and Bolingbroke, given his choice of departments, elected to move to the South. "You will judge right, Monsieur," he wrote to Torcy, "that I did not hesitate a moment to declare for the one which includes France."[108] Bolingbroke's fondness for France and his great success there did not advance his popularity at home. His close association with France not only lent credence to the Whig charge that the government was conspiring with the enemy against Britain's allies—to an extent this was true, but in Bolingbroke's view the government was driven to concert with France by the intractability of the allies—it also made him an object of suspicion to the backbenchers in the House of Commons who regarded all things foreign with mistrust and all

---

[106] Torcy to Bolingbroke, 29 Août 1712, N.S. *Bolingbroke Correspondence*, III, 41–2.
[107] Prior to Bolingbroke, 6–17 October 1713, *ibid.*, IV, 322.
[108] Bolingbroke to Torcy, 29 September 1713, *ibid.*, p. 311.

things French as frivolous, dissolute, and corrupt. Prior wrote to Harley from Paris: "Monsr de Torcy constantly drinks your health, and Madame de Torcy who has a great deal of good humour and witt, drinks to Robin et to Harry, mais Je croy, dit Elle, que Robin est trop serieux pour Nous."[109] For the same reason that Madame de Torcy preferred Bolingbroke, the English squirearchy in this respect preferred Harley, who never seems to have traveled abroad and had no taint of foreignness about him.

III

Bolingbroke was dismissed from his post as Secretary of State in August 1714, shortly after the Queen's death. Though half his life still lay ahead of him, his formal political career was over. In the spring of 1715 he left England for France under threat of impeachment and joined the Pretender's service. Impeached in his absence and attainted of high treason, he was condemned to death and his property and titles were forfeit. He remained with the Pretender less than a year but long enough to be convinced of the hopelessness of a Stuart restoration under James's leadership. James dismissed him in February 1716, and he immediately set about negotiating his return to England. In May 1723, his pardon passed the Great Seal: the death penalty was revoked but the Act of Attainder still stood. Bolingbroke could return to England, but deprived of his estates and titles he had no means of support and he could not regain his seat in the House of Lords. Two years later Parliament acted to restore his property but not his peerage. Barred from the House of Lords, he was effectively prevented from resuming an active role in politics.

Now from the moment Bolingbroke left the Pretender's service, while he worked steadily first for his pardon, then for

---

[100] Prior to Oxford, 29 August–9 September 1712, BM, Portland Loan, 29/154.

the full restoration of his estates and titles, he never stopped insisting that his ambition was dead, that he welcomed retirement and regretted only the years he had spent in the world. "The retirement I propose to myself is not only what I chuse but what I languish after," he wrote to his friend Charles Ford in 1717.[110] In 1723 he and Pope penned a joint letter to Swift, in which Pope remarked that a "Glutt of Study & Retirement" in the first part of his life had cast him into his present "infinitely more various & dissipated" existence. Bolingbroke continued the letter:

I am under no apprehensions that a Glut of Study and Retirement should cast me back into the Hurry of the World; on the contrary, the single Regret which I ever feel, is that I fell so late into this Course of Life: My Philosophy grows confirmed by Habit. . . . Reflection and Habit have rendred the World so indifferent to me, that I am neither afflicted nor rejoiced, angry nor pleased at what happens in it, any farther than personal Friendships interest me in the Affairs of it, and this Principle extends my cares but a little Way: Perfect Tranquillity is the general Tenour of my Life.[111]

Swift was not impressed. "I have no very strong Faith in you pretenders to retirement," he replied to Pope, and his response was just.[112] To his most intimate friends Bolingbroke admitted how much he wanted to secure full restoration and how difficult he found the continuing uncertainty of his situation. "I hope that this winter will decide my fate," he wrote his sister Henrietta, "for in truth a longer delay would not be bearable. . . . It is true that I am resigned to exile, and to all the other events of life. But it is also true that I have neglected nothing at all that a man of affairs ought to do to bring about the end of

---

110 Bolingbroke to Ford, 17 April 1717, *The Letters of Jonathan Swift to Charles Ford*, ed. by D. Nichol Smith (Oxford: The Clarendon Press, 1935), p. 232.
111 Bolingbroke and Pope to Swift, August 1723, *Swift Correspondence*, II, 461–2.
112 Swift to Pope, 20 September 1723, *ibid.*, p. 464.

that exile."[113] However much he proclaimed his indifference to the world—and as his hopes for a return to politics faded, he did so ever more insistently—his actions belied the assertion. And this remained true to the end of his life. Within months of his return to England in 1725 he joined the opposition to Walpole, the archenemy, now first minister, who had moved his impeachment in 1715, who had effectively blocked his full pardon and would continue to do so as long as he headed the government. Excluded from Parliament, Bolingbroke functioned behind the scenes as theorist and master strategist for the opposition, lending his craft and his formidable pen to the full-scale attack on Walpole's Whig administration. Yet in the thick of his successful campaign against Walpole's Excise Bill, he wrote the Earl of Essex that all he desired was "retreat and quiet. . . . I have so little concern in the world that it concerns me little who governs it or how it is governed."[114] Determined that his enemies were not to triumph in his misfortunes, he had, in the spring of 1733, to provide against all eventualities. If Walpole fell, Bolingbroke's full restoration might follow; if Walpole survived the crisis, Bolingbroke had to contemplate his continued exclusion from politics and possible withdrawal from England. When the second alternative came to pass, he could fall back on those repeated assertions that retreat and quiet were "the innocent and sole objects of my ambition."[115] He expected the world to believe them, and in later years he believed them increasingly himself.

When he returned to France in 1735—vaguely threatened by Walpole's savage counterattack, his services no longer welcome to a now fragmented opposition—he struck up the same theme with renewed frequency and force. To Lord Essex he wrote that his walk of life would "probably be in absolute

[113] Bolingbroke to his half-sister, 23 December 1723, N.S., Sichel, *Bolingbroke and His Times*, II, 505-6.
[114] Bolingbroke to Essex, 12 March 1733, *ibid.*, p. 535.
[115] Bolingbroke to Sir Philip Yorke, 23 May 1733, *ibid.*

retreat, not from my friends, but from the world, the rest of my days. And in that walk I do assure your Lordship I shall have no other regret than this one, that I ever left it."[116] "You would be sorry, I am sure," he told Wyndham, "if I wanted the courage to say to myself, thy part in public life is over. . . . I neither expect nor desire power, and as to my being restored, I am perfectly indifferent."[117] But while he addressed his friends in this manner, the same letters revealed that his interest in the world was far from dead and that he was not convinced his part in public life was over. "If you see a prospect of uniting on principles of conduct for the interest and honor of Britain," he wrote Marchmont the year following Walpole's resignation, "and if you and three or four of my friends think I can be any way serviceable in the scheme, I will come to you, though I come on crutches."[118] But the call to action never came, and when he settled in England in 1744 he was again—and still—resolved to retire from the world as if for the first time. Again the reality was rather different, so that in 1746 he could write Marchmont:

I have not left off, since I came to resettle here, advising and exhorting, till long after you saw it was to no purpose, and smiled at me for persisting. It is time I should retire for good and all from the world, and from the very approaches to business. . . . If I have shewed too much zeal, for I own that this even in a good cause may be pushed into some degree of ridicule, I can shew as much indifference; and surely it is time for me to shew the latter, since I am come to the even of a tempestuous day, and see in the

---

[116] Bolingbroke to Essex, 25 June 1735, N.S., *ibid.*, p. 538.

[117] Bolingbroke to Wyndham, 5 January 1736, N.S., Coxe, *Walpole*, II, 336–7.

[118] Bolingbroke to the Earl of Marchmont, 2 October 1743, N.S., *A Selection from the Papers of the Earls of Marchmont, in the Possession of the Rt. Honble. Sir George Henry Rose. Illustrative of Events from 1685 to 1750* (London, 1831), II, 324. Hereafter cited as *Marchmont Papers*. For Bolingbroke's continuing interest in politics and foreign affairs, see his other letters printed in this volume; also the letters in Coxe, *Walpole*, II, 333–42, and III, *passim;* and in Sichel, *Bolingbroke and His Times*, II.

whole extent of our horizon no signs, that to-morrow will be fairer.[119]

Four months later, he said that he was plunging himself "deeper and deeper into that retreat from persons, and abstraction from the concerns of the world, which becomes a man, who is destined to pass the remainder of his days out of it, and to live as if he were dead."[120] But Bolingbroke was far too deeply committed to the world to abstract himself from it: he was incapable of living as if he were dead. In April of 1751, a month after his wife's death, he wrote:

The world, dear sister, may very well spare a man so useless in it as I am, and I do assure you, I can as easily spare the world. I can do it so easily that I think not only of retreating from it, and of excluding it from my Retreat, which is to die civilly before I die naturally; but that this thought gives me more comfort than any other, and that I hasten to put it into execution.[121]

Within the year Bolingbroke was dead. Swift's judgment stands: "But as to his breathing after retirement, I fear he will hardly find it till he breaths his last."[122]

I V

The question is why Bolingbroke chose to insist upon the satisfactions of a life of retirement so far beyond the bounds of credibility. He was a man of enormous energy and capacity; he thrived at the center of affairs and in the society of the great capitals; he aspired to be, by his own definition, a whole man, equally engaged in business and in pleasure. That he should be

---

[119] Bolingbroke to Marchmont, 24 July 1746, *Marchmont Papers*, II, 350.
[120] Bolingbroke to Marchmont, 25 November 1746, *ibid.*, p. 357.
[121] Bolingbroke to his half-sister, 11 April 1751, Sichel, *Bolingbroke and His Times*, II, 585.
[122] Swift to Pope, 12 May 1735, *Swift Correspondence*, IV, 334.

content entirely removed from the spheres in which he flourished was unlikely in the extreme. He did enjoy the country, he did find satisfaction in intellectual pursuits; and doubtless it was true that in his later years his thirst for sensual pleasures diminished, making way for the quieter delights of retirement and study. Yet for all this, he never ceased to crave the world, never ceased to resent his exclusion from politics, never succeeded in retreating from the world or excluding it from his retreat. He could not in retirement, any more than when he was Secretary of State, "help saying thus much" on the matter at hand. The hurried apologies at the end of his official dispatches come to mind: "I am warm with this thought, and having taken the pen into my hand, was not master of stopping the tide of ink."[123] As Goldsmith observed:

There is not, perhaps, a stronger instance in the world than his lordship, that an ambitious mind can never be fairly subdued, but will still seek for those gratifications which retirement can never supply. . . . it was in vain that he attempted to take root in the shade of obscurity, he was originally bred in the glare of public occupation, and he secretly once more wished for transplantation.[124]

Bolingbroke's celebration of the blessings of retirement was then a pose, and one which he struck well before 1715. In 1709, when he was out of office and out of Parliament as well, he had written to Orrery:

Whether it is owing to Constitution or to Philosophy I can't tell, but certain it is, that I can make myself easy in any Sort of Life. . . . Happiness, I imagine, depends much more on desiring little, than enjoying much; & perhaps the surest road to it is Indifference. If I continue in the Country, the Sports of the Field & the Pleasures of my Study will take up all my Thoughts, and serve to amuse me as long as I live. If any Accident should call me again to

---

[123] Bolingbroke to Lexington, 1 August 1713, *Bolingbroke Correspondence*, IV, 220-1.

[124] Goldsmith, "The Life of . . . Bolingbroke," *Collected Works of Oliver Goldsmith*, III, 465.

the Pleasure & Business of London, I shall be as eager as ever I was in the pursuit of Both.[125]

Allowing for some change in emphasis and some embellishment, this was the language of the years of proscription. It was the rhetoric of Bolingbroke out of office, of Bolingbroke politically disabled and in exile; it was the pose to which he reverted in every degree of misfortune and adversity. The pose served well enough before 1715 when Bolingbroke out of Parliament and out of office was certain to be in again. He was scarcely indifferent, but no doubt he did enjoy his interval of leisure, sure in the belief it would not last long. The rhetoric to some extent represented the reality. But in the latter part of his life, particularly in the years after 1735, the gap between assertion and reality widened; unable to accept the reality, he had to insist upon the pose as the only means by which he could preserve his public reputation and thus his self-esteem. "The transition from a minister of State to an Hermit is a very great one in the eye of the world," he had written to Ford in 1724.

But there is nothing in it hard to be bore by a man, who whilst he is in the first station, supposes he may one time or other fall into the second, and who takes care, even amidst the dissipations of pleasure and of business, to temper & harden his mind by philosophy. Repulses and disappointments, diminution or loss of Estate & Rank, Exil & Calumny itself, are unable to make a painful impression upon such a man, and to constitute him unhappy.[126]

Bolingbroke believed himself to be such a man: he had to persuade the world that it was so; he had also to reassure himself.

Bolingbroke throughout his life was preoccupied with his public reputation. He viewed life as a play, himself as an actor before an audience, whether an individual, the House of

---

[125] St. John to Orrery, 1 September 1709, Bodleian Library, MS Eng. Misc. e. 180. See also Bolingbroke to Baron de Seckingen [?], 22 August 1711, *Bolingbroke Correspondence,* I, 330–1.

[126] Bolingbroke to Ford, 10 October 1724, *The Letters of Jonathan Swift to Charles Ford,* p. 239.

Commons, or the larger political and social world. His language abounded in theatrical imagery: habitually he spoke of acting a part, of stages and prompters, and tragic and comical scenes. In 1729, speaking of himself and his wife, he wrote: "Both of us have closed the 10th Luster, and it is high time to determine how we shall play the last act of the Farce. might not my life be entituled much more properly a *What d'ye call it* than a Farce? Some Comedy, a great deal of Tragedy, and the whole interspersed with Scenes of Harlequin, Scaramouch, and Doctor Baloardo, the prototype of your Hero Oxf--d."[127] In 1735 he told Wyndham he was considering how to conduct the last act of his life, "and to wind up the whole piece. . . . My part is over, and he who remains on the stage after his part is over, deserves to be hissed off."[128] The following spring he observed of his life that "two acts are over att least; and the farce, you know, consists but of three."[129]

The actor was always conscious of his role. Commenting on Wyndham's account of the latest ludicrous episode in the quarrel between the King and the Prince of Wales, Bolingbroke remarked: "It gave you inwardly, I suppose, much the same emotion as a scene of Tom Thumb would have done. But you are too wise not to know, that they who are on the stage must keep the countenance their parts require in a tragicomical farce, whilst they who are in the pit may laugh their fill."[130] Bolingbroke was on the stage all the time, in office and out, at home and in exile; and throughout his life he strove to keep the countenance his part required, whatever the part may have been. Hence the poses, hence, after 1715, the compelling

---

[127] Bolingbroke to Swift, 27 September 1729, N.S., *Swift Correspondence*, III, 348, and note: *What d'ye call it* was the title of a farce by John Gay; Harlequin, Scaramouch, and Doctor Baloardo are Commedia del Arte characters.

[128] Bolingbroke to Wyndham, 29 November 1735, N.S., Coxe, *Walpole*, II, 333–4.

[129] Bolingbroke to Wyndham, 18 March 1736, N.S., *ibid.*, III, 319.

[130] Bolingbroke to Wyndham, 13 October 1737, N.S., *ibid.*, p. 495.

need to justify himself. He claimed not to need the applause of the world: "I agree with your Lordship, that it is better to be clapped on the stage, than hissed. . . . But the applause of the world is a very uncertain tenure; and a wise and good man will secure to himself another, that inward, conscious applause, which will never fail him when he has deserved it."[131] But Bolingbroke's preoccupation with justifying both the past and the present, with transmitting his reputation unblemished to posterity, suggests that for him inward applause was not enough: he was obsessed with clearing his name before the world.

In a number of works Bolingbroke dealt at some length with his years in office, and from his own writing his political career emerges as a tale of virtue unrewarded and innocence betrayed.[132] His theme was always the same: his motives had always been pure, he had been ill-used and misunderstood, deserted by all but a few faithful friends. Those mistakes he admitted to—or could not afford not to admit to—were made for the right reasons and not from iniquity. And he appeared to believe that the act of admitting them in itself absolved him of blame. Thus he claimed credit in all eventualities: he was virtuous and right or virtuous in admitting he was wrong. Forced to recognize his misjudgment in joining the Pretender, he ended by asking for praise because he later sought to warn the Jacobite Tories of the hopelessness of the Stuart cause.[133] In this view the second action canceled the first, and he avoided responsibility for the consequences of his actions. A point made earlier comes to mind: his repeated failure, particularly where his own fortunes were concerned, to anticipate the conse-

---

[131] Bolingbroke to Marchmont, 28 March 1747, *Marchmont Papers,* II, 364–5.

[132] See especially Letter VIII of the "Letters on the Study and Use of History" for his defense of the Treaty of Utrecht; "A Letter to Sir William Windham"; "Of the State of Parties at the Accession of George the First"; Bolingbroke, *Works,* I and II.

[133] See "A Letter to Sir William Windham," *ibid.,* I, 111–80.

quences of his actions. His rashness and natural impetuosity supply part of the explanation, and his tendency to immerse himself so thoroughly in the action itself that he thought too late of what was to follow. But there is another consideration, and this relates to the quality of his self-consciousness. For though Bolingbroke was supremely conscious of himself, he was curiously unintrospective. And there is perhaps a relationship between introspectiveness and the capacity for self-deception: the unintrospective man is a prey to self-deception and conversely, the man inclined to deceive himself cannot afford introspection.

Bolingbroke's sense of himself was public: he existed in terms of his public reputation. But his concentration on the part he was acting insulated him from the demands of his audience. The roles he chose to play offended as often as they pleased, hindered as much as they helped his political career. He often chose the wrong role in terms of political England, and he erred again in being too obviously a performer. For Bolingbroke the private and the public man were never far apart; and in the latter part of his life, in his own eyes at least, they became one, which is to say that he believed his image of himself.

CHAPTER III

Early Associations: "Dear Master" and "Faithful Harry"

SWIFT dated the breach between Harley and St. John from the attempt made on Harley's life in March 1711. "I have some very good reasons to know," he wrote, "that the first misunderstanding between Mr. Harley and Mr. St. John, which afterwards had such unhappy consequences upon the public affairs, took it's rise during the time that the former lay ill of his wounds, and his recovery doubtful."[1] Elsewhere he remarked that "some Things happened during Mr. Harley's Confinement, which bred a Coldness and Jealousy between those two great Men; and these increasing by many subsequent Accidents could never be removed."[2] Auditor Harley concurred, observing that "Mr. St. John and others now began to form a party against the Chancellor, while he lay ill of his wounds."[3] But Harley himself disagreed: "The

---

[1] Jonathan Swift, "Memoirs, Relating to That Change Which Happened in the Queen's Ministry in the Year 1710," *Political Tracts, 1713–1719*, ed. by Herbert Davis and Irvin Ehrenpreis (Oxford: Basil Blackwell, 1964), p. 128. Hereafter cited as Swift, "Memoirs."

[2] Swift, "An Enquiry," pp. 145–6.

[3] Edward Harley, "Memoirs," HMC, *Portland MSS*, V, 655.

beginning of February 1710–11, there began to be a division among those called Tories in the House, and Mr. Secretary St. John thought it convenient to be listing a separate party for himself."[4] While it is doubtless true that the weeks following the assassination attempt saw the first blatant and public manifestation of the ministers' dissensions, their misunderstanding "took it's rise" long before. St. John's conduct during the period of Harley's convalescence exacerbated but did not create their difficulties. The evidence suggests that these were of long standing and stemmed from differences of political tradition and practice as well as from the collision of two utterly dissimilar personalities.

Harley's political origins were Whig but when, in the last decade of William's reign, he emerged as leader of the New Country party, his appeal was to backbench Tories as well as those "Old Whigs" of 1688 who in varying degrees opposed the policies of William and the influence of the Whig Junto—the small and powerful group of Whig leaders who, with their followers, constituted the most significant element in the Whig party after the Revolution.[5] His preeminence in the Commons was early established, and by 1700 his power was such that the King moved to enlist his support on the government side. Harley's election as Speaker with the backing of the Crown, in February 1701, marked his move to the Court. As Speaker he managed the safe passage of the Act of Settlement establishing the Hanoverian succession and, a year later, of the abjuration oath which reinforced it, requiring office-holders and members of Parliament to forswear the Pretender. And he backed William's call for renewed military action against France. By the Auditor's account, Harley "endeavored by all means to prevent" the impeachments brought by the Tories against the Whig lords, Halifax, Somers, and Orford, for their acquies-

---

[4] Earl of Oxford, "A brief Account of Public Affairs, since August 8, 1710, to this present 8th of June, 1714," *Parliamentary History*, VI, ccxlv.

[5] For Harley's political background and his early career, see McInnes, *Robert Harley*, chaps. 2 and 3.

cence in the negotiation of the partition treaties by which William, without consulting Parliament, and Louis XIV, anticipating the death without heirs of Charles II of Spain, sought to deal with the problem of the Spanish inheritance; but the evidence suggests that, on the contrary, Harley did what he could to further the proceedings.[6] To this extent, at least, he remained a member of the opposition.

The ministerial changes that brought Harley into the Court interest brought Godolphin into the Cabinet, and the close association that began then assumed the first importance when, on the accession of Queen Anne in March 1702, Godolphin became Lord Treasurer. Godolphin and Marlborough, now Captain-General and Master of the Ordnance, shared first rank in the ministry, but Harley played an enormously important role.[7] He remained in the Speaker's chair continuously until April 1705, including the first year he was Secretary of State, and his correspondence with Godolphin in these years and beyond is remarkable for the deference the Treasurer showed to Harley's opinion and to his convenience. Godolphin would be glad to see the Speaker "at my house tomorrow at five if it be no constraint to you & if it bee, my business is not so pressing but that I may take another time." And if he "could bee sure it wd not bee uneasy to you," Godolphin hoped Harley would call on his way to Kensington or on his return. "I should bee very glad to stay at home, to expect you, but I hope you will bee so kind as never to Constrain yr Self wth your humble Servt."[8] The two first ministers consulted Harley at every turn: they sought his views on appointments, elections, parliamentary strategy. Godolphin wrote to say that he would not

[6] Edward Harley, "Memoirs," HMC, *Portland MSS*, V, 646. McInnes, *Robert Harley*, pp. 59–60. The evidence McInnes cites appears to be conclusive.

[7] McInnes feels that from 1702 on, the administration should properly be called a triumvirate, at least until the divisions of 1706–7 which led to Harley's dismissal early in 1708. McInnes, *Robert Harley*, p. 67.

[8] Godolphin to Harley, 10 April [?], "Saturday at one," n.d., Longleat, Portland Misc. MSS, ff. 3, 19.

see Harley until the meeting of Parliament: "I depend upon you for thinking in ye mean time of what is to bee done, of all kinds, preparative to its meeting, as well, as of what is to bee fixed, when it Comes; I must also pray you to send mee a list, or memorand-- of such persons as you wish might bee Consider'd upon occasion of any vacancys betwixt this and that time."[9] It is a sweeping charge.

Recent studies concur in regarding Harley's extraordinarily close relationship with Godolphin and Marlborough as stemming from the latters' limitations as political men.[10] Neither had the particular abilities nor the inclination to deal at first hand with the day-to-day workings of the political world: Godolphin was thin-skinned, stiff, inaccessible; Marlborough, equally sensitive to public criticism, was primarily a soldier. Out of the country much of the time, he was in any case better suited to the diplomacy of foreign courts than to the machinations of domestic politics. In the circumstances, Harley's talents were essential to the two ministers. His presence in the House of Commons, his skill as a parliamentary manager, his contacts among powerful groups outside the House, particularly the City of London and the Church, made him a necessary and invaluable associate. The ministers relied upon him and trusted him completely. "Now I have vented myself, & eased what was upon my heart," Godolphin concluded a letter, "to show you that I am in charity, will you dine with mee, & my Lord chief Justice?"[11]

A further reason for Harley's close association with Godolphin and Marlborough was their common aversion to government by party. All three regarded themselves as servants of the

[9] Godolphin to Harley, 13 August [1703], *ibid.*, ff. 166–7.

[10] See McInnes, *Robert Harley*, pp. 63–7; and H. L. Snyder, "Godolphin and Harley: A Study of Their Partnership in Politics," *Huntington Library Quarterly*, XXX (1966–7), 241–71. Snyder speaks also of Harley's desire "to direct or influence government policy without bearing full responsibility for it" in accounting for his side of the relationship (p. 244).

[11] Godolphin to Harley, "Tuesday morning," n.d., Longleat, Portland Misc. MSS, f. 65.

Queen, not of a party: their function was to insure that the Queen's business was done. As "managers" they sought to check the extremes of both parties and to enlist moderate support for the policy of the Crown.[12] And moderation was the key to Harley's politics.[13] For him party was "faction," self-serving in motive, in practice destructive of the foundations of government. "As for Parties in generall," he wrote in 1702, "it hath long been my opinion, that Parties in the State is Knavery and Parties in Religion is Hypocrisy."[14] The leaders of party used the trust placed in them by honest men to serve their own selfish interests, thereby enslaving both Crown and nation: "Parties . . . have prov'd to us like a whip-saw, which soever Extream is pull'd, the Nation is still miserably sawn between them."[15] In Harley's view, government should center on the sovereign served by able and loyal men recruited from both parties. The Crown, standing above the heats of party warfare, alone could unify the nation. "I am satisfied to a demonstration there can be no other centre of union but the Queen, . . ." he wrote Godolphin in 1707,

and there the bulk of the nation will fix themselves if they may be suffered, all other expedients are very wretched things and will

---

[12] For the "managers," see G. S. Holmes, *British Politics in the Age of Anne*, pp. 188–94, 414–18; and G. S. Holmes and W. A. Speck, eds., *The Divided Society* (London: Edward Arnold, 1967), pp. 6–7.

[13] For Harley's politics see McInnes, *Robert Harley*, pp. 102–10 and *passim*, and his article, "The Political Ideas of Robert Harley," *History*, L (October 1965), 309–22.

[14] Robert Harley to William Heysterman, 13–24 January 1702, BM, Portland Loan, 29/146.

[15] [Simon Clement], *FAULTS on both SIDES* (London, 1710), p. 55. This pamphlet was written by Clement at Harley's dictation. The same points are emphasized in a pamphlet written in Harley's hand entitled *Plaine English to all who are Honest or would be so if they knew how*. The style Harley chose was that of an Old Testament prophet denouncing the wicked and recalling men to the paths of righteousness. It begins: "Men, Brethren, Fathers, & Country Men! I beseech you give eare while I write to you the words of truth and soberness . . . But my words shal be of the uprightness of my Heart, & my Lips shal utter knowledge clearly." BM, Portland Loan, 29/10.

end but very ill; and I dread the thought of running from the extreme of one faction to another which is the natural consequence of party tyranny, and renders the government like a door which turns both ways upon its hinges to let in each party as it grows triumphant, and in truth this is the real parent and nurse of our factions here.[16]

But while Harley rejected government by party and consistently upheld the independence of the Crown, he realized that government without party was impossible. The Crown's business could not be carried forward without parliamentary support, and favorable majorities could not be secured without regard to party allegiances. Harley believed that the country members were the crucial element in controlling the House of Commons; and while these men prided themselves on their independence, he knew that among them party loyalties were strong and the influence of party leadership considerable. To gain backbench votes and to prevent the formation of a backbench coalition in opposition to the Court, the government had to make some commitment to one party, without, he hoped, totally alienating the other. But it was central to Harley's scheme that no alliance between Court and party should ever be imposed upon the Queen against her will; and further, that party leaders should never be able to control the policy of the Crown. In practice, this was reasonable enough when the parties were more or less evenly balanced in the House of Commons and the Court could throw its weight to either side. But the situation was entirely different when one party held a clear majority, for then the Court had no such latitude in choosing its allies. Particularly when highly controversial questions embroiled the House, the government's best hope of carrying its measures lay in establishing connections with the majority party. But here precisely was the greatest threat to Harley's scheme, for the party leadership, backed by a large

[16] Robert Harley to Godolphin, 10 September 1707, HMC, *Bath MSS*, I, 181.

majority in the Commons, could exert great pressure on the Queen and her ministers, could in fact control the policy of the Crown. It was to avoid this situation that Harley resolved to maintain, insofar as he could, the goodwill of the minority party by echewing extreme measures and by retaining in office all those moderate men he considered loyal to the Queen.

The pursuit of moderation lasted all his political life. "As near as I can guess by the elections," he wrote Godolphin in 1702, "though there are many Violent Whigs left out, yet, those who come in their places wil be for moderate & safe counsels, unless deceiv'd by the artifice of some few hot men, whom I hope the Government wil take care to prevent, by applying proper antidotes."[17] Four years later his theme was the same: "I have with grief observed that the leaders (or zealots rather) of both parties are frequent even now, in their reflections on the Queen's ministers, . . . I cannot but apprehend danger from both sides in the extreme, and therefore I am humbly of opinion to increase the number of those who would devote themselves to the Queen's and your service would be best."[18] When in April 1704 Harley joined the Godolphin-Marlborough ministry as Secretary of State, replacing the High Tory Earl of Nottingham, his Whiggish friend Sir Rowland Gwynne sent his congratulations: "I have seen your moderation in Parliament and you have seen my conduct there. . . . I am glad that My Lord Treasurer will choose moderate men to carry on his Ministrye, which is approved by all people hithertoe, but those who are very much inclined to passion, and Selfe Interest."[19] Ten months later, at the time of the General Election following the defeat of the "Tack," the High Tory attempt to join the bill against occasional con-

[17] Robert Harley to Godolphin, 9 August 1702, BM, Add. MSS, 28, 055, f. 3.

[18] Robert Harley to Godolphin, 15 October 1706, HMC, *Bath MSS*, I, 111.

[19] Sir Rowland Gwynne to Robert Harley, 11 July 1704, BM, Portland Loan, 29/137.

formity to the Land Tax bill as a means of forcing it through Parliament, Gwynne wrote again: "I doubt not but you will be supported by the next Parliament, if you will employ only moderate men and pursue moderate counsels. . . . We have sufficient experience that no violent party in England could ever stand long."[20] But the question for Harley was not so much whether a violent party could stand, but how a moderate government allied with the Tories could deal with its own violent men. For if the danger from Whig side was domination by the Junto, on the Tory side the difficulty lay in controlling the country gentlemen, generally of extreme political views, who constituted the majority of the party in the House of Commons.[21] Every government, whatever its political coloring, was hard-pressed when the country members joined forces against it: "The Embodying of gentlemen (country gentlemen I mean) against the Queen's service is what is to be avoided," Harley warned Godolphin in 1705.[22] But for a Tory government the problem was more difficult in that these gentlemen supplied its voting strength and, conscious of their power, sought to exert what influence they could on the policy of the Tory ministers. The question was how to keep them in check without entirely losing their support; and here the distribution of places became an issue of importance.

In Harley's view the proper qualification for office was willingness to serve the Queen. To give out places as enticement or reward for party loyalty shifted the emphasis from the Queen's service to the service of party and led ultimately to government by party. On the other hand, to allow those loyal to the Queen to remain in office regardless of ministerial

---

[20] Gwynne to Robert Harley, 15 May 1705, HMC, *Portland MSS*, IV, 181.

[21] For the Country Tories and their significance in Parliament, see Holmes, *British Politics in the Age of Anne*, pp. 249–52; also pp. 171, 372–6. He terms them "invariably the largest and usually the most significant constituent of the party in every Parliament of this period" (p. 249).

[22] Robert Harley to Godolphin, 4 September 1705, HMC, *Bath MSS*, I, 74–5.

changes and shifting majorities in the House of Commons provided a check to the predominant party and at the same time prevented the formation of a solid and troublesome opposition of the dispossessed. "If persons who serve without reproach be turned out for not being of a party," he observed after the election of 1705, when the Tories lost their clear majority in the Commons, "it will increase the jealousy that a party who have been once narrow spirited will be so again, and they will need all the assistance imaginable to keep them from running into their old error."[23] The next year he warned Godolphin "to increase the number of those who would devote themselves to the Queen's and your service. . . . I the rather mention this because so many who have been lately obliged pay their acknowledgments to and real dependence on other people." He was "humbly of opinion that whoever would come in a volunteer to the service should be accepted as far as he would go"; and he could not forbear saying that the ensuing session of Parliament "may be made very easy or very difficult by either giving or sparing a few good words without any further engagement than to let those who are not stigmatised by any particular folly know that they need not be desperate."[24]

Harley's policy suited the gentlemen of England very well when it worked in the interests of Tory placeholders under a predominantly Whig government; it displeased them extremely when it benefited the Whigs. They were not sympathetic to the notion that a loyal Whig was as good as a loyal Tory: they expected a Tory administration to remove all Whigs from office, clearing the way for the appointment of their own men. "One side will not be contented with less than all," an observer commented, "and it is not to be expected the other will bear being excluded."[25] When in 1705, the year following the

23 *Ibid.*, p. 75.
24 Robert Harley to Godolphin, 15 October 1706, *ibid.*, p. 111.
25 James Vernon to the Duke of Shrewsbury, 18 August 1704, *Letters Illustrative of the Reign of William III. From 1696 to 1708. Addressed to the*

defeat of the Tack, the Court backed a Whig for Speaker of the new House of Commons over his High Tory opponent, Sir Robert Davers, a Tory and himself a Tacker, wrote Harley an angry letter saying he hoped Harley's interest would not come into choosing the Whig candidate.

Do you not remember that you told me my Lord Treasurer bid you tell me and all your friends he would not suffer a Whig to come into place nor a "leagh torry." I will not launch out but will say we have been most barbarously used by one that we have not deserved it from. I have often told you that those vile wretches the Whigs only watch for an opportunity to tear you and that Lord to pieces, and you have always agreed with me in that matter.[26]

The Tackers had not forgiven Godolphin and Harley for enlisting moderate Tory support to defeat their motion —"the side that lost it . . . are still more and more incensed against the ministry, who they say have debauched their party from them"[27]—and the issue of the Speaker enraged them further. Harley's interest did come into choosing the Court candidate, and his reply to Davers illuminates some of the difficulties he had to contend with. "I do assure you I have the same principles I came into the House of Commons with," he declared; "I have never willingly nor never will change them." He defied the world "to say I have directly or indirectly done anything against the common interest of the Church or Monarchy of England." But

it hath been my misfortune for twelve years past almost every session to get the ill word upon one occasion or other of both parties; for the good word of one side I did not court it, and that of the other I lost it only upon such occasions by which they ran into those extraordinary things which gratified none but their

---

Duke of Shrewsbury, by James Vernon, Esq., ed. by G. P. R. James, Esq. (London, 1841), III, 267. Hereafter cited as *Vernon Correspondence*.

26 Sir Robert Davers to Robert Harley, 2 October 1705, HMC, *Portland MSS*, IV, 256. Could a "leagh torry" be a *Low* Tory conceivably?

27 James Vernon to Shrewsbury, 1 December 1704, *Vernon Correspondence*, III, 275.

enemies, as appeared by many instances. . . . I have laboured with the utmost application to prevent our friends doing anything unreasonable. . . . but tares have been sown in the wheat, and impracticable measures suggested by those, who whatever else they meant, did not intend the public good. As to what I mean by reasonable—it is this, the Queen hath nothing to ask for herself, she will protect nobody in doing ill; therefore it is easy to agree what is reasonable to defend ourselves.[28]

Chief among the extraordinary things to which Harley referred was, of course, the Tack; but he had in mind also the consistent attempts of the High Tories to obstruct government policy and embarrass the Queen's ministers. Davers and his High Tory friends had their own definition of what was reasonable, and it did not include cooperation with the Whigs.

Harley's principles inevitably brought on him the accusation of trimming. In November 1704 Defoe reported that the Whigs were cheerfully predicting his imminent fall. " 'Both sides are against him,' " the Whig propagandists maintained.

"he has trimmed so long on both sides, and caressed both Parties, till both begin to see themselves illtreated, and now as he loves neither side, neither side will stand by him. All the Whigs of King William's reign expected to have come in play again, and had fair words given them, but they see it was but wording them into a Fools' Paradise, and now the two ends will be reconciled to overturn the middle way."[29]

The same theme, turned to more flattering account, ran through a lengthy communication from a correspondent in Tunbridge Wells, who asked leave "to acquaint you with my observation of people's opinion of your Honour."

You are entirely master of two opposite parties, both think you to be theirs and confide in you as such, to promote their several

---

[28] Robert Harley to Sir Robert Davers, 16 October 1705, HMC, *Portland MSS*, IV, 261.
[29] Defoe to Robert Harley, 2 November 1704, HMC, *Portland MSS*, IV, 147.

different interests: whatever distinguishing favour you show to either side, doth not lessen your esteem in the other party, 'tis all ascribed to a depth of policy which they cannot comprehend and which they say is peculiar to yourself, but is not a leaving the party; and in such an unprecedented manner do you manage the heads of both parties, that both sides believe, at a proper time and occasion you will show yourself entirely in their distinct interests.[30]

This was August 1704, before the Tack, and Harley had been in office only four months. Admiration for the deep policy they could not comprehend soured on the part of many of Harley's Tory followers when, with the passage of time, he failed to make all things clear by showing himself entirely in their interest. "Depth of policy" now appeared simply as trimming and an indication of Harley's unwillingness wholeheartedly to support sound Tory principles.

Harley was not daunted by such criticism and complaint. When in the summer of 1710 he unseated the Godolphin–Marlborough ministry, he came into office on the principles he had consistently maintained. A pamphlet written on his instruction to justify the change of ministers declared that he designed to free the Queen from "the formidable Power of a few Men" who "have entered into Confederacies, and taken Resolutions to govern both Queen and Nation according to their own pleasure."[31] The subtitle of the pamphlet summarized Harley's views on the proper course of government:

An Essay upon the Original Cause, Progress, and Mischievous Consequences of the Factions in this Nation.

Shewing, That the Heads and Leaders on both Sides have always imposed upon the Credulity of their respective Parties, in order to compass their own Selfish Designs at the Expence of the Peace and Tranquillity of the Nation.

Sincerely intended For the allaying the Heats and Animosities of the People, and persuading all Honest, Well-meaning Men to compose their Party-Quarrels, and unite their Hearts and Affec-

[30] Stanley West to Robert Harley, 29 August 1704, *ibid.*, pp. 118–19.
[31] [Simon Clement], *FAULTS on both SIDES*, p. 36.

tions for the promoting the Publick Good, and Safety of their Queen and Country.[32]

The Junto, the "Whig" author contended, inflamed the minds of their admirers by telling them that "nothing less is intended than a total Change of hands, all *Whigs* to be turn'd out of the Ministry, and the *Tories* to rule all; then the Dissenters must expect another Occasional Conformity Bill, nay even their precious Liberty of Conscience will be taken away." But these reports were altogether fictitious and false.

Her Majesty is as firmly resolv'd against all Extreams as they [honest men] can wish, that She will bear equal regard to Men that behave themselves well of either side, and desires that the Names of Parties and Factions may be buried in oblivion, and that we may have no other Mark of Distinction among us than that of Knaves from honest Men; that they will find such of the *Tories* (as people still call them) as shall be admitted into the Ministry, will come into moderate measures, and when any of them act otherwise they will be laid by.[33]

There was not "the least Reason to doubt, but that all those of the *Whig* Party who shall abandon the ill Designs of the *Junto*, and heartily concur (according to their own Principle) in the Promotion of the publick Good, will be as freely admitted to Employments, and as well regarded as ever."[34] The writer defended Harley against the accusation of trimming, describing him as "much more a Patriot and a true *Whig* than his Adversaries." He joined the Tories only when the Whigs deserted "the true interest of their Country" in the late reign, "and, as St. *Paul* became all unto all that he might gain some, if this Gentleman has employ'd the Dexterity of which he is so great a Master, to draw off the best Men of that Party from the extream which they had formerly fallen into, and to win them into the true Interest of the Nation," he should be applauded

[32] *Ibid.*, title page.
[33] *Ibid.*, pp. 43–4.
[34] *Ibid.*, p. 36.

by both parties and looked upon "as the happy Instrument that is content to Sacrifice his own ease, to pass through good Report and bad Report, and to labour constantly to destroy Faction, and to reconcile the honest Men of all sorts who really design the good of their Country."[35]

FAULTS on both SIDES was a piece of propaganda specifically designed to allay the fears of moderate Whigs and Dissenters and to attract their support to Harley's government. Harley's "Plan for conducting the Business of the Public," proposed to the Queen after the General Election of 1710, reflected equal concern with the need to rescue the Crown from faction and to pursue a moderate course. Dealing with domestic affairs, he pointed out that, while "in all places the Faction have been for many years possessed of the Power,"

the Queen has had an opportunity of seeing where the true strength, and inclination of the People are. . . . The great care should be, that this Bent and Disposition of the people should be guided and directed for the Queen's service and the public good, and not be at the disposal of particular persons.[36]

The greater part of the "Plan" was devoted to a more detailed consideration of the means by which this end could be accomplished. Ministers must avoid open dissension:

The Faction have no hope but from Divisions at Court, and at this time it will be of very ill consequence, if by the Behaviour of any of those who have credit with the Queen there should be a Pretence in either House to doubt what the Queen's mind is—

The Queen is the Center of Power and Union, if a Breach be suffered to be made in her Ministry, the Enemy will enter at that Breach.

As for Parliament, in the House of Lords, where "the Faction have most of their Strength . . . and most of their able Men, . . . no time should be lost in securing those who are to be had before they are engaged too far the other way." In the House

[35] Ibid., p. 33.

[36] "Mr. Harley's Plan for conducting the Business of the Public as proposed to the Queen in a Conference with H. M., Oct. 30th 1710," BM, Stowe MSS, 248.

of Commons, where there was a clear majority, "the Queen's servants must have directions to be prudent in conducting this Majority, and the Pleasing the Clergy, avoiding giving Jealousies, and the hopes of Places after will render that House easy this Session."

Thus Harley at the threshold of his ministry: a man of moderation, only reluctantly a man of party and this largely as a matter of expediency. Nominally a Tory, his moderate principles separated him from the zealous majority within the party. His Toryism was suspect, and rightly so. Apart from his opposition to the power and pretension of the Junto and his desire to bring the war to an early conclusion, he held no distinctly Tory views. And while he strongly supported the Established Church, his sympathy for Dissent did not endear him to those High Tories who cried "the Church in danger" and urged that the party must become the Church party if it was to establish itself on a strong foundation. "Though now he passes for a tory he was formerly a great dissenter," an observer commented in 1710;[37] and the mistrust reflected in that remark was confirmed by his refusal, even after the great Tory electoral victory in October 1710, to remove all Whigs from office. From one point of view the story of Harley's ministry and of his ultimate failure turns around the efforts of his High Tory associates to make him into a party leader. His steadfast rejection of this role made his position difficult from the outset and increasingly so when, impatient with moderation, the Tory gentlemen, organized into the October Club, lent their weight to the urgings of their leaders.

I I

Prudence, the avoiding of giving jealousies, were the watchwords of Harley's policy; they did not figure so largely in the

[37] Lord Raby, "Caracteres de plusieurs Ministres de la cour d'Angleterre," *The Wentworth Papers, 1705–1739*, ed. by J. J. Cartwright (London, 1883), p. 133.

politics of St. John. His political connections were Tory from the beginning, and it was as a spokesman for High Tory interests that he embarked on his parliamentary career.[38] He plunged into the impeachment of the Whig lords in 1701, and as a Commissioner of Public Accounts in the new reign—one of a group Burnet described as "the hottest men in the House" —he was active in investigating charges of mismanagement in William's time.[39] In 1702–3 he supported his friend William Bromley in introducing the first two bills against what Bromley termed "that abominable Hypocrisie, that inexcusable Imorality of Occasional Conformity."[40] It was not until the following year, when he had joined the ministry as a Harleyite, that he changed sides, voting with the government to defeat the Tack. St. John considered himself a good Tory and when, after 1715, he was under attack from the Tory side, he took particular pains to defend his unswerving commitment to the principles of his party. In the "Letter to Sir William Windham," he began his account of "the state of affairs in Britain" with the year 1710: "I go no farther back because the part which I acted before that time, in the first essays I made in public affairs, was the part of a tory, and so far of a piece with that which I acted afterwards."[41] And there is no reason to question his claim. He shared the Tory resentment of the "moneyed interest," the Bank of England, the great trading corporations, and all those lesser companies and individuals engaged in commerce and finance who, in the Tory view, grew rich at the expense of the gentlemen of England. Finance was associated with Whiggery—in general a fair association—and

[38] For Bolingbroke's politics and his early parliamentary career see Dickinson, *Bolingbroke*, chaps. 1 and 2.

[39] Burnet, *History*, V, 6. For the impeachments, see St. John to Sir William Trumbull, 22 June 1701, HMC, *Downshire MSS*, I, 803, where St. John heatedly denounces the House of Lords' acquittal of Somers.

[40] Bromley to Dr. Charlett, 22 October 1702, Bodleian Library, MS Ballard 38/137.

[41] Bolingbroke, *Works*, I, 114.

the Bank in particular denounced as an instrument of Whig domination. But the Tory complaint was loudest on the matter of taxation, for while hostilities dragged on and the gentry continued year after year to pay a land tax of four shillings in the pound, the "moneyed men," the bankers, the stock-jobbers and speculators, made spectacular profits out of the exigencies of a nation at war.[42] Speaking of 1710, Bolingbroke pointed to

the prodigious inequality between the condition of the moneyed men and of the rest of the nation. The proprietor of the land, and the merchant who brought riches home by the returns of foreign trade, had during two wars bore the whole immense load of the national expenses; whilst the lender of money, who added nothing to the common stock, throve by the public calamity, and contributed not a mite to the public charge.[43]

In 1709 he had written to Lord Orrery:

We have now been twenty years engaged in the two most expensive Wars that Europe ever saw. The whole Burthen of this Charge has lain upon the landed Interest during the whole Time. The Men of Estates have, generally speaking, neither serv'd in the Fleets nor Armies, nor meddled in the public Fonds, & management of the Treasure.

[42] For the landed versus the moneyed interest in Anne's reign, see Holmes, *British Politics in the Age of Anne,* chap. 5; W. A. Speck, "Conflict in Society," in Holmes, ed., *Britain after the Glorious Revolution;* also J. H. Plumb, *The Growth of Political Stability in England,* pp. 138–51. For Bolingbroke's views in particular, see Dickinson, *Bolingbroke,* pp. 22–3, 186–91. Isaac Kramnick, in his study of Bolingbroke's political ideas, sees Bolingbroke as a "reactive conservative," a defender of the traditional political, economic, and social order against the encroachments of the moneyed interest. He opposed the war because "the war and the new moneyed order that subsidized and supported it were, he thought, bringing destruction to the landed gentry and subverting the traditional constitutional and hierarchical structure of society" (p. 10). Kramnick finds this opposition to the moneyed men "the thread of continuity that runs through Bolingbroke's entire career" (*ibid.*). Isaac Kramnick, *Bolingbroke and His Circle: The Politics of Nostalgia in the Age of Walpole* (Cambridge, Mass.: Harvard University Press, 1968).

[43] Bolingbroke, "A Letter to Sir William Windham," *Works,* I, 116.

A new Interest has been created out of their Fortunes, & a sort of Property, wch was not known twenty years ago, is now encreased to be almost equal to the Terra firma of our Island. The Consequence of all this is, that the Landed Men are become poor & dispirited. . . . In the mean while those Men are become their Masters, who formerly with joy would have been their Servants.[44]

The notion that money concentrated in the Bank and the great joint-stock companies was displacing the power and prestige of land was a fundamental tenet of Tory orthodoxy. So was the view that England should stay clear of expensive continental wars; and, if they must be fought, should wage them at sea rather than on land. Here again Bolingbroke showed himself a good Tory. His conviction that England's interest—determined by her insularity—cast her as a bystander in European affairs, except when her security was threatened, underlay all his diplomatic correspondence and informed much of his later writing. "An island, under one government," he declared in his "Remarks on the History of England," "advantageously situated, rich in itself, richer by its commerce, can have no necessity, in the ordinary course of affairs, to take up the policy of the Continent, to enter into the system of alliances we have been speaking of; or, in short, to act any other part than that of a friendly neighbour or a fair trader."[45] But given the fact that England had been forced by extraordinary circumstances to act another part—and Bolingbroke did not question the necessity for fighting France—he pushed steadily for more vigorous action at sea, urging that England could humble the enemy most effectively by striking at her colonies and overseas trade. This "blue-water" school of thought commanded strong support in Tory circles: St. John's sponsorship of the Quebec expedition in 1711 stemmed from his commitment to its principles, however much, as Harley suspected, he

[44] St. John to Orrery, July 1709, Bodleian Library, MS Eng. Misc. e. 180, ff. 4–5.
[45] Bolingbroke, *Works*, I, 386.

may have hoped to bolster his financial and political fortunes as well.

St. John was, then, a thorough Tory and a ringing spokesman for the gentlemen of England. He was vastly more sophisticated than his backbench followers and his espousal of the High Church cause at least was purely political, but he believed as fervently as they that the future belonged in Tory hands. He was not, but for the first years of his association with Harley, in the least sympathetic to nonparty government: "A coach may as well be driven with unequal wheels, as our Government be carried on with such a mixture of hands," he observed in 1701.[46] And in the "Letter to Sir William Windham," he wrote of 1710:

I am afraid that we came to court in the same dispositions as all parties have done; that the principal spring of our actions was to have the government of the state in our hands; that our principal views were the conservation of this power, great employments to ourselves, and great opportunities of rewarding those who had helped to raise us, and of hurting those who stood in opposition to us.[47]

This may have been St. John's disposition, but it was not Harley's: for while both strove "to have the government of the state in our hands," St. John looked forward to exactly that government by party which Harley hoped to avoid. On this ground alone, it is hardly surprising that their partnership did not prove durable.

I I I

The association between Harley and St. John dates at least from the late summer of 1701, when Sir William Trumbull

[46] St. John to Trumbull, 14 September 1701, HMC, *Downshire MSS*, I, ii, 807.
[47] Bolingbroke, *Works*, I, 114.

offered to approach Harley about an employment for St. John. "Our bantering friend [the Speaker]," he wrote, "has answered my expectation by not coming, though he thought fit to send me word every week that he designed to call here. If the blessing comes unlooked for, 'tis great odds that you will be mentioned."[48] St. John replied with thanks: "If our bantering friend has once in his life deviated from that laudable custom of never meaning what he says, you must have seen him by this time. . . . It is strange a man of his sense cannot stop at secrecy without making a step into falsehood."[49] A month later St. John dined with the Speaker, presumably for the first time, reporting to Trumbull that "there was so much company all the time with him that he never laid his banter one minute aside."[50] But shortly thereafter, following the dissolution of Parliament, he wrote in terms suggesting more familiarity: "The L. C. Justice and our *quondam* Speaker are very much your servants."[51] By the end of the year he was writing to Harley himself: "To tell you that I long extremely to see you is doing a very unfashionable thing, for it is professing a great truth."[52]

Their correspondence continued in much the same style over the next two years. St. John maintained a deferential and rather formal tone. "I give you frequent opportunities of showing your virtues," he concluded a letter in September 1703, "your patience I often exercise, your charity will appear in forgiving the length and impertinence of this letter, and your justice in believing me, Dear Mr. Harley, your . . . etc."[53] In December he explained that he had not written sooner "because I thought it unreasonable to interrupt the pleasures of so

[48] Sir William Trumbull to St. John, 22 September 1701, HMC, *Downshire MSS*, I, ii, 807.
[49] Trumbull to St. John, 30 September 1701, *ibid.*, p. 808.
[50] St. John to Trumbull, 31 October 1701, *ibid.*, p. 810.
[51] St. John to Trumbull, 12 November 1701, *ibid.*, p. 811.
[52] St. John to Harley, 26 December 1701, HMC, *Bath MSS*, I, 54.
[53] St. John to Harley, 25 September 1703, *ibid.*, pp. 55–6.

keen a sportsman as you are, in this season. . . . That you may return quickly to town and bring up, the only good thing a man can go into the country for, health and fresh recruits of vigour, is what I ardently wish, who am from my soul, dear Mr. Harlay your faithful unalterable friend etc."[54] Predictably, Harley was a poor correspondent. "Yesterday I saw Mr. St. John, who complained that he wrote to you three weeks since, but could get no answer," Henry Guy reported to Harley in 1702. "To mollify him I told him I was much longer before I had one. Pray write to him, for he seems to take it unkindly."[55]

St. John was more substantially mollified when he took office in the spring of 1704 with Harley's backing if not demonstrably by his design.[56] By 1705 "Harry" St. John was in constant communication with his "dear Master" and making affectionate reference to the famously obscure Harley style. "I came back yesterday from Wiltshire to this place [Bucklebury], where I found the letter my good natured Robin writ me. Part of it, translated into English, I take to signify that the Queen thinks well of my services. . . . Adieu dear Master no man loves you more entirely than Harry."[57] It is clear that St. John's attachment to Harley in these years was much more than a matter of political convenience and that he was, for a time at least, unreserved in his devotion to his master.

St. John took office as Secretary-at-War in April 1704. In May Harley replaced the High Tory Earl of Nottingham as Secretary of State. Both appointments followed more or less directly from the obstructionist tactics of the Tory majority in the House of Commons and the Tories' refusal wholeheartedly to back the government's war policy. Disappointed in their

[54] St. John to Harley, 16 October 1703, HMC, *Portland MSS*, IV, 73.

[55] Henry Guy to Harley, 17 September 1702, *ibid.*, p. 47.

[56] Dickinson, *Bolingbroke*, p. 37; McInnes, *Robert Harley*, p. 71 and n. 29.

[57] St. John to Harley, 15 May 1705, HMC, *Portland MSS*, IV, 180. For other letters from "Harry" to his "dear Master," see *ibid.*, IV, *passim*; and BM, Portland Loan, 29/156.

expectations for place and favor following the accession of a Tory queen and their electoral victory in the summer of 1702, the Tories were more interested in proceeding with their own projects, in harassing the ministers and denouncing the men and measures of the last reign, than in voting supplies to carry on the war. The ministry could rely on a certain amount of Whig support, but the success of the government program required that at least some of the High Church following be brought over to the Court. This Harley set about doing, and chief among his converts was Henry St. John.[58] St. John's shift to the Court seems to have been motivated by a combination of political ambition and admiration for Harley. Dickinson writes that his conversion "owed much to his desire to hold office,"[59] and the path to advancement lay in support of the ministry. At the same time St. John had made it clear that, left to lead the Tories in the Commons, he could be extremely troublesome: he had demonstrated to the ministers that he was worth buying off. He was shrewd enough to see as well that continued Tory obstructionism could only lead to increased ministerial reliance on the Whigs. He had no intention of abandoning the Tories; on the contrary, he wanted to save the party from its own extremists in order to preserve its power, and his own political base. His move to the government side was no doubt made easier for him by his consistent support of Marlborough's conduct of the war.[60] In 1702 he had written that his "great dependance" was on Marlborough's "admirable good sense"; and a year later he told Trumbull that the Duke's reasons for attacking the French "are such as I can not imagine can be fairly and strongly answer'd."[61] His confidence in Marlborough contributed significantly to his willingness to support the ministry.

[58] For St. John's conversion to the Court see Dickinson, *Bolingbroke*, pp. 28–38. Also McInnes, *Robert Harley*, pp. 70–1.

[59] Dickinson, *Bolingbroke*, p. 34.

[60] *Ibid.*, pp. 34–5.

[61] St. John to Trumbull, 13 October 1702, 24 September 1703, Berkshire R.O., Downshire Papers, Trumbull Add. MSS, 133/13,24.

Shortly after St. John joined the ministry, the Earl of Nottingham resigned his post as Secretary of State for the Southern Department.[62] Displeased with Marlborough's conduct of the war and by the ministers' continued refusal to support High Tory measures—he was particularly stung by the defeat of the second bill against occasional conformity—Nottingham issued an ultimatum calling for the removal of all Whigs from office.[63] Presumably he thought he had strength enough to force a confrontation from which he would emerge the victor. But the Queen responded by dismissing a number of his High Tory supporters, and Nottingham's own resignation followed. As St. John wrote to Trumbull, "Nottingham sacrific'd himself because his point could not be carryed."[64]

Harley replaced Nottingham as Secretary of State, apparently with some reluctance. He may have felt that taking office would limit his freedom of action, making it more difficult for him to act as an intermediary and negotiator; and his inclination to work behind the scenes rather than in the public eye might well have made him hesitate.[65] In any case, in the middle of May he agreed to serve. His appointment gave formal recognition to his influence at Court rather than increasing it; and, together with St. John's accession to office, it marked the ministry's break with the High Tories. A number of St. John's friends were given places, as was Harley's friend Thomas

[62] For Harley's appointment, see A. McInnes, "The Appointment of Harley in 1704," *The Historical Journal*, XI (1968), 255–71, and his *Robert Harley*, pp. 67–75. Also Snyder, "Godolphin and Harley," pp. 244–6, 252–4.

[63] For the occasional conformity bills, see H. L. Snyder, "The Defeat of the Occasional Conformity Bill and the Tack: A Study in the Techniques of Parliamentary Management in the Reign of Queen Anne," *Bulletin of the Institute of Historical Research*, XLI (1968), 172–92. Godolphin and Marlborough, not wishing to antagonize either their Whig support or the Queen, voted for the second bill, as they had for the first, but they would not canvass for it and Godolphin secretly worked for its defeat. See also Burnet, *History*, V, 106–9.

[64] St. John to Trumbull, 9 May 1704, Berkshire R.O., Downshire Papers, Trumbull Add. MSS, 133/28.

[65] On Harley's reluctance, see Snyder, "Godolphin and Harley," pp. 253–4; McInnes, *Robert Harley*, pp. 191–2.

Mansell, a moderate Tory. The solid Tory front was broken. Backed by a majority in the Commons composed of Whigs and Court Tories, the ministers hoped the Queen's business could be carried forward without undue delay.

In his new courtier's role St. John did not disappoint them. He hastened to align himself with the moderates against his erstwhile High Church colleagues, and he began to use the language of Harleian moderation. Commenting on the dismissal of Lord Jersey, Nottingham's friend and supporter, St. John, wrote that Jersey was one of a group who sought to impose their measures on the Queen and her ministers: "This gang was to be broken & disabled," and Jersey was the first to fall. At the same time he assured Trumbull, rather self-consciously, that men, not measures, had changed: "We are far from being in a Whig interest." Those who had gone out pretended to serve the Church of England party but in reality they served only themselves. He added that he saw signs of "a better spirit" among some of the warmest Tories.[66]

But while Harley's recruitment of St. John and his following had reduced the threat from the Tory right, it had not removed it; and in the autumn of 1704, Parliament opened under the threat of a High Tory offensive. St. John urged his old friend Thomas Coke not to linger in the country, "because it is most certain our patriots design some gallant thing to open the session with, and this is what, out of kindness to them, every one should oppose."[67] The attack focused on a third attempt to put through a bill against occasional conformity; and this time, determined to avoid another defeat in the Whiggish House of Lords, which had twice blocked their efforts, the High Church leaders proposed to attach it to the Land Tax bill, the Crown's principal revenue measure. This was the infamous Tack. By tradition the Lords could not amend a money bill; assuming the combined measure passed the Com-

[66] St. John to Trumbull, 9 May 1704, 16 May 1704, Berkshire R.O., Downshire Papers, Trumbull Add. MSS, 133/28,29.

[67] St. John to Thomas Coke, 16 October 1704, HMC, *Cowper MSS*, III, 49.

mons, the Lords would be faced with accepting it or rejecting it, thus endangering supply. Given these alternatives, the Tories reasoned the Lords would take the first course rather than jeopardize the funds needed to carry on the war. All that was required was safe passage through the Commons.[68] But early in November Harley and Godolphin, alerted to the danger, moved to stem the attack. By their direction meetings were held, votes were canvassed, strategy was planned.[69] Godolphin regretted "that so unreasonable a thing as this Tack shd need so much sollicitation & industry to prevent it, however I shall omitt nothing in my power."[70] In the event, solicitation and industry brought success, and the Tack went down to defeat. The ministerial Tories, St. John, Harcourt, the Solicitor-General, Mansell, and their friends all voted with the Court, though a number of them, probably including St. John, supported the bill itself, without the Tack.[71] The defeat was a signal victory for the government. At the same time it alienated the High Church Tories from their brethren who had voted with the Court. The Tackers would not for a long time forgive the betrayal but, ever optimistic, they were not prepared to give up. "We are told, that if the next H. of C. shall desire the

[68] For the Tack, see Snyder, "The Defeat of the Occasional Conformity Bill and the Tack"; Burnet, *History*, V, 179–82.

[69] See the series of letters from Godolphin to Harley in November and December 1704, Longleat, Portland Misc. MSS, ff. 124–7, 132–8, 140, 199–200; also Patricia M. Ansell, "Harley's Parliamentary Management," *Bulletin of the Institute of Historical Research*, XXXIV (1961), 92–7, on Harley's efforts to detach potential supporters of the bill.

[70] Godolphin to Harley, "Sunday past 2," n.d., Longleat, Portland Misc. MSS, f. 138.

[71] The day after the Commons voted to bring in the bill Godolphin wrote to Harley: "I find plainly it was in the power of the Queen's servants to have kept out the Occasional bill." The bill "might have been prevented if these gentlemen had thought fit." Godolphin to Harley, 16 November 1704, HMC, *Bath MSS*, I, 64–5. See also the letters dated "Monday noon" and "Sunday 19 at 2," Longleat, Portland Misc. MSS, ff. 124–5, 199–200. Mrs. Burnet reported to the Duchess of Marlborough that St. John had voted to bring in the bill, c. 14 November 1704, Blenheim MSS, F-30, quoted in Snyder, "The Defeat of the Occasional Conformity Bill and the Tack," p. 179.

same Security for our Ch. & Religion, they cannt be withstood," Bromley wrote in December. "This, with other Considerations that are very obvious, will I hope engage all that are
Freinds to our Establishmt. to use their utmost Endeavours in
the approaching Elections, our Enemies will nt be wanting in
theirs."[72]

The elections in the spring of 1705 in fact brought heavy
gains for the Whigs, making the parties roughly equal in the
Lower House. "I take it for granted that no party in the House
can carry it for themselves without the Queen's servants join
with them," Harley wrote to Godolphin in September, a
month before the new Parliament met; "That the foundation
is, persons or parties are to come in to the Queen, and not the
Queen to them."[73] St. John, echoing his master, told Thomas
Coke he

should be glad to know what temper you find gentlemen in:
whether they will think it reasonable to support the Queen, who
has nothing to ask but what we are undone if we do not grant: and
who, if she does make use of hands they do not like, has been
forced to it by the indiscretion of our friends. The real foundation
of difference between the two parties is removed, and she seems to
throw herself on the gentlemen of England, who had much better
have her at the head of 'em than any ringleaders of fashion. Unless
gentlemen can show that her administration puts the Church or the
State, in danger, they must own the contest to be about persons:
and if it be so, can any honest man hesitate which side to take.[74]

The gentlemen of England did not agree. Party strife continued unabated, and in the new parliamentary situation the
ministry had to decide how best to consolidate its position.
This was the issue on which the ministers ultimately split. Godolphin and Marlborough, ever fearful of losing support for the
war, moved toward an accommodation with the Whigs. Har-

---

[72] William Bromley to Dr. Charlett, 23 December 1704, Bodleian Library,
MS Ballard 38/142.
[73] Harley to Godolphin, 4 September 1705, HMC, *Bath MSS*, I, 74.
[74] St. John to Coke, 19 September 1705, HMC, *Cowper MSS*, III, 63–4.

ley viewed this as the first step in putting the government into the Junto's hands. He felt that alliance with the Tories offered much the safer course. They were less united, their leadership was less strong: fewer concessions would have to be made. Still, Harley's policy of cooperation with the Tories called for the support of moderate Whigs as well. It was largely through his efforts that the Duke of Newcastle came into the ministry in March 1705, replacing the High Tory Duke of Buckingham as Lord Privy Seal.[75] Newcastle, a Whig peer of great wealth and great electoral influence, was an important addition to the ministry. But, as McInnes points out, his appointment seemed to mark the end of Harley's active attempts to bring more Whigs into the government.[76] The Whig gains in the elections later in the spring gave the Junto a stronger base in the Commons, and Harley had reason to fear the resurgence of Whig domination at Court.

The divergence in policy between Harley and the principal ministers was apparent from the beginning of the new Parliament. Godolphin's decision to nominate John Smith, a moderate Whig, as Court candidate for Speaker was not happily received by Harley and St. John, though both supported him, and he was duly elected.[77] In the same month—October— William Cowper, another moderate Whig, replaced the Tory Lord Keeper, an appointment pressed upon the Queen by Godolphin and the Marlboroughs, though with Harley's eventual acquiescence.[78] There is evidence of a rift between Harley and the two ministers in the summer of 1705, possibly over the

[75] A number of Harley's letters to Newcastle are printed in HMC, *Portland MSS*, II; and see *ibid.*, IV, for Newcastle's side of the correspondence.

[76] McInnes, *Robert Harley*, p. 95.

[77] W. A. Speck, "The Choice of a Speaker in 1705," *Bulletin of the Institute of Historical Research*, XXXVII (1964), 20–46. Dickinson, *Bolingbroke*, p. 41.

[78] Cowper, *Diary*, pp. 1–2, 4; William Coxe, *Memoirs of John Duke of Marlborough* (London, 1820), II, 234–7, hereafter cited as Coxe, *Marlborough*; Burnet, *History*, V, 223–5. Elizabeth Hamilton, *The Backstairs Dragon: A Life of Robert Harley, Earl of Oxford* (London: Hamish Hamilton, 1969), pp. 82–3.

choice of Smith for the Speaker's chair. In July Harley protested his devotion to the Treasurer in terms suggesting that his
loyalty had been questioned. His letter set the pattern for a
number of others to follow over the next three years, and
judging by the revisions and corrections of an earlier draft, the
writing of it caused him some difficulty. He was, he told
Godolphin,

justly conscious to myself that the utmost service I can perform to
her Majesty falls infinitely short of what the Queen deserves, nor
can it bear any proportion to the reverence and affection I have
for your Lordship and the Duke of Marlborough, by whose indulgence and too kind recommendation I have those marks I now
enjoy of the Queen's favour; and as I cannot be without fear lest
her service should suffer in my hand, so I shall always have a
concern that I may not do anything unworthy of your favour.
. . . I have no other views, no other passions, than to be subservient
to your Lordship, if I go astray it shall be only for want of your
direction. I confess I am too apt to tell my own opinion, but then
with good reason I suspect myself so much that I double my
diligence to bring about what is better designed by others.[79]

This was all very well, but the following year brought a
further disagreement between Harley and the Treasurer when
the Whig leadership claimed as further reward for its support
of the Crown the appointment of the Whig Earl of Sunderland
as Secretary of State. Sunderland was Marlborough's son-in-
law, and as the Duchess of Marlborough later wrote, "they
[the Whigs] chose to recommend him to her Majesty, because,
as they expressed themselves to me, they imagined it was driving the nail that would go."[80] Godolphin and Marlborough

[79] Harley to Godolphin, 21 July 1705, HMC, *Bath MSS*, I, 72-3. The
earlier draft, undated, is in Longleat, Portland Misc. MSS, ff. 113-4. Speck's
evidence makes it clear that Godolphin's choice of Smith was known at
least as early as 25 July, so that this could well have been the occasion of
Harley's letter. Speck, "The Choice of a Speaker in 1705," pp. 26-7.

[80] *Memoirs of Sarah, Duchess of Marlborough*, ed. by William King (New
York: E. P. Dutton and Co., 1930), p. 113. For Sunderland's appointment,
see *ibid.*, pp. 113-20; Coxe, *Marlborough*, chaps. 51 and 52; *Private Corres-*

were prepared to concede. In the previous session of Parliament the Court's measures had been carried with Whig votes. The ministers believed that the government's war policy could not be carried on without continuing Whig support and that this support could not be assured without further concessions to the Junto: Whig votes must be paid for with Court favor. But they believed that this could be done without putting the government into the hands of the Whigs. The Tories, said Godolphin, had behaved with "as much inveteracy and as little sense as was possible." He would "be always of opinion to receive such of them as would come off, but I see very little reason to depend upon that or upon them afterwards." The Whigs had, but for one occasion, voted with the Court, and "is it not more reasonable and more easy to preserve those who have served and helped us than to seek those who have basely and ungratefully done all that was in their poor power to ruin us."[81] Harley, for his part, held to the view that further concessions to the Whigs would lead inevitably to government by party. Sunderland, unlike Newcastle and Cowper, both moderates, was a Junto leader: his appointment would herald the return of Whig domination. Harley thought it was still possible to retain the support of moderate Whigs without bowing to the Junto. He was certain "many of the most staunch Whigs . . . have, and do frequently lament the fury of their leaders, and have rejoiced when their presumption was humbled." The Whigs were "the inferior number, . . . they will not follow those who make themselves their leaders, but yet may be united in the Queen's service by her ministers." But he assured Godolphin he had "no measures, nor will have any but what shall be submitted to the test of your better judgment."[82] Earlier he had written:

---

pondence of Sarah, Duchess of Marlborough (London, 1838), I, 38–9, 60, 65–85; also Snyder, "Godolphin and Harley," pp. 260–2.

[81] Godolphin to Harley, 22 March 1706, HMC, *Portland MSS*, IV, 291.

[82] Harley to Godolphin, 15 October 1706, HMC, *Bath MSS*, I, 110–11.

I have no consideration nor thought but promoting the Queen's service. . . . I have no obligations to any party I list myself of none, ever since I was able to do any thing in Parliamt it has been to oppose & expose the extravagancys & heats of both Partys. . . . To prevent . . . the rocks on both sides is to be the Care of ye Government and that it may not be like a door wch turns upon its Hinges from one side to another, or to shut out always somebody, ought to be ye care of those yt love ye Governmt: for it is certain in such a Country as ours the going over to the extreams of one Party onely makes way to go again to another. For if a man can be turnd out or put in for being of a Party, that Party is the Government and none else.[83]

In November he told Godolphin "that all that has been done has not obliged the party [the Whigs]; whether it has their pretended leaders will be shewn hereafter." He hoped the Treasurer would "rescue us from the violence of either party; and I cannot forbear saying, I know no difference between a mad whig and a mad tory."[84]

Sunderland's appointment would not have been delayed so long had the Queen herself not opposed it, and on much the same grounds as Harley. Anne disliked Sunderland personally; she disliked still more the fact that he was a Whig. "I do fear, for the reasons I have told you, we shall never agree long together," she told Godolphin,

and the making him secretary, I can't help thinking, is throwing myself into the hands of a party. They desire this thing to be done, because else they say they can't answer that all their friends will go along with them this winter. If this be complied with, you will then in a little time, find they must be gratified in something else, or they will not go on heartily in my business. You say yourself, they will need my authority to assist them, which I take to be the bringing more of their friends into employment, and shall I not

[83] Harley to [?], draft, 25 August 1706, Nottingham University Library, Portland Collection, Pw2, Hy 662.
[84] Harley to Godolphin, 16 November 1706, Coxe, *Marlborough*, III, 123–4. See also Harley to Marlborough, 20 September–1 October 1706, Longleat, Portland MSS, V, f. 101.

then be in their hands? If this is not being in the hands of a party, what is?[85]

But Marlborough and Godolphin were unmoved, though Marlborough had, to begin with, been loath to press the Queen against her will.[86] The Captain-General put the point succinctly: "Madam, the truth is, that the heads of one party have declared against you and your government, as far as it is possible, without going into open rebellion. Now, should your majesty disoblige the others, how is it possible to obtain near five millions for carrying on the war with vigour, without which all is undone."[87] The Queen at last relented, but only after months of resistance and under threat of Godolphin's resignation.

The breach between Harley and the two ministers was covered over for the present at least. But Harley's loyalty had been questioned. "Lady Marlborough told me this morning," the Treasurer reported to Marlborough in October, "that Mr. Harley, Mr. St. John, and one or two more of your particular friends, were underhand endeavouring to bring all the difficulties they could think of upon the public business in the next sessions." Godolphin was "apt to think they may have made some steps toward this," and he was not convinced by Harley's declarations to the contrary: "I have had a long letter this very day, full of professions of being guided in these measures, as in all others, by you and me; but at the same time, I doubt so much smoke could not come without some fire."[88] Harley and St. John had in fact been seeking a rapprochement with the

[85] Queen Anne to Godolphin, 21 September 1706, Coxe, *Marlborough*, III, 104.

[86] *Private Correspondence of Sarah, Duchess of Marlborough*, I, 60; *Memoirs of Sarah, Duchess of Marlborough*, p. 113.

[87] Marlborough to Queen Anne, 24 October 1706, N.S., Coxe, *Marlborough*, III, 118.

[88] Godolphin to Marlborough, 18–29 October 1706, Coxe, *Marlborough*, III, 129. The letter Godolphin refers to may have been Harley's letter of 15 October, quoted above, p. 125.

Tories, though not necessarily with a view to creating difficulties in the next session. This was hardly surprising. Harley had declared himself in favor of closer cooperation with the Tories, and he and St. John had greater reason to cultivate the Tory leadership when the ministry relied increasingly on Whig support. Neither would be particularly welcome in a Whig ministry, though Harley more so than St. John; and St. John in any case had no wish to abandon his Tory connections. "I am glad you find the same disposition where you have been as I believe is in other places," he wrote to Harley in November, congratulating him on his approach to the Tory leaders.

It will be one of the greatest pleasures I can have to be instrumental under you in making a proper use of it; in order to this, sure we must have a little more commerce with some gentlemen than has been of late kept up. I did not believe when I writ last to you that the application made to Mr. B[romley] and Sir T. H[anmer] was the effect of your advice, but I do imagine in fact there has been some negotiation of that sort. . . . Adieu! make haste to town, where the public as well as your friends wants you. No man is more entirely, dear Master, yours, than H.[89]

The following year brought another crisis, comparable in its outlines to the one occasioned by the appointment of Sunderland. The difficulties of 1707 were a continuation of those of 1706. In this instance the dispute turned around a number of ecclesiastical appointments, principally the question of who should succeed to the sees of Exeter and Chester.[90] The Queen had promised these to two clerics of her own choosing, both Tories; the Whigs, again claiming their due reward for support of the Court, put forward their own candidates. Harley, with Abigail Hill, the Queen's dresser, his supposed accomplice, was thought to have managed the Queen's

[89] St. John to Harley, 5 November 1706, HMC, *Bath MSS*, I, 121.
[90] For the bishoprics crisis, see G. V. Bennett, "Robert Harley, the Godolphin ministry, and the bishoprics crisis of 1707," *English Historical Review*, LXXXII (1967), 726–47.

choices, but this both he and the Queen denied. "I believe you have been told, as I have, that these two persons were recommended to me by Mr. Harley," Anne told Marlborough, "which is so far from being true, that he knew nothing of it, till it was the talk of the town: I do assure you these men were my own choice."[91] And Harley protested to Godolphin: "I have told you nothing but truth. I scorn to deny anything I have done, and if I had ever directly or indirectly, by myself or any other, recommended these two persons . . . I am not so mean as to deny it, which I solemnly do."[92] There is no particular reason to question Harley's denials; at the same time the Queen's stand was consonant with his own, and it is reasonable to assume that he encouraged her. Once again the Queen and Harley were aligned against Godolphin and Marlborough. Again the Whig leadership threatened to lead their forces into opposition if their demands were not met; again the two ministers urged the Queen to comply lest the war effort be jeopardized.

But the Queen stood firm, unmoved even by a threatened parliamentary attack on the Admiralty, a peculiarly sensitive target since Prince George, the Queen's consort, was Lord High Admiral and George Churchill, Marlborough's brother, the effective head of the department. The Whigs had thought the Queen would wish to avoid embarrassment to either. Her resolution was ascribed by the Whigs to Harley's treachery: Sunderland and the Duchess of Marlborough in particular fed the suspicions of the two first ministers. "I am afraid there is too much conversation between the queen and Mr. Harley," Marlborough wrote the Treasurer in July. And in August he was "a good deal concerned at a letter I received by the last

[91] The Queen to Marlborough, [August 1707], Coxe, *Marlborough*, III, 371-2. For further correspondence on the bishoprics crisis, see *ibid.*, chaps. 58, 62-3.
[92] Harley to Godolphin, 17 September 1707, HMC, *Bath MSS*, I, 182. Harley made the same declaration to Marlborough: Coxe, *Marlborough*, III, 395-6.

post from lady Marlborough, in which she tells me that Mr. Harley has the entire confidence of the queen."[93] In all of this Harley repeatedly declared himself innocent of any attempt to undermine the ministers or their policy. "I crave leave to profess to you most solemnly," he wrote to Godolphin, "that I have made it. my study to serve the Queen upon an honest principle, that I have no attachment to any other person in the world but your lordship and the Duke of Marlborough." He was prepared to resign whenever Godolphin thought him "a burden to the service or uneasy to anyone."[94] Godolphin replied: "I never had, nor ever can have, a thought of your being out of the Queen's service while I am in it; but I am as sure I neither desire nor am able to continue in it, unless we can agree upon the measures by which she is to be served both at home and abroad."[95]

It is difficult to know how much the two ministers believed Harley's assurances or, indeed, how much they should have. Marlborough talked of Harley's "scheme," Godolphin replied that there was no scheme.[96] According to Burnet, Harley, St. John, and Harcourt tried unsuccessfully to enlist the High Tory leaders "in the queen's interest; assuring them, that her heart was with them, that she was weary of the tyranny of the whigs, and longed to be delivered from it."[97] At the same time Harley was working to detach dissident Whigs from the Junto.[98] All this was consistent with Harley's policy, whether or not he was secretly plotting to alter the ministry.

[93] Marlborough to Godolphin, 18 July 1707, 29 August 1707, Coxe, *Marlborough*, III, 279, 368-9. See also Sunderland's letter of 8 October, *ibid.*, p. 387.

[94] Harley to Godolphin, 10 September 1707, HMC, *Bath MSS*, I, 180.

[95] Godolphin to Harley, 18 September 1707, HMC, *Bath MSS*, I, 183.

[96] Marlborough to the Duchess of Marlborough, 11 July 1707; Marlborough to Godolphin, 29 September 1707, Coxe, *Marlborough*, III, 273, 381; Godolphin to Marlborough, 7 October 1707, *ibid.*, p. 400.

[97] Burnet, *History*, V, 340.

[98] Harley to Newcastle, 11 September 1707, HMC, *Portland MSS*, II, 200; Newcastle to Harley, 17 September 1707, *ibid.*, IV, 448.

When Parliament met at the end of October the Junto leadership, still unsatisfied in their demands, made good their threats, joining with the High Tories in an attack on Admiralty affairs and on a number of other questions opposing the Court. Early in December, presumably in an attempt to find a way out of this situation, it appears that Marlborough and Godolphin attempted to reach some agreement with Harley on the basis of a moderate nonparty government. "I am just come from the two great men," Harley wrote to Newcastle. "I believe they are fully sensible of their danger, and that there are number of men enough to support them, who are ready and willing to do it, if they will but create a confidence in them."[99] A meeting of moderate Whigs was called; and the two ministers may also have approved a renewed approach to the Tories.[100] At the end of the month James Brydges reported that "the Tories (I mean the reasonable ones) have been kept in temper, and by the steadiness of my Lord Marlborough &c. we have all been preserved from the violence of the Whigs, whom nothing would satisfy (at least as some affirm) but a total extirpation of us all." The Court Whigs had declared "they would never come in to press the Queen and the ministry" to unreasonable measures. And, according to the Lord Treasurer, the Queen had given Harley "authority to say, that she is for the future firmly resolved to govern upon such principles as will incline her to side with the violence neither of Whig or Tory; that she will never make bargains with either party to persuade them to do that which a sense of their duty alone ought to lead them to but that those shall always be the object of her countenance and favor, who without expecting terms come voluntarily into

[99] Harley to Newcastle, [5 December 1707], HMC, *Portland MSS*, II, 200. Snyder points out that this letter is misdated September in the HMC report: "Godolphin and Harley," p. 265, n. 80.

[100] For the meetings of early December, see *ibid.*, pp. 264-7, and Bennett, "Robert Harley, the Godolphin ministry, and the bishoprics crisis of 1707," pp. 743-6. According to Bennett, Harley asked for and received permission to approach the Tories (pp. 743-4).

the promoting of her service."[101] Brydges's report is confirmed by Archbishop Sharp, the Queen's confessor, who wrote that on December 16 the Queen told him "she meant to change her measures, and give no countenance to the Whig Lords, but that all the Tories, if they would, should come in, and all the Whigs likewise, that would show themselves to be in her interests, should have favour."[102] The Queen prevailed on the matter of the bishoprics; and it appeared that Harley's counsels had prevailed with the Queen.

Yet within two months Harley was out of office. At the end of January 1708 an open rupture occurred between Harley and Godolphin. This time the Treasurer had no use for Harley's professions of innocence and submission; and Marlborough's decision to stand by his partner forced the crisis which resulted in Harley's resignation.[103] It is impossible to know exactly what happened in the weeks before Harley's fall, but several points seem clear. To begin with, the rapprochement of early December, however real it had been—and one does not know with how much enthusiasm Godolphin and Marlborough entered into it or what exactly had been promised—had not resolved the ministry's difficulties. Parliament recessed over Christmas, but in January the opposition resumed the offensive, turning its attention to the war in Spain and in particular to the defeat suffered by the British forces at Almanza the previous April. St. John had been asked in December for figures on the number of English troops in the Peninsula at the time of the battle of Almanza, but debate was postponed until January to give him time to assemble the

[101] Brydges to Cadogan, 24 December 1707, quoted in Godfrey Davies, "The Seamy Side of Marlborough's War," *Huntington Library Quarterly*, XV (1951-2), 38-9.

[102] Thomas Sharp, *The Life of John Sharp, D.D., Lord Archbishop of York*, ed. by Thomas Newcome (London, 1825), I, 323.

[103] In general I follow G. S. Holmes and W. A. Speck, "The Fall of Harley in 1708 Reconsidered," *English Historical Review*, LXXX (1965), 673-98. See also Snyder, "Godolphin and Harley," pp. 263-70; McInnes, *Robert Harley*, chap. 5.

information.[104] Now it appeared that St. John's figures accounted only for 8,660 of the 29,295 men authorized by Parliament, a discrepancy which gave the opposition grounds for what promised to be a direct onslaught against the ministry.[105] The Almanza inquiry did not cause the rift between Harley and St. John and the two first ministers, but it can only have strained the relationship further. It is probable that Godolphin and Marlborough felt St. John could have handled the disclosure of the missing troops with less embarrassment to the government and that Harley could have done more on the ministers' behalf in the crucial debates of January 29 and February 3, when the Commons passed an address critical of the ministry. At the same time it is likely that the two Secretaries were themselves surprised by the figures, and laid the blame on Godolphin and Marlborough.[106]

The government's position had, since Christmas, been made still more uncomfortable by an entirely adventitious circumstance. At the end of December William Greg, a clerk in Harley's office, was taken up for selling secrets to the French. From his arrest until the moment of his execution he denied Harley's complicity in his crime; but the Whigs were bound to make what capital they could out of the affair, to use it if they could to bring about Harley's dismissal. The discovery of Greg's treason increased the pressure on the ministers, making them more vulnerable to Whig attack. Harried by the Junto on one side and the High Tories on the other, the ministry's situation was becoming untenable, and it was presumably the impossibility of continuing on the same foot that led Marlborough and Godolphin to reconsider Harley's proposal for an

104 St. John to Harley, 24 December 1707, Longleat, Portland MSS, VI, f. 217, and 14 January 1708, HMC, *Bath MSS*, I, 189.

105 Addison to Lord Manchester, 10 January 1708, *Court and Society from Elizabeth to Anne*, edited from the Papers at Kimbolton by the Duke of Manchester (London, 1864), II, 272.

106 Holmes and Speck, "The Fall of Harley in 1708 Reconsidered," pp. 675-8, 693-4; Dickinson, *Bolingbroke*, pp. 55-7.

alliance with the Tories. In mid-January two meetings were held to explore Harley's scheme: a number of Court Whigs were among the government leaders present, reflecting Harley's hope that a reorganized ministry could retain the support of moderates from both parties.[107] What Marlborough and the Treasurer thought of Harley's plan is not known, but it seems certain that Harley moved ahead in any case, negotiating underground with key Tory leaders; and it seems equally certain that he did so with the approval of the Queen.[108] At the time of Harley's dismissal James Vernon told Shrewsbury he had heard "that messages have been carried as from the Queen to several leading men among the Tory party, to engage them to stand by her Majesty against the Whigs, whose management she was dissatisfied with, and no less with the influence they had upon her ministers. This is laid to the charge of Mr. Attorney [Harcourt] and Mr. St. John, but more particularly the latter, so that they are looked upon as a triumvirate that were framing a new scheme of administration."[109] What Harley intended remains an open question. He consistently denied then and subsequently that he ever plotted to unseat either Godolphin or Marlborough.[110] But at the end of January Godolphin apparently became convinced that Harley had betrayed him. Nothing less than the revelation of Harley's supposed treachery could account for the letter the Treasurer delivered to him January 30: "I have received your letter, and am very sorry for what has happened to lose the good opinion I had so much inclination to have of you, but I cannot help seeing and hearing, nor believing my senses. I am very far from having deserved it from you. God forgive you!"[111]

It is generally thought that in the crisis Marlborough was,

[107] Holmes and Speck, "The Fall of Harley in 1708 Reconsidered," pp. 683–4.

[108] *Ibid.*, pp. 684–6, 690–1.

[109] Vernon to Shrewsbury, 10 February 1708, *Vernon Correspondence*, III, 345. Harcourt was promoted Attorney-General in April 1707.

[110] McInnes, *Robert Harley*, pp. 101–2.

[111] [Godolphin to Harley], [30 January 1708], HMC, *Bath MSS*, I, 190.

for a time at least, prepared to work out some means of cooperating with Harley, though Marlborough had reasons of his own to mistrust the Secretary.[112] Harley had offended him in something he had said to the Queen, presumably critical of Marlborough and perhaps of Godolphin as well,[113] though Harley denied this had ever been his intention. He begged that Marlborough would "not let me Continue under the Anxiety I am, but that you wil vouchsafe me an opportunity to wait upon you to clear my Self, for I never did entertain a thought that was prejudicial to your Grace."[114] And he went on to ask that Marlborough intercede for him with the Lord Treasurer. For another week Harley continued to hope that the Duke might fall in with his plans, even if the Treasurer did not.[115] But Marlborough decided to stand with Godolphin, influenced no doubt by Harley's less than vigorous defense of the ministry when on February 3 the Commons voted an address critical of the conduct of the war in Spain. He joined the Treasurer in declaring his intention to resign if Harley was not dismissed. He told the Queen that as he had been unable to convince her of "the false and treacherous proceedings of Mr. secretary Harley to lord treasurer and myself," he found himself "obliged to have so much regard to my own honour and reputation, as not to be every day made a sacrifice to falsehood and treachery, but most humbly to acquaint your majesty that no consideration can make me serve any longer with that man. And I beseech your majesty to look upon me, from this moment, as forced out of your service, as long as you think fit to continue him in it."[116]

The Queen, apparently, was prepared to sacrifice Godolphin. According to Swift, "the Queen told Mr. St. John a week

[112] But see Snyder, "Godolphin and Harley," for an alternative view: p. 270 and n. 93.

[113] Harley to Marlborough, 28 January 1708, draft, BM, Portland Loan, 29/12.

[114] *Ibid.*

[115] See Harley's letters to Marlborough of 1 and 6 February 1708, BM, Portland Loan, 29/12.

[116] Marlborough to the Queen, February 1708, Coxe, *Marlborough*, IV, 24.

ago, that she was resolved to part with Lord Treasurer; and sent him with a letter to the Duke of Marlborough, which she read to him, to that purpose; and she gave St. John leave to tell it about the town, which he did without any reserve."[117] Godolphin was expendable; but Marlborough's continuance as Captain-General was essential to the ministry, however it might be reconstituted. His ultimatum meant Harley's defeat. Still, the Queen gave way only when a number of Cabinet ministers made clear their refusal to serve under Harley and the Commons expressed their dissatisfaction by delaying the vote on a pending bill of supply. At the same time the Whigs in the House of Lords moved an inquiry into the Greg affair which could well have proved dangerous to Harley. There seems to have been a good deal of truth in Burnet's report that the Queen "would have put all to the hazard, if Harley himself had not apprehended his danger, and resolved to lay down."[118] And Swift perhaps understated the case when he observed that "the Queen, who had then a great Esteem for the Person and Abilityes of Mr. Harley . . . was deprived of his Service with some Regret."[119]

Harley's protestations to the contrary, contemporary observers were inclined to believe that he meant to force the Lord Treasurer's resignation. Swift wrote that "Mr. Harley had been some time, with the greatest art imaginable, carrying on an intrigue to alter the Ministry, and began with no less an enterprise than that of removing the Lord Treasurer." According to Joseph Addison, Sunderland's Under-Secretary, "It is said Mr Harley and his friends had laid schemes to undermine

[117] Swift to Archbishop King, 12 February 1708, *Swift Correspondence*, I, 69–70. See also Swift, "Memoirs," p. 113, and Lord Raby to Cadogan, 10 March 1708, N.S., *Wentworth Papers*, p. 20.

[118] Burnet, *History*, V, 354. And see *ibid.*, pp. 353–5 and Coxe, *Marlborough*, IV, 25–7.

[119] Jonathan Swift, "Some Considerations upon the Consequences hoped and feared from the Death of the Queen," *Political Tracts, 1713–1719*, ed. by Herbert Davis and Irvin Ehrenpreis (Oxford: Basil Blackwell, 1964), p. 101. Hereafter cited as Swift, "Some Considerations."

most of our Great officers of State and plant their own party in the room of 'em. If we may believe common fame he himself was to have bin a Peer and Ld Treasurer." Addison was not sure if Rochester and Bromley would be provided for; but Harcourt and St. John were to be promoted and a number of other Tories taken into the ministry.[120] "Common fame" may of course have been mistaken; but whether or not Harley's scheme from the outset required, or at least regarded with equanimity, Godolphin's resignation, there is no question that the eleven days between the Treasurer's "God forgive you" note and Harley's fall constituted a contest of strength between the two men. It seems probable that Harley wished to avoid a showdown, but events overtook him, and the break with Godolphin at the end of January forced the issue. In the crisis, Harley discovered that, even with the backing of the Queen, he could not by himself command enough support to lead the ministry.

Harley resigned on February 11. In a gesture of loyalty extremely unusual for the time his particular friends, St. John, Harcourt, and Mansell, left office with him. St. John's resignation especially was greeted with surprise as he was known to be well thought of by Marlborough. "I thought you told me that Harry St. Johns and his gang were all entirely my lord Duke's," Lord Raby inquired of Cadogan.[121] It was no accident that St. John carried the Queen's letter to the Duke informing him that she was prepared to part with Godolphin. And Cadogan must have reflected his commander's sentiments at least to some extent when he told James Brydges that he was "beyond expression concerned and surprised at our friend Harry St John's resigning. I had a letter from it [him] on that

---

[120] Swift to Archbishop King, 12 February 1708, *Swift Correspondence*, I, 69; Addison to Manchester, 13 February 1708, *The Letters of Joseph Addison*, ed. by Walter Graham (Oxford: The Clarendon Press, 1941), p. 91. See also Addison's letter of 27 February, *ibid.*, p. 95.

[121] Lord Raby to Cadogan, 10 March 1708, N.S., *Wentworth Papers*, p. 20. See Dickinson, *Bolingbroke*, pp. 59–62, for St. John's resignation in 1708, and chap. 3, esp. pp. 45–9, for Marlborough's high opinion of him.

subject to justify the resolution he had taken. I am sorry he
thought he had reason for it. I am sure the whole army and
particularly those that know him will have reason to regret
it."[122] Given Marlborough's support, St. John could certainly
have remained in his post in spite of his connections with
Harley and the important role he had played in the negotiations with the Tories. But in the circumstances principle and
personal interest conjoined in his decision to resign. He had not
abandoned his commitment to Tory principles: he had never
wished to cut himself off from his Tory base. Since 1706 he
had encouraged Harley in his approaches to the Tories, but the
ministry's drift to the Whigs made his position increasingly
precarious with regard to his Tory supporters. By Brydges's
account, the Tory ministers said they had resigned

because Mr Harley was turned out, which they looked upon as a
full declaration of the ministry's intentions to join entirely with
the Whigs, which they thought was inconsistent with the declaration they had made to them, and the assurances which by the
authority and permission as also by the Queen's commands they
had given the Tories that no such thing should be done.[123]

So long as St. John conceived of his political role in terms of
Tory leadership, he could not afford to stay on in a predominantly Whig ministry. He may have thought as well that even
with Marlborough's backing, he would himself be purged in
due course. But most probably St. John's Tory principles and
the dictates of Tory politics were sufficient to compel his resignation. He knew well enough what Harley would discover to
his cost, that the Tory gentlemen had little use for a minister
who behaved like half a Whig.

[122] James Brydges to Cadogan, 8 March 1708, N.S.; Davies, "The Seamy
Side of Marlborough's War," p. 40.
[123] Brydges to Cadogan, 12 February 1708, Davies, "The Seamy Side of
Marlborough's War," p. 40.

CHAPTER IV

Harley
Heads the Ministry

N the months following his resignation, Harley continued to pursue the policy he had earlier embarked upon. Helped on by a Whig victory at the polls in May, by the year's end his efforts to form an alliance with the Tories had met with considerable success. Writing to Bromley in August, he deplored the present state of affairs, in which "those who are ye smaller part of the Nation have made themselves formidable & terrible to the greater: They have taken advantage of ye mistakes of others, and tho' they hate one another yet they unite together to carry on their design; Why may not ye same thing be done to preserve the whole & for good purposes wch they do to destroy & overturn every thing?" And he assured Bromley "that those who you conversed with last Winter are resolved most heartily to enter into measures with you and those other Gentlemen."[1] A month later Bromley replied:

I can now assure you of my own very sincere disposition to enter into measures with you and the gentlemen you mention, for serving our common interest, and that I verily believe you will find the like in others. . . . I am determined, notwithstanding anything past, to join with you, not as you observe they do on the other

[1] Harley to Bromley, 20 August 1708, BM, Portland Loan, 29/128.

side, though they hate one another, but in affection as well as zeal to preserve the whole, and for the service of the public.

He would be in town in another week and hoped that Harley would then be more particular about his plans and "more free and open, which will be necessary to unite us, and to create that confidence that I desire may be among us."[2]

While he was wooing Bromley, Harley remained in touch with his Whig friends, particularly with Newcastle, and at the same time set about gathering additional Whig support, a task made easier by the divisions within the party.[3] During the summer he appears to have gained the Duke of Shrewsbury to his side.[4] Secretary of State in William's reign, a man of weight and reputation, Shrewsbury had earlier quarreled with the Junto. He had been on cordial terms with Harley for some time; politically, Harley's moderate scheme appealed to him and, according to Cowper, he had shown his willingness to act with Harley in 1707–8. Writing in 1710, Cowper quotes Harley as saying that Shrewsbury, at Marlborough's instigation, had entered into "proper Measures" with himself, Harcourt,

---

[2] Bromley to Harley, 18 September 1708, HMC, *Portland MSS*, IV, 504–5. See also Harley to Harcourt, 16 October 1708, HMC, *Bath MSS*, I, 193, for Harley's support of Bromley's unsuccessful candidacy for Speaker.

[3] A number of Harley's letters to Newcastle are printed in HMC, *Portland MSS*, II, and of Newcastle's to Harley in *ibid.*, IV. See also Harley to Newcastle, 22 October 1708, Nottingham University Library, Portland Collection, Pw2, 95: "ye state & condition of ye Country is too plain to escape any ones knowledge; & it must owe it to your Graces penetration steadiness & Virtue to avert ye miseries wch wil inevitably follow unless a speedy care be administred." For the divisions among the Whigs, see Sunderland to Newcastle, 19 October, 4 November 1708, printed in Trevelyan, *England under Queen Anne*, II, 414–16. In October Cowper urged Newcastle to come to town to assist in "the good and now necessary work of preventing a division among honest men." Cowper to Newcastle, 4 October 1708, HMC, *Portland MSS*, II, 205.

[4] Harley to Shrewsbury, 27 July 1708, HMC, *Buccleuch and Queensberry MSS*, II, 702; Shrewsbury to Harley, 6 May, 29 July 1708, HMC, *Bath MSS*, I, 191. A number of earlier letters from Shrewsbury to Harley, dating from 1694, are printed in HMC, *Bath MSS*, I. See also Godolphin to Marlborough, 29 July 1709, Coxe, *Marlborough*, V, 213–14.

and St. John in an effort to check the tyranny of the Junto. But the "D. of Marlb: never renew'd any Conversation of Business with D. Shrews:. This taken ill; and of a sudden the D. of Marlb: and ld. Tr. closed with Juncto, & obliged Harley, &c. to go out."[5] If Harley's account is correct, and if Cowper reported it accurately, Shrewsbury had reason to distrust Marlborough as well as the Junto. It is not surprising to find him again entering into proper measures with Harley and his friends. He was, in any case, an enormously significant recruit to Harley's forces.

St. John urged on Harley's negotiations with the Tories, but after the elections in the spring of 1708 he had to do so from outside the House of Commons. A quarrel with his father, who opted to stand himself for the family seat at Wootton Bassett, in Wiltshire, left the younger St. John without a constituency, and neither his own efforts nor those of his friends succeeded in finding him another.[6] "I neither have omitted, nor would omit, any trouble, care or expense in my power since my friends think I might be of some little use to them and to my country, but I know not which way to turn myself," he told Harley, reporting on three boroughs where his prospects appeared hopeless.[7] "When I parted with our friend Harry, he seemed pretty confident of succeeding in some place or other," George Granville wrote to Harley several weeks later, "and I own I took it for granted he knew himself secure. I join with you in being under the greatest concern for this disappointment."[8]

St. John's difficulties seem to have stemmed largely from

[5] Cowper, *Diary*, p. 43.

[6] For St. John's failure to find a seat and its significance, see H. T. Dickinson, "Henry St. John, Wootton Bassett, and the General Election of 1708," *Wiltshire Archaeological and Natural History Magazine*, LXIV (1969), 107-11.

[7] St. John to Harley, 1 May 1708, HMC, *Bath MSS*, I, 190.

[8] Granville to Harley, 20 May 1708, HMC, *Portland MSS*, IV, 489. See also Harcourt to Harley, 28 May 1708, and Granville to Harley, 17 July 1708, *ibid.*, pp. 491, 495.

the short time left to him to find another seat once he knew of his father's resolve and decided not to challenge it, though in at least one instance his earlier desertion from the High Church cause weighed against his candidacy.[9] But he seems to have blamed Harley at least in part for his exclusion from Parliament. With characteristic affectation, he told James Grahme that while he took "this event to be of very small moment to the publick, and no great misfortune to me, . . . I did all I could to get myself elected in some other place, but found it utterly impossible." He added: "If I could have been of any great use, that which was impossible for me to compass in my circumstances had been brought about by those whom it is my inclination and my principle to serve and since they have left me out I conclude they do not want me."[10] The reference to those who "have left me out" would seem to be to Harley—Dickinson feels it is clearly so. And while the evidence suggests that Harley was greatly concerned for St. John's plight, St. John was, by his own admission, quick to resent and he must have felt Harley could have done more to provide for him.[11]

St. John did not return to Parliament until 1710. He proclaimed himself content in his life of retirement: "Could I Enjoy you & a very few more friends as frequently at this Place as it is Easy [to] do in Londo.," he wrote to James Brydges, "I wd. not only make people beleive I intended to Spend the remr. of my days here but I would steadily resolve to do so."[12] But his actions belied his indifference. He tried

---

[9] At Weobly, where Lord Weymouth was the High Church patron. Dickinson, "Henry St. John, Wootton Bassett, and the General Election of 1708," p. 108. For St. John's failure to gain Weymouth's support at Weobly, see Harcourt to Harley, 28 May 1708, HMC, *Portland MSS*, IV, 491; Edward Harley to Abigail Harley, 15 December 1708, *ibid.*, p. 515.

[10] St. John to Grahme, 18 July 1708, H. T. Dickinson, ed., "Letters of Bolingbroke to James Grahme," *Transactions of the Cumberland & Westmorland Antiquarian & Archaeological Society*, LXVIII N.S. (1968), 127–8.

[11] Dickinson, *Bolingbroke*, pp. 64–5.

[12] St. John to Brydges, 29 July 1708, G. Davies and M. Tinling, eds., "Letters of Henry St. John to James Brydges," *Huntington Library Bulletin*,

again to find a seat at one of several by-elections in December, again without success.[13] And he waited with ill-concealed impatience for the moment when his political fortunes would change. "In this obscure and private life I am perfectly easy," he assured Harley, "and shall with the same ease return to the noise and business of an active public life, whenever the service of my country or of my friends calls me forth."[14]

St. John could not be certain when the occasion would arise; but he saw the best hope of returning to power in an outright commitment to party government. No advantage could be gained from further cooperation with the Whigs. "I have thought a good while that you could expect from one quarter nothing but that you have met with," he told Harley, "and this prepossession used to make me very uneasy when we were building up the power of a faction which it was plain we should find it necessary in a short time to pull down, and when we entered into some engagements which would prove clogs and fetters upon us whenever we came in our own defence to play a contrary game." He continued:

There is no hope I am fully convinced but in the Church of England party, nor in that neither on the foot it now stands, and without more confidence than is yet reestablished between them and us. Why do you not gain Bromley entirely? The task is not difficult, and by governing him without seeming to do so, you will influence them. . . .

You broke the party, unite it again, their sufferings have made them wise, and whatever piques or jealousies they may entertain at present, as they feel the success of better conduct these will wear off, and you will have it in your power by reasonable measures to lead them to reasonable ends.[15]

---

no. 8 (1935), p. 159. See also, St. John to Orrery, 1 September 1709, Bodleian Library, MS Eng. Misc. e. 180.

[13] Edward Harley to Abigail Harley, 15 December 1708, HMC, *Portland MSS*, IV, 515; St. John to Harcourt, 20 December 1708, 20 January 1708, *ibid.*, pp. 515, 517.

[14] St. John to Harley, 17 September 1709, HMC, *Bath MSS*, I, 196.

[15] St. John to Harley, 11 October 1708, HMC, *Bath MSS*, I, 191-2.

The talk of "reasonable measures" and "reasonable ends" may have been for Harley's benefit at least in part, to lend persuasiveness to the appeal; at the same time St. John presumably believed the interests of the party required that its violent men be kept in check. He returned to the same theme a month later when he again entreated Harley to take up the leadership of the party.

No one living is able to do so much as you towards removing our present evils, and towards averting those which a very short-sighted man may perceive to impend over us. But you are the mark at which every dart of faction is levelled, and it is impossible either that you should be safe from daily insults, or that the least progress should be made towards those views which you propose, unless a number of gentlemen be satisfied of their danger, unless they be convinced that to preserve themselves they must follow you, unless you inspire your party with industry and courage, which at present seem only to be possessed of the factions.

He added by way of encouragement: "The fiery trial of affliction has made the gentlemen of the Church of England more prepared to form such a party than from their former conduct it might have been expected." He had heard "what you have done to gain Mr. B[romley], and how well you have succeeded. I make no question but you will unite and govern the whole body of gentlemen to their own and to your good."[16] Yet for all the optimism these words expressed, the urgency of St. John's tone reflected some anxiety. He may have feared that Harley would not move quickly enough, doubted that he could ever be brought to pursue a thoroughly Tory policy. His resentment at Harley's supposed failure to find him a seat in the Commons can only have undermined his former trust. Whatever the nature of his apprehensions, it was clear that he no longer had full confidence in Harley.

Outwardly, the relationship had changed. After 1708 St. John's letters were less affectionate, more reserved, markedly

16 St. John to Harley, 6 November 1708, *ibid.*, pp. 193-4.

different from the "Dear Master" correspondence. His compliment to Harley on the marriage of one of his daughters in 1709 was correct and formal but without warmth.

Do me . . . the justice to believe that I wish the young couple happy in each other, and you so in both of 'em.

It is great satisfaction to me to consider that this happiness must needs attend a match, where you have brought into your family one who by his good sense, his knowledge, his probity, and his modesty seemed to be akin to you even before his marriage.[17]

At the same time, in the autumn of 1709, it appears that St. John was rumored to be scheming against his former master, an allegation he was quick to deny. From the country he protested his innocence: "I should have been very glad to have known the particulars of this noble project, since it's hard to imagine what air of probability could be given to any story calculated for such a purpose. But there is an ill nature in the world which makes men incapable of submitting to the laws of friendship themselves, and of patiently seeing it prevail among others."[18] George Granville was at Bucklebury with St. John and, writing to Harley several days later, he put in a word on behalf of his friend. Assuring Harley of his own loyalty and support, Granville added: "I am much mistaken if I cannot likewise answer in the same manner for the friend with whom I am, notwithstanding any suggestions that may have been, etc."[19]

What St. John was plotting, if indeed he was plotting anything at all, is not known. But the fact that the rumor existed is further evidence of a rift between the two men, and St. John's

[17] St. John to Harley, 14 August 1709, *ibid.,* p. 195.
[18] St. John to Harley, 17 September 1709, *ibid.,* p. 196.
[19] Granville to [Harley], 22 September 1709, HMC, *Portland MSS,* IV, 527. Granville's letter is not dated "Bucklebury," but he was certainly there September 9: St. John to James Grahme, 9 September 1709, Dickinson, "Letters of Bolingbroke to James Grahme," p. 129; and the sense of Granville's letter taken with St. John's of 17 September 1709 makes it nearly certain that "the friend with whom I am" was St. John.

disclaiming letter failed to conceal his exasperation, even his contempt.

Since you are so indifferent as not to trouble yourself either about the peace or about the measures which our governors at home will pursue, my indifference will increase upon me, and I will likewise wait with patience for that something which is not much expected.

Adieu, dear Sir, may you still continue involved in your virtue and shielded by your innocence, safe from every dart of malice. May all your designs for the good of your country prosper, and every other blessing light upon you.[20]

Indifference, patience, safety within the shield of innocence, none of these appealed to St. John. A year earlier he had congratulated Harley on timing his return to the country so that he escaped a severe storm. "But 'tis in your fate to do so. You have before now been in dangers of this kind and have yet been so prudent and so lucky both, as to receive only some sprinkling drops and to gain shelter before the whole tempest could overtake you." On that occasion St. John had been neither prudent nor lucky: "I got home without any misfortune but that of being wet twice a day to the skin."[21] But St. John preferred getting wet to the skin. If Harley's fate was to escape, his own was to be at the center of the tempest. Impetuous and extravagant in his own actions, he came to despise Harley's prudence and caution.

It is clear, then, that before the end of 1708 the Harley–St. John alliance exhibited many of the strains under which it would eventually break. Their differences were both personal and political. The question facing them after February 1708 was how best to strengthen their position in order to regain power and office, and here their policies diverged. St. John resumed his commitment to government by party, though as a matter of expediency he believed the extremists on the Tory right must be kept in check. To this extent he remained a

[20] St. John to Harley, 17 September 1709, HMC, *Bath MSS*, I, 196.
[21] St. John to Harley, 11 October 1708, *ibid.*, p. 191.

moderate. But he abandoned the principle of nonparty government. As a Harleyite minister, he had supported Harley's
moderate nonparty scheme, but the evidence suggests that he
was always more of a Harleyite than a moderate. His commitment was to the man rather than the principle, and his enthusiasm for moderation faded with his enthusiasm for Harley. He
had come into the ministry in 1704 prepared to support moderate measures because of his regard for Harley and because he
believed this was the best means of advancing Tory fortunes,
including his own. But by 1708 the Whigs had triumphed:
moderation had failed in its own terms, and at the same time
the Tories had lost ground. The lesson seemed to be that
government by party was inevitable; and if party was to rule,
better the Tories than the Whigs.

But Harley learned a different lesson from 1704–8. In his
view, moderate policies had failed only because of Godolphin's
—and to a lesser extent Marlborough's—bad judgment. Had
they followed his advice and formed a connection with the
Tories rather than the Whigs, they could have escaped capitulation to the Junto. In Harley's eyes his scheme of government
had been subverted rather than discredited. He hoped to return
to office on the basis of his former plan: he looked to an
alliance with the Tories, but his ultimate aim was to establish a
moderate government not subject to the dictates of either
party. He held consistently to his earlier principles; and so,
really, did St. John. Originally committed to High Tory
policies, for a time St. John tried another course. But there is
little to suggest that he ever abandoned his former convictions:
he seems rather to have pushed them aside, so that, when the
moderate experiment failed, he had only to reembrace them.
His support for Harley's moderate scheme of government was
an aberration from an otherwise consistent approach to politics. The political division between St. John and Harley was
fundamental, but in the end it was the combination of personal
and political dissension that doomed the partnership. Had St.
John been less impatient with Harley's methods, had his antip-

athy been less extreme, they could perhaps have resolved their differences in policy; and had those differences been less significant, personal animosities would have mattered less to an effective working alliance.

II

In his "Commentarys" on the year 1709, the Jacobite George Lockhart wrote that "Mr. Harly in the mean time was not idle; for as one of his chief talents lay in plodding and carrying on intrigues to undermine others, he found a way to enter into a correspondence with the Queen, who, tho forc'd against her will to lay him asyde from being Secretary of State, still retain'd a kindness for and a favourable opinion of him. This correspondence was conveyed by messages through the hands of Mrs. Masham, one of her Majesties dressers, and formerly introduced to Court by the Dutches of Marlburrow."²² Virtually all the contemporary accounts of Harley's dismissal in 1708 remark upon the Queen's reluctance to part with her minister and nearly all of them ascribe to Mrs. Masham a major conspiratorial role in Harley's scheme. Lord Coningsby, a loyal follower of Godolphin and a hostile witness to be sure, spoke of "the assurances wch the Queen most certainly gave to Harley at parting of a speedy restoration" and of Mrs. Masham's "unbounded influence over her unhappy mistress's will in all things whatever."²³ There is no evidence for Coningsby's first assertion, and the second is demonstrably untrue. But Harley's relationship with the Queen was of the first importance to his political career and thus requires some elaboration; and as Mrs. Masham figured so largely in the imagination of contemporaries, it is proper to inquire into the nature of

²² *The Lockhart Papers*, ed. by A. Aufrere (London, 1817), I, 309.
²³ "Lord Coningsby's Account of the State of Political Parties during the Reign of Queen Anne," ed. by Sir Henry Ellis, *Archaeologia*, XXXVIII (1860), 8.

her connection with Harley and of her influence with the Queen.

To take first the matter of Harley's standing with the Queen. While the monarchy had since 1689 been parliamentary in the literal sense that the sovereign reigned by act of Parliament, and so limited that the royal prerogative could no longer successfully challenge the authority of Parliament, it remained a powerful constitutional force, especially in the person of a ruler determined to assert the royal authority to the full. The prestige of the Crown was great, its traditions remained strong: monarchy, though limited, still inspired awe. With the weight of its prestige and the judicious use of the patronage at its disposal, the Crown could exercise considerable influence on political affairs, particularly at election time; but it was in the matter of appointments that the prerogative was most often and most crucially asserted. Queen Anne's insistence on her right to name her own servants gave her an enormously important, sometimes decisive role in the formation of ministries and thus in the shifting balance between factions and parties. For this reason primarily, but also because the sovereign retained the right to dissolve Parliament, favorable majorities in the House of Commons were no guarantee of a ministry's continuing tenure of office. Directly subject to the personal and political dispositions of the monarch, ministers rose and fell independently of parliamentary support; and this meant that in practice no ministry could survive without the backing of the Crown. As Harley observed, "there is no one party, nay not both of them, can stand agst. the Queens frowns."[24] But the realities of eighteenth-century politics limited to an extent the sovereign's freedom of choice, for without favorable majorities the government's business could not move forward, and there were occasions on which the Queen was forced to give way in order to gain—or retain—the support of

[24] Blenheim MSS, F. 2–16, 12/23 September 1704. Quoted in Holmes, *British Politics in the Age of Anne*, p. 210.

an unruly Parliament: the appointments of Cowper and Sunderland are cases in point. But more often she did not. As a rule, the royal favor was in some degree necessary to every seeker after place and power, and it was Harley's great good fortune to be both personally and politically pleasing to his Queen.

Anne was by all accounts a conscientious monarch with a strong sense of the dignities and privileges attaching to her high office.[25] Cautious and deliberate, sensible rather than intelligent, she bore her responsibilities with all the fortitude chronic ill-health allowed and she worked hard at the business of ruling, attending Cabinet meetings, diligently reading dispatches, going "incognito" to the House of Lords to listen to debate.[26] Not given to conversation, she disliked society and presided, when her health permitted, over an oppressively dull and dowdy Court. "I don't make you a compliment," Lady Orkney wrote to Lady Harriet Harley, "to say you are wanted at Windsor, for after the respectful thoughts seeing the Queen gives there is nothing but ceremony, no manner of conversation. . . . We played after dinner, drank tea, bowed extremely and so returned. Reflection, how vain is ambition if these are the ornaments of Courts."[27] Physically incapacitated much of the time, without social or intellectual pleasures, the Queen found what comfort she could in strong personal attachments and in her religion. These were the solaces of a lonely and pain-ridden existence made sadder still by the death in 1700 of her last surviving child and in 1708 of her husband. There was pathos in the figure of the Queen, in her peculiar isolation, and in her physical suffering. But she had great strength as well, and tenacity bordering on stubbornness. She

[25] For the Queen, see David Green's recent biography: *Queen Anne* (New York: Scribner's, 1970).

[26] "Incognito" meant that the Queen attended as an observer without her robes and the ensigns of her office. She was officially unrecognized. Holmes, *British Politics in the Age of Anne*, pp. 390–1.

[27] Lady Orkney to Lady Harriet Harley, June 1714, HMC, *Portland MSS*, V, 463.

knew her own mind; moreover, she knew that she was right. "I have the same opinion of Whig and Tory that I ever had," she wrote to the Duchess of Marlborough. "I know both their principles very well, and when I know myself to be in the right nothing can make me alter mine. It is very sertin there are good and ill people of both sorts, and I can see the faults of the one as well as of the other."[28] Marlborough, who had reason to know, observed that "when she thinks herself in the right, she needs no advice to help her to be very firm and positive."[29]

The Queen set high store on her independence of judgment, but poor health and limited intellectual capacity made her unusually dependent on her principal ministers and the small circle of her friends. Extreme dependence brings with it extreme vulnerability, and this accounts at least in part for her continuing fear of falling into the hands of party. Aware that perforce she must be in some hands, she feared lest they be unfriendly; and the leaders of party were, in her view, less interested in serving the Crown than their own selfish ends. "I must own to you I dread the falling into the hands of either party," she wrote Godolphin, protesting against Cowper's appointment as Lord Keeper, "and the Whigs have had so many favours showed them of late, that I fear a very few more will put me insensibly into their power, which is what I'm sure you would not have happen to me no more than I. . . . I do put an entire confidence in you, not doubting but you will do all you can to keep me out of the power of the *merciless men of both parties*."[30] Strong-willed the Queen might be, but she craved protection and she was reluctant to part with those she had come to trust. There was comfort and safety in familiarity and much to be feared from the unknown. Politics alone cannot

[28] Queen Anne to the Duchess of Marlborough, 17 November 1704, HMC, *Eighth Report*, Appendix, Part I, 51b.

[29] Marlborough to the Duchess of Marlborough, 9 August 1706, N.S., Coxe, *Marlborough*, III, 89.

[30] Queen Anne to Godolphin, 11 July 1705, BM, Add. MSS, 28070, ff, 12–13. Quoted in Trevelyan, *England under Queen Anne*, II, 31–2.

explain the intensity of her opposition to the Sunderland appointment. "All I desire," she wrote Godolphin,

is my liberty in encouraging and employing all those that concur faithfully in my service, whether they are called whigs or tories, not to be tied to one, nor the other; for if I should be so unfortunate as to fall into the hands of either, I shall not imagine myself, though I have the name of queen, to be in reality but their slave, which as it will be my personal ruin, so it will be the destroying all government; for instead of putting an end to faction, it will lay a lasting foundation for it.

She begged him "to consider how to bring me out of my difficulties, and never leave my service, for Jesus Christ's sake; for . . . this is a blow I cannot bear."[31] Three weeks later she implored him again: "This is a thing I have so much at my heart, and upon which the quiet of my life depends, that I must beg you, for Christ Jesus' sake, to endeavour to bring it about." In conclusion she invoked Marlborough's support: "Let his words plead for her, who will be lost and undone, if you pursue this cruel intention, and begs that you would neither think of it, nor mention it any more to one, that is so affectionately and sincerely your humble servant."[32] There is no mistaking the passion of these appeals. The issue was the inviolability of the Crown, but it was the Queen who wore the crown. Godolphin's intransigence was for her a personal as well as political betrayal: "as it will be my personal ruin, so it will be the destroying all government." Small wonder that she never forgave Godolphin or that in 1708 she was ready to sacrifice him for Harley, who had opposed the Sunderland appointment and the policy it represented.

The Queen was Tory in politics and High Church in religion, but her fear of being enslaved by the leaders of party made her sympathetic to the principles of moderation.

---

[31] Queen Anne to Godolphin, 30 August–10 September 1706, Coxe, *Marlborough*, III, 91–2.
[32] Queen Anne to Godolphin, 21 September 1706, *ibid.*, p. 106.

Schooled first by Godolphin and Marlborough and then by Harley, she responded to a scheme of government which sought to avoid the extremes of party; and when, in the years after 1705, the ministerial partners seemed to be abandoning moderation, she placed her confidence in Harley, whose belief in the central importance of the Crown accorded with her own and strengthened her resolve to assert her independence against both High Tory and Junto leaders. In Swift's view, the Queen became more of a moderate than Harley, a circumstance which "put him upon innumerable difficulties" later on.[33] In any case, by 1710 "She had entertained the Notion of forming a moderate or comprehensive Scheam, which She maintained with great firmness, nor would ever depart from untill about half a Year before her Death."[34]

But the Queen's confidence in Harley was based on personal as well as political considerations. She admired his piety, his devotion to his family, the exemplary character of his private life. Swift spoke of "that incurable disease, either of negligence or procrastination, which influenced every action both of the Queen and the Earl of Oxford,"[35] and doubtless the Queen liked Harley because he rarely pushed her. "As he was a Lover of gentle Measures, and inclined to Procrastination, so he could not with any decency press the Queen too much against her Nature," Swift observed, "because it would be like running upon the Rock where his Predecessors had Split."[36] While Harley was not immune from the royal rebuke, the Queen's affection for him was deep and lasting.[37] She signed her letters "your very affectionett friend," and the

---

[33] Swift, "Memoirs," p. 117.
[34] Swift, "An Enquiry," p. 143.
[35] Swift, "Memoirs," p. 110.
[36] Swift, "Some Considerations," p. 103.
[37] See Anne to Oxford, 27 November 1712 and 21 August 1713, HMC, *Bath MSS*, I, 223, 227, for two instances in which he pressed the Queen too far. And a draft in Oxford's hand in which he relates that when he raised the question of a peerage for Mrs. Masham's husband, the Queen "took me up very short . . . only for mentioning it." BM, Portland Loan, 29/10.

concern she showed for him over the years makes clear that this was not an empty formula. In 1707, St. John wrote Harley:

I cannot finish this note without telling you that when I waited on the Queen yesterday she enquired after your health, and expressed her concern for your illness in such terms as I am sure came from the bottom of her heart. She said so much of your having prejudiced your health in her service, and showed so much trouble, that I thought it was proper for me to tell you particularly of it.[38]

She continued to inquire after his health as long as she lived, and in terms that came from the bottom of her heart. "I am exstream sorry to heare you have bin out of order since I saw you," she wrote from Windsor in the autumn of 1711,

and therefore I desire you would not think of going any journey till you are perfectly well. I intend, an it please God, to be at Hampton Court next Teusday or Wensday next which will be nearer to you; however I desire you would not com thither till you are easy, which I hope will be soon, and in the mean time be soe kind to your freinds as to give them an account of your health, and be assured of my being sincerly your very affectionate friend.[39]

She feared troubling him too often with letters when he was not well, "and I beg if it is not easy to you to writt not to give me any answer to this till it is."[40] She would continue her prayers for "the perfect recovery and confirmation" of his health. In the meantime, she begged him "to be carefull of yourself and not to fatigue yourself with buisnes till you are better able to beare it."[41] As Harley's illnesses were frequent, so were the Queen's prayers for his perfect recovery.

The Queen's affection implied loyalty as well as concern, and when in 1708 she failed to save Harley, she did not aban-

[38] St. John to Harley, 30 January 1707, HMC, *Bath MSS*, I, 157.
[39] Anne to Oxford, 19 October 1711, *ibid.*, p. 213.
[40] Anne to Oxford, 26 October 1711, *ibid.*, p. 214.
[41] Anne to Oxford, 3 November 1711, *ibid.*, p. 215.

don him. He continued to enjoy her confidence when he was out of office, and it is unlikely that he could have returned to the ministry in 1710 without her concurrence and favor. Harley's political advancement depended to a considerable extent on his relationship with the Queen, and this was generally recognized. "I hope in a little time the Nation will have as good an opinion of you as her Majesty," a cousin wrote, congratulating him on his appointment in the summer of 1710.[42] And Bolingbroke observed with some bitterness in the "Letter to Sir William Windham" that "he [Harley] was the first spring of all our motion by his credit with the queen."[43] Just as Harley profited greatly from the Queen's favor, it was Bolingbroke's liability that he never succeeded in gaining her trust.

Abigail Masham, the Queen's dresser, was related to Harley as well as to the Duchess of Marlborough, who had first secured her a place in the royal bedchamber. By 1708 she had clearly replaced the Duchess in the Queen's affections—though it appears that Sarah had been losing ground for some time[44]— and it is equally clear that she had formed an alliance with Harley. Sarah herself gives 1707 as the year in which she "discovered the base returns made me by Mrs Masham, upon whom I had heaped the greatest obligations."[45] Her suspicions aroused by the secrecy surrounding Abigail's marriage that summer to Mr. Masham, equerry and gentleman of the bedchamber to Prince George, Sarah found, upon inquiry, "that

[42] Richard Foley to Harley, [?]1710, BM, Portland Loan, 29/135.
[43] Bolingbroke, *Works*, I, 119.
[44] Swift wrote in 1710 that "the Dutchess of M's Removall has been 7 years working," Coningsby that when Harley became Secretary of State in 1704, Mrs. Masham "was then, upon my Lady Marlborough's losing ground on account of her insolent behaviour to the Queen, a growing favourite with her." Swift to Archbishop King, 10 October 1710, *Swift Correspondence*, I, 186 (He repeats this view in his *History*, p. 8.); "Lord Coningsby's Account," p. 6. Churchill thought the Duchess's influence was declining by the end of 1705 (*Marlborough*, V, 29–30, 317). David Green places the first signs of strain in 1703, when Sarah launched her campaign to enlist the Queen's sympathies on the Whig side, *Queen Anne*, pp. 122–3.
[45] *Memoirs of Sarah, Duchess of Marlborough*, p. 125.

my cousin was become an absolute favourite; that the Queen
herself was present at her marriage. . . . And I likewise then
discovered beyond all dispute Mr Harley's correspondence and
interest at Court by means of this woman."[46] While the
Duchess had her own reasons to denounce "the black ingrati-
tude of Mrs. Masham," and Dartmouth later described the new
favorite as "exceeding mean and vulgar in her manners, of a
very unequal temper, childishly exceptious and passionate," a
relative of Harley's had "heard her greatly commended for a
sober woman,"[47] and Swift, who knew her well, praised her
most generously.

My Lady Masham was a Person of a plain sound Understanding, of
great Truth and Sincerity, without the least Mixture of Falshood
or Disguise; of an honest Boldness and Courage superiour to her
Sex; firm and disinterested in her Friendship, and full of Love,
Duty, and Veneration for the Queen Her Mistress; Talents as
seldom found or sought for in a Court, as unlikely to thrive while
they are there.[48]

If Swift's characterization is just, it is easy to see why the
Queen trusted Abigail Masham; the more difficult question is
how much Mrs. Masham was able to sway her royal mistress.
Contemporaries evidently thought her influence was considerable. When Harley was dismissed in 1708, Addison wrote: "It
is said he [Harley] had hopes of working his Ends by the
Assistance of a Bedchamber-woman, whom, it seems, he had
found out to be his Cousin."[49] James Vernon spoke of the
triumvirate of Harley, St. John, and Harcourt "that were framing a new scheme of administration, and Mrs. Hill [Mrs.

[46] *Ibid.*, pp. 130–1. By some accounts, Harley is said to have smoothed
the path for the marriage. Boyer, *History*, p. 322; Lord Raby, "Caracteres,"
Wentworth Papers, p. 132.

[47] Duchess of Marlborough to Trumbull, 13 November 1707, HMC,
Downshire MSS, I, 855; Burnet, *History*, VI, 37, Dartmouth's note; Lady
Pye to Abigail Harley, 12 May 1707, HMC, *Portland MSS*, IV, 406.

[48] Swift, "An Enquiry," p. 153.

[49] Addison to Lord Manchester, 13 February 1708, *The Letters of Joseph
Addison*, p. 92.

Masham], the dresser, is said to be engaged with them in the project."[50] Swift wrote from London that Harley had nearly succeeded in removing the Lord Treasurer, "by the help of Mrs. Masham, one of the Queen's dressers, who was a great and growing favourite, of much industry and insinuation." He added that it was said "Mrs. Masham is forbid the Court; but this I have no assurance of."[51] The Queen had no intention of parting with her dresser. Nor had she two years later when several Whig leaders proposed that Parliament address the Queen to remove Mrs. Masham from her service. The occasion was the Queen's promise of a regiment, against Marlborough's wishes and without consulting him, to Mrs. Masham's brother, Jack Hill.[52] Angry and humiliated by the slight, Marlborough could not but think "that the Nation wou'd be of opinion that I have deserv'd better then to be made a sacrifice to the unreasonable passion of a bedchamber woman."[53] He wrote as much to the Queen, begging leave to remind her "of what I writ to you the last campaign, of the certain knowledge I had of Mrs Masham's having assured Mr Harley that I should receive such constant mortifications as should make it impossible for me to continue in your service." And he asked that she allow him to retire.[54] The Queen relented and the crisis passed: Marlborough stayed on, and so did Mrs. Masham. The issue was, of course, broader than the influence of the favorite alone: Marlborough and the Whigs meant to strike at Harley through Mrs. Masham. But the whole episode is an indication

[50] James Vernon to Shrewsbury, 10 February 1708, *Vernon Correspondence*, III, 345. Vernon refers to Mrs. Masham as Mrs. Hill, though she had married the previous summer.

[51] Swift to Archbishop King, 12 February 1708, *Swift Correspondence*, I, 69.

[52] For the dispute over Hill's regiment and the proposed address, see Coxe, *Marlborough*, V, 126–48; *Memoirs of Sarah, Duchess of Marlborough*, pp. 162–7; *The Lockhart Papers*, pp. 316–17; Boyer, *History*, p. 472.

[53] Marlborough to Cowper, 18 January 1710, Hertfordshire R.O., Panshanger MSS, D/EP, F63.

[54] *Memoirs of Sarah, Duchess of Marlborough*, p. 166.

of the credit she was thought to have with the Queen, particularly by the Marlboroughs, who blamed her for their loss of favor.[55]

The reality appears to have been rather different. Mrs. Masham was in fact in close touch with Harley at least by the summer of 1707, but it was after his dismissal the following February that their correspondence took on a conspiratorial rather than merely confidential tone.[56] They wrote in cipher, and Mrs. Masham's letters reveal that she shared Harley's political views and was prepared to do all she could to advance them with the Queen.[57] In practical terms she functioned as a channel of communication between Harley and the Queen, reading Anne his letters when she would allow it, conveying messages, and arranging secret meetings between them. Through Mrs. Masham Harley had access to the Queen, but only at the Queen's pleasure. He had no communication with the Queen between February and October 1708, and this can only have been because she did not choose to consult him.[58] "I shall be glad to have your opinion upon things that I may lay it before her," Mrs. Masham wrote Harley in July, "for that is all that can be done. I trust in God and beg him to supply her, that she may not be so blinded but save herself while it is in her power."[59] Mrs. Masham often despaired of influencing her

[55] Coxe, *Marlborough*, III–VI; *Private Correspondence of Sarah, Duchess of Marlborough; Memoirs of Sarah, Duchess of Marlborough, passim.*

[56] Abigail Masham to Harley, 29 September 1707, HMC, *Portland MSS*, IV, 454, describing an encounter with the Duchess of Marlborough in the Queen's drawing room, makes clear that by this time Mrs. Masham and Harley were already allies. This is in accord with Sarah's chronology. *Memoirs of Sarah, Duchess of Marlborough,* pp. 130–1.

[57] There is a copy of the key to the cipher in Harley's hand dated 12 May 1708, in BM, Portland Loan, 29/38/10. For Mrs. Masham's letters to Harley in the 1708–10 period, see HMC, *Portland MSS*, IV, 495–540, *passim;* and BM, Portland Loan, 29/38/10. For Harley's to Mrs. Masham, see Longleat, Portland MSS, X, 51, 55–6, 59.

[58] "It is now Eight months since, I have had no sort of communication with her [the Queen]" Harley to Cozen K. Stephens [Mrs. Masham], 16 October 1708, Longleat, Portland MSS, X, f. 55.

[59] Abigail Masham to Harley, 27 July 1708, HMC, *Portland MSS*, IV, 499.

mistress. "I can't tell you what use my friend has made of the advice was given her in your letter," she told Harley, "but she heard it over and over. She keeps me in ignorance and is very reserved, does not care to tell me any thing."[60] Some months later she complained that "because I am still with her people think I am able to persuade her to anything I have a mind to have her do, but they will be convinced to the contrary one time or another. I desired her to let me see you, she would not consent to that, and charged me not to say anything to you of what passed between us."[61]

Mrs. Masham herself, then, had no illusions about the extent of her influence with the Queen; neither, for that matter, did Harley. From his point of view she was an extremely useful friend in 1708–10 when he would not otherwise have had regular access to the Queen, and her presence in the bedchamber facilitated the negotiations leading to his return to office. But Harley recognized the limitations of Mrs. Masham's role. After 1710 he seems to have consulted her on political matters only in times of crisis, and it was not until the last year of his ministry that he again had need of her assistance with the Queen.

III

Harley's messages to the Queen, whether conveyed by Mrs. Masham or by himself, dwelt upon the evil consequences of government by party, deplored the increasing tendency of the ministers to accede to the Junto's demands, urged the Queen to free herself from the dictates of party leadership. The arguments were familiar: the Whigs would not be contented with less than all; Marlborough and the Treasurer, under cover of

---

[60] Abigail Masham to Harley, 14 September 1709, *ibid.,* p. 525.
[61] Abigail Masham to Harley, 10 March 1710, *ibid.,* p. 536.

necessity, had thrown in their lot with the Junto; the Queen must act if she would save herself from ruin.[62] By Swift's account, Harley "told her of the dangers to her crown as well as to the church and monarchy itself, from the councils and actions of some of her servants: That she ought gradually to lessen the exorbitant power of the Duke and Duchess of Marlborough, and the Earl of Godolphin, by taking the disposition of employments into her own hands: That it did not become her to be a slave to a party; but to reward those who may deserve by their duty and loyalty, whether they were such as were called of the High or Low-Church."[63]

The Queen was inclined to listen to Harley. She was sympathetic to the views he put forward; and she seems to have been increasingly unhappy with Godolphin and Marlborough. Burnet was probably right in saying that after Harley's dismissal in 1708, "the queen seemed to carry a deep resentment of his [Marlborough's] and the lord Godolphin's behaviour on this occasion; and though they went on with her business, they found they had not her confidence."[64] Relations were not improved when, in 1709, Marlborough proposed to the Queen that he be made Captain General for life, in spite of Lord Chancellor Cowper's advice that there was no precedent for such a grant.[65] The Queen refused: she was, said Swift, "highly alarmed at this extraordinary proceeding in the Duke, and talked to a person whom she had then taken into confidence, as if she apprehended an attempt upon the crown."[66] Whatever Marlborough's motives, and one can only assume that he thought both to restore his credit and secure his future,

[62] Harley to Cozen K. Stephens [Mrs. Masham], 10, 16, 31 October 1708, Longleat, Portland MSS, X, ff. 51, 55–6, 59. See also *The Lockhart Papers*, I, 309–10.

[63] Swift, "Memoirs," p. 116.

[64] Burnet, *History*, V, 355. See also "Lord Coningsby's Account," p. 9.

[65] Coxe, *Marlborough*, V, 116–17.

[66] Swift, "Memoirs," p. 114. According to Dartmouth, Marlborough tried to get the House of Commons to make the proposal, "without so much as mentioning of it to the queen." Burnet, *History*, V, 416, Dartmouth's note.

his action was ill-timed and ill-advised, and it was hardly resassuring to his sovereign.

Still, the Queen was not prepared to lend her support to Harley's scheme until the spring of 1710. As McInnes points out, she had backed the losing side in 1708 and she did not wish to do so again. This time she would not act until she was reasonably certain Harley could succeed.[67] In the circumstances, a number of factors worked in Harley's favor. Divisions among the Whigs continued, and Marlborough and Godolphin were on uneasy terms with the Junto. "At home everything goes as the ministry would have it, I suppose," Harley wrote in 1709, "and they seem to be endeavouring to patch up entirely with the Junto, though underhand they do what they can to ruin the credit of the latter."[68] At the same time, feeling against the war was growing throughout the country. The hardships of long years of fighting had begun to tarnish the splendor of Marlborough's victories; the government, finding it increasingly difficult to raise men and money, resorted to increasingly unpopular methods of taxation and recruitment. Poor harvests and high prices in the summer of 1709 exacerbated popular discontent; and the collapse of the peace negotiations at The Hague in August dashed existing hopes for a permanent end to hostilities.[69] Harley and his friends now joined the majority of Tories in calling for an early peace. St. John in particular spoke for the Tory squires, denouncing the fat profits reaped by the moneyed men while the land paid—and suffered.[70] "Peace is at this time the most desireable publick or private Good if you will not think yt. I putt on to much of the Country Esqr.," he

[67] McInnes, *Robert Harley*, p. 121.

[68] Harley to Newcastle, 15 September 1709, HMC, *Portland MSS*, II, 208. See also Coxe, *Marlborough*, V, chap. 85 and pp. 162–5; *Private Correspondence of Sarah, Duchess of Marlborough*, I, 118–296, *passim;* "Lord Coningsby's Account," pp. 9–14.

[69] Trevelyan, *England under Queen Anne*, II, 387–8; III, 33–5. P. G. M. Dickson, *The Financial Revolution in England* (London: Macmillan, 1967), pp. 62, 362.

[70] See above, pp. 112–14.

wrote to Brydges in June of 1709. "Ile Venture to tell you, that wee want it more then perhaps any man out of the Country can Imagine. Glorious successes and the hopes of a last Campaine are Soveraigne Cordials. They Elevate the few Spirits we have left and wee are not seen to pine or Languish; but should the Distemper Continue the strings of Life may Crack at once." "Peace is as much our Interest as theirs," he told Orrery two months later. "I am so firmly persuaded of this, that I will continue to hope the Winter may ripen this glorious Fruit, wch: the Summer could not."[71]

The glorious fruit did not ripen that winter. Had it done so, the government's position would have been considerably stronger, Harley's much less so, in the spring of 1710. But an altogether different issue provided the Queen with reasonable assurance that Harley's plan could succeed. On November 5, 1709, Guy Fawkes Day and also the anniversary of William's landing in 1688, the High Tory cleric Dr. Henry Sacheverell preached an inflammatory sermon at St. Paul's before the Lord Mayor and Court of Aldermen of the City of London.[72] "He asserted the doctrine of non-resistance in the highest strain possible," said Burnet. "He poured out much scorn and scurrility on the dissenters, and reflected severely on the toleration; and said the church was violently attacked by her enemies, and loosely defended by her pretended friends."[73] In its content and the violence of its language the sermon was sensational—the congregation shook "at ye Terrours of his Inveterate Expressions," wrote the Jacobite Thomas Hearne[74]—and though the Court of Aldermen refused to desire it to be

[71] St. John to Brydges, 26 June 1709, Davies and Tinling, "Letters of Henry St. John to James Brydges," p. 161; see also the letters of 26 July, 8 September 1709, ibid., pp. 162–4. St. John to Orrery, 1 September 1709, Bodleian Library, MS Eng. Misc. e. 180, f. 7.

[72] For Sacheverell, see Geoffrey Holmes's recent study, The Trial of Doctor Sacheverell (London: Eyre Methuen, 1973).

[73] Burnet, History, V, 434–5.

[74] C. E. Doble, ed., Remarks and Collections of Thomas Hearne (Oxford, 1886), II, 306. Hereafter cited as Hearne.

printed, forty thousand copies flowed from the London presses and were circulated throughout the country.[75] The ministry, regarding the sermon as an attack upon themselves—Godolphin in particular took personal offense[76]—and, by implication, upon the Revolution and the succession, resolved to impeach Sacheverell for high crimes and misdemeanors. In so doing they committed an indiscretion far more damaging to themselves than the sermon could ever have been. "So solemn a prosecution for such a scribble," observed Harley's friend Dr. Stratford, "will make the Doctor [Sacheverell] and his performance much more considerable than either of them could have been on any other account."[77]

In mid-December the Whiggish House of Commons voted the impeachment and on February 27, 1710, the trial began, moved from the House of Lords to Westminster Hall so that the full membership of the Commons and the public could attend.[78] The government evidently assumed the prosecution would redound to their credit both within and outside Parliament: they would appear in the role of defenders of the Revolution settlement and the Queen's lawful title to her throne.[79] But in this they miscalculated badly. By the time the trial began, Sacheverell was already something of a hero.

[75] *Ibid.;* Abel Boyer, *The History of the Reign of Queen Anne, Digested into Annals* (London, 1703-12), VIII, 205, hereafter cited as Boyer, *Annals;* Burnet, *History*, V, p. 435.

[76] Swift, "Memoirs," p. 155 and *History*, p. 9; Burnet, *History*, V, 443, Dartmouth's note.

[77] Dr. Stratford to Harley, 21 December 1709, HMC, *Portland MSS*, IV, 530.

[78] Sir Christopher Wren was ordered to construct scaffolds to accommodate the spectators. *Hearne*, II, 343-4; Burnet, *History*, V, 440. See also Boyer, *Annals*, VIII, 217-45, 254-335 for a full account of the trial.

[79] Though not all the Whig leaders had favored the impeachment. Swift quotes Somers, the Lord President, as saying "That He was against engaging in the foolish Prosecution of Dr. *Sacheverell;* as what he foresaw was likely to end in their Ruin." Swift, *History*, p. 6. He says the same in "Memoirs," p. 115. And according to Burnet there were others who spoke for less drastic methods of censure. Burnet, *History*, V, 435, and Hardwicke's note.

People of quality vied for seats in Westminster Hall—
"Secheverell will make all the Ladys turn good huswivs, they
goe att seven every mornin," Lady Wentworth wrote[80]—and
the Doctor was acclaimed by the London populace as he
traveled there and back every day. According to Burnet,
"great crowds ran about his coach, with many shouts, expressing their concern for him in a very rude and tumultuous
manner."[81] "The Mob," said Hearne, "both in London and
elsewhere (as well as the most considerable Persons of Distinction that are fam'd at all for Integrity) are altogether for the
Doctor, and they express'd themselves with the utmost fury
when he was convey'd to Westminster Hall and from thence
against the Presbyterians, Whiggs and all that large Tribe."[82]
Before the trial was over, the crowds had expressed their
enthusiasm by yet more violent means, destroying several meeting houses and menacing those bystanders who refused to doff
their hats to the Doctor as he passed or shout for "The Church
and Sacheverell."[83]

The prosecution of Sacheverell served as a catalyst for the
discontents that had been building against the ministry. Godolphin soon wished "this uneasy trial of Sacheverell . . . had
never begun; for it has occasioned a very great ferment."[84]
Lockhart claimed he had "good reasons to affirm that the
Ministry, before the end of the tryal, wish'd they had not
drove matters so farr, but having begun they thought themselves oblig'd to go on." He added: "and indeed nothing did
more contribute to their ruine, for the measure was universally
distasteful to all England and created the Ministry many enemies."[85] Swift agreed. The trial, he said, "drew the Populace as

[80] Lady Wentworth to Lord Raby, 6 March 1710, The Wentworth
Papers, p. 113.
[81] Burnet, History, V, 440.
[82] Hearne, II, 350.
[83] Ibid., pp. 350–1, 354–5; Burnet, History, V, 444–5; Boyer, Annals, VIII,
264–8.
[84] Godolphin to Marlborough, 5 March 1710, Coxe, Marlborough, V, 154.
[85] The Lockhart Papers, I, 315.

one Man into the Party against the Ministry and Parliament."[86]

The Lords judged Sacheverell guilty by a vote of 69–52, hardly a sweeping victory for the government. And they were content to censure him with the lightest of punishments: he was forbidden to preach for three years and his sermon was ordered to be burned by the common hangman. "When this mild judgment was given," wrote Burnet, "those who had supported him during the trial expressed an inconceivable gladness, as if they had got a victory; bonfires, illuminations, and other marks of joy appeared, not only in London, but over the whole kingdom."[87] Addresses in support of Sacheverell, the Church, and the monarchy poured in from all parts of the country, even from the Whiggish City of London, "which we are much surprised at," James Brydges observed, "not having expected it from thence."[88] "All that has passed in that whole affair," Godolphin observed, "must needs bee a very great heartning of the opposition party as well as a great mortification to her Matys. ministers."[89]

The close votes in the Lords revealed the government's weakness in that House. There had, moreover, been a number of key defections. The Duke of Somerset, the Master of the Horse, threw his influence against the ministry and absented himself from the House the day Sacheverell was voted guilty; the Duke of Argyll was in the majority against the Doctor on the first vote but left the government on the question of his punishment, declaring against severe censure.[90] Most significantly, Shrewsbury voted against the ministry. Marlborough, who knew "the cautious temper of the duke," was certain he would not have acted as he did "but that he knew the inclina-

---

[86] Swift, "Some Considerations," p. 102. See also his *History*, p. 34.

[87] Burnet, *History*, V, 450.

[88] Brydges to Cadogan, 7 April 1710, Davies, "The Seamy Side of Marlborough's War," p. 43. For the addresses, see also Burnet, *History*, V, 449–51; Hearne, II, 364–5, 367, 369; Boyer, *Annals*, IX, 158–85.

[89] Godolphin to Marlborough, 23 March 1710, Blenheim, Marlborough Papers, BII, 8.

[90] Coxe, *Marlborough*, V, 153–9.

tions of the queen."[91] In fact, though the Queen was sufficiently interested in the proceedings to be in regular attendance
at Westminster Hall, she told Burnet "that it [Sacheverell's]
was a bad sermon, and that he deserved well to be punished for
it."[92] But whatever her feelings on the matter of Sacheverell's
guilt, she can only have been impressed by the great outpouring of sentiment in his favor and, by implication, against the
government. At the same time a number of her servants had
demonstrated their dissatisfaction with the present administration. The Sacheverell trial provided the Queen with exactly
those assurances she had sought.[93] In January she had appointed Lord Rivers, a Whig supporter of Harley, Lieutenant
of the Tower of London against the wishes of Marlborough.[94]
Within a month of the conclusion of the trial, shortly after
Parliament was prorogued, the Queen dismissed the Marquis of
Kent and gave the Lord Chamberlain's staff to Shrewsbury.
The change of ministers had begun.

IV

Though Harley himself did not take office until August, the
appointment of Shrewsbury signaled the Queen's determination to act upon Harley's scheme. Godolphin was informed,
not consulted, about the change. He had no doubt that Harley
was behind it; and while he resolved to get on with Shrewsbury as best he could, he warned the Queen that the path she

[91] *Ibid.*, pp. 158–9.
[92] Burnet, *History*, V, 446.
[93] According to Swift, "It was the Issue of Doctor Sacheverall's Tryall,
that encouraged her to proceed so far." Swift, "An Enquiry," p. 142. Following Godolphin's dismissal, James Brydges wrote that "the Prosecution of Dr.
Sacheverell, . . . has contributed the most to bring this Revolution about."
Brydges to Mr. Morice, 21 August 1710, C. Buck and G. Davies, eds.,
"Letters on Godolphin's Dismissal in 1710," *Huntington Library Quarterly*,
III (1939–40), 234.
[94] Swift, "Memoirs," p. 117.

appeared to be taking would compass her own ruin and destruction.[95] But Anne was no longer much interested in her Treasurer's advice. Weeks of speculation as to her further intentions ended in June with the dismissal of Sunderland, a removal Godolphin had earlier described as "insupportable" to Marlborough and consequently to himself.[96] Informing Lord Somers of her decision, the Queen assured him "that she was entirely for moderation, yt she did not intend to make any other alterations, but this was a resolution yt she had taken for a long time, and that nothing could divert her from it." The Lord President represented to her the ill consequences of the step, and also of a change of Parliament, in which, he told Godolphin, "she seem'd pretty much to Concurr."[97] This at least was some comfort, for as long as the present Whig Parliament continued, there could be no Tory triumph. Nonetheless, however sincere the Queen's commitment to moderation, the Tories were inclined to regard the ministerial changes in rather a different light. Reporting the news of Shrewsbury's appointment, James Brydges wrote: "The Tories are very high upon it and give out 'tis but the first step of what the Queen intends and that there's to be a new Parliament."[98] And when Sunderland was removed, Abel Boyer observed: "the High-Church Party were wonderfully pleas'd, and elated, upon this Alteration, which they look'd upon as a sure Earnest, and Forerunner of greater Changes."[99]

Some ten days before Sunderland's dismissal, Shrewsbury had told Godolphin the step had been delayed so long only

[95] Godolphin to Marlborough, 18, 25 April, 16 May 1710, Blenheim, Marlborough Papers, BII, 8; Godolphin to the Queen, 15 April 1710, *Memoirs of Sarah, Duchess of Marlborough*, p. 177. For the Queen's letter to Godolphin, 13 April 1710, see Coxe, *Marlborough*, V, 215–16.

[96] Godolphin to Marlborough, 12 May 1710, Blenheim, Marlborough Papers, BII, 8.

[97] Godolphin to Marlborough, 13 June 1710, *ibid*.

[98] Brydges to Cadogan, 18 April 1710, Davies, "The Seamy Side of Marlborough's War," p. 44.

[99] Boyer, *History*, p. 472.

because a replacement could not be agreed upon.[100] The post went at last to Lord Dartmouth, a moderate Tory and a man well liked by the Queen; the interesting point is that it did not go to St. John, who in fact seems not even to have been among those considered. St. John had been engaged in Harley's negotiations at least since the winter; and in May, when James Brydges wrote Cadogan about the changes at Court, he spoke of "your friend Mr. St. John, who is very high in this affair."[101] Yet in return for his services Harley had offered him a minor place as secretary to the Duke of Marlborough, replacing Adam de Cardonnel. "I am indifferent what employment is reserved for me," he told Harley in March, "but I must own that to succeed Mr. Cardonnel, upon the same foot as Mr. Cardonnel was, is not coming into the service a second time with so good a grace as I came in the first; and keeping one's present situation is a good deal better than sinking whilst one affects to rise."[102] By one account, attributed to George Granville, Harley, subsequently perhaps, offered St. John his old job of Secretary-at-War. St. John refused, insisting that he be made Secretary of State; when he threatened to go off to Oxfordshire, leaving Harley to manage matters as best he could, Granville interceded, telling Harley "that if he went on at this rate, he would lose all his friends, and nobody would have anything to do with them."[103]

[100] Godolphin to Marlborough, 2 June 1710, Blenheim, Marlborough Papers, BII, 8. See also Godolphin to the Duchess of Marlborough, 1 June 1710, Coxe, *Marlborough*, V, 245–8; Burnet, *History*, VI, 9, Dartmouth's note.

[101] Brydges to Cadogan, 20 May 1710, Davies, "The Seamy Side of Marlborough's War," p. 44. See also St. John to Harley, 8, 9 March 1710, HMC, *Portland MSS*, IV, 535–6.

[102] St. John to Harley, 8 March 1710, HMC, *Portland MSS*, IV, 536.

[103] "Mr. Carte's Memorandum-book," James Macpherson, ed., *Original Papers* (Dublin, 1775), II, 531. Carte cites as his source a conversation with Granville, then Lord Lansdowne, in 1725. This was fifteen years after the event, reason enough to question the accuracy of Lansdowne's memory. On the other hand, Lansdowne was a close friend of St. John and of Harley; and he came into Harley's ministry as Secretary-at-War in September 1710. His story could well have been correct.

Whatever the truth of the story, the evidence suggests that St. John was not happy with the arrangements proposed for him in the spring of 1710—"I have heard that Mr. St. John said yesterday, in a rant, that he would go into the country, and stay there," Arthur Maynwaring wrote to the Duchess of Marlborough in May, "so that I believe, upon the whole, there scheme is upon a full stop for the present."[104] Equally, it appears that he did want to be Secretary of State. "Mr. St. John's heart will be at ease, he will be in the post he has long wished for," Dr. Stratford remarked when St. John's appointment was rumored later in the summer. "I pray God he consider himself under his new character, a Secretary of State must not take all those liberties one of War might think perhaps proper to his station."[105] But Harley was in no hurry to satisfy his old associate. The Secretaryship of State was a Cabinet office while the War Secretaryship was not, and as Harley hoped to persuade the other Secretary of State, Henry Boyle, to stay on, it appears that he had thoughts of keeping St. John out of the Cabinet entirely. Mistrust had entered the relationship on both sides: it was neither as close nor as solid as it once had been. At the same time it is likely that Harley was reluctant to appoint so able and eloquent a spokesman for High Tory views to so prominent a place in his ministry.

For while St. John recognized that Harley alone could accomplish a change of administration, as before he followed a more narrowly Tory line. Writing to Trumbull in June to ask for his support whenever a new election should take place, St. John declared that he was resolved to "neglect nothing in my power wch may contribute towards making ye Church interest the prevailing one in our County." At the end of August he told Trumbull that he saw every day more reason to pursue the first principles he established and the first views he held. He

---

104 Mr. Maynwaring to the Duchess of Marlborough, May 1710, *Private Correspondence of Sarah, Duchess of Marlborough*, I, 320.

105 Dr. Stratford to Edward Harley, 17 August 1710, HMC, *Portland MSS*, VII, 12.

could say "with great truth, and a little pride," that he had never deviated from either. He conceded, rather apologetically, much as he had when he took office six years before, that appearances do change; but a pilot must often steer a west course to arrive at a port to the north.[106] To Orrery he wrote that while it would not be possible in every respect "to play the Game just as We would wish to do, or as We at first propos'd, yet certainly with common Address, & uncommon Steadiness, We may be able to build up as well as We have been to pull down." He thought the Tories could "be made to proceed reasonably; . . . tho' I must think that We do not take these in with the best Grace, & with the greatest Advantage to Ourselves." But those who feared "the utmost Violence" from that quarter would come into Harley's measures when they found the Tories kept in order "and the true Interest pursued."[107] St. John was no more impressed than he had ever been by the prospects of cooperation with the Whigs. "The treaty you mention I was not let into ye secret of," he wrote to Brydges. "I can only say that it seems to me very difficult, if not utterly impossible to carry on with success a negociation of that kind between partys, amongst whom there is not ye least confidence remaining."[108] But he knew that the path to office lay through Harley's scheme. No doubt he hoped that, in time, Harley could be persuaded to pursue a thoroughly Tory policy; and it is reasonable to suppose that he had already begun to consider what his own role would be should Harley continue to resist this course. For the present, expediency dictated St. John's support of Harley's dealings with moderate Whigs as well as Tories. In any event, his immediate wish was gratified in September, when he replaced Henry Boyle as Secretary of State.

106 St. John to Trumbull, 2 June, 31 August 1710, Berkshire R.O., Downshire Papers, Trumbull Add. MS 133, 39/1–2, 41/1–5.

107 St. John to Orrery, 22 August 1710, Bodleian Library, MS Eng. Misc. e. 180, ff. 9–10.

108 St. John to Brydges, 1 August 1710, Davies and Tinling, "Letters of Henry St. John to James Brydges," p. 168.

One is left to wonder what alternatives would have been offered him had Boyle agreed to stay on.

Following Sunderland's removal, the Queen had told Somers she intended to make no other alterations in the ministry. She had occasion to offer the same reassurances to a delegation from the Bank of England which came to represent to her the dire consequences to the public credit of further changes: "all credit would be gone, stock fall, and the Bank be ruined, which included the ruin of the nation."[109] "To which her answer is very differently reported," Brydges wrote, "but I have had it [?] from so good hands that I cannot doubt she was pleased to express at least that she had not come to a determination of making more."[110] The fears of the financial community were real enough. The government's indebtedness had reached a new high yet the need for funds continued to increase. The growing unpopularity of the war together with the widespread economic distress of 1709–10 made it difficult to raise public loans. The Treasury was hard-pressed to meet its obligations; government securities changed hands at higher and higher discounts, Bank stock fell. In this situation, the City men, large-scale creditors of the government, in any case feared for their future, but they feared even more a future in Tory hands. Traditionally Whiggish in their politics, mindful of Tory hostility to them, they felt their interests were best secured by a Whig administration; and they had great confidence in Godolphin.[111] As Abel Boyer put it, "the *Whiggs* or *Moderate Party*, were the more alarm'd and cast down, in that the best Part of their Wealth was lodg'd in the Exchequer and

109 Harley to Arthur Moore, 19 June 1710, HMC, *Portland MSS*, IV, 545.

110 James Brydges to Lord Stair, 3 July 1710, Buck and Davies, "Letters on Godolphin's Dismissal in 1710," p. 232. See also Hertfordshire R.O., Panshanger MSS, Sir David Hamilton's Diary, f. 14: "I set down from her [the Queen's] own Mouth, wt she sd to ye Commissioners of ye Bank who came to suplicate her not to Change ye Ministry nor dissolve ye Parlt. Viz. *I Have no thoughts of making any further alterations.*" Also Boyer, *Annals*, IX, 231–3.

111 Dickson, *The Financial Revolution in England*, pp. 59–64, 361–3.

Publick Funds; and that they rightly consider'd, that the Removal of the Earl of *Sunderland*, was but a Step to come at the Lord Treasurer, in whose Capacity, Punctuality, and Integrity, as the Merchants and Money'd-men repos'd an entire Confidence, so they foresaw that his being laid aside would very much affect Publick Credit."[112] Both Harley and the principal ministers thought the continual reports of Godolphin's removal and the imminent dissolution of Parliament were put out by the Whigs to convince the Queen that such steps would indeed bring financial ruin. "On Thursday a report was maliciously and industriously spread that the Parliament was dissolved and the proclamation for it in the press," Harley wrote to Newcastle at the beginning of July. "Some think it was done with a design to lower stock. If it was that, it had the effect to sink it about two per cent; but there being orders come by post from Holland to buy stock it will quickly be up again. It is certain the report came from the Whigs."[113] A few days earlier Godolphin had told Marlborough that the rumors of a new Parliament had begun to affect the credit, "and I am afrayd some very well meaning people, may have in some measure Contributed to that, out of kindness and good will, as they think it, to [Marlborough] and [Godolphin], and beleiving they shall show [the Queen], the Credit fails upon the Mortifications given to them, but wthout considering that when it is once broken, it is not to be recovered again, but by length of time, and in the mean time the whole must be ruined, and they for whose sake it is pretended to bee done, ruined, among the rest, if not the first of any."[114] But the rumors continued to circulate, and stocks continued to fall.

Through the summer months Harley, "obliged to almost daily attendance on [the Queen]," was at the same time work-

[112] Boyer, *Annals*, IX, 231.

[113] Harley to Newcastle, 1 July 1710, HMC, *Portland MSS*, II, 211.

[114] Godolphin to Marlborough, 27 June 1710, Blenheim, Marlborough Papers, BII, 8. See also Marlborough to Godolphin, 17, 31 July 1710, N.S., *ibid.*, BII, 9.

ing through his own connections in the City to allay these financial alarms.[115] It was a difficult task. By Addison's account, Tories as well as Whigs feared the consequences of a dissolution. "The bank have represented that they must shut up on the first issuing out of new writs; and . . . the monied citizens on the Tories side, have declared to the Duke of Shrewsbury, that they shall be ruined, if so great a blow be given to the public credit, as would inevitably follow upon a dissolution."[116] At the beginning of August the Bank refused to advance additional funds to the Treasury without renewed assurances that the Queen intended no further changes in the ministry nor the dissolution of Parliament. The Queen responded by dismissing her Lord Treasurer.[117] The Treasury was put into commission—Shrewsbury had earlier declined the Lord Treasurer's staff, protesting that the employment was one "I do not in the least understand and have not a head turned for,"[118]—and Harley took office as Chancellor of the Exchequer. He had a place on the Treasury commission as well; of the four remaining members, all Tories, three were moderates[119] and the fourth, Sir Thomas Mansell, was a loyal Harleyite. From this point on, Harley was the effective head of the ministry. In part because Shrewsbury chose to remain in the background, Harley's leadership was never in question. Swift wrote that "Mr. *Harley* is looked upon as First Minister, and not my Lord *Shrewsbury*, and his Grace helps on the

[115] Harley to Newcastle, 1 July 1710, HMC, *Portland MSS*, II, 211. John Carswell, *The South Sea Bubble* (Stanford, California: Stanford University Press, 1960), pp. 40–1; Holmes, *British Politics in the Age of Anne*, pp. 167–8.

[116] Addison to Joseph Keally, 5 August 1710, *The Letters of Joseph Addison*, p. 229.

[117] James Brydges to Mr. Sencerf, 17 August 1710, Buck and Davies, "Letters on Godolphin's Dismissal in 1710," p. 232, and n. 31 for the Court minutes of the Bank of England of 3 and 8 August 1710; Brydges to Mr. Drummond, 24 August 1710, *ibid.*, pp. 235–6; also *ibid.*, p. 228, for the Treasury minute of 3 August 1710.

[118] Shrewsbury to Harley, 22 July 1710, HMC, *Bath MSS*, I, 198.

[119] The moderates were Henry Paget, William Benson, and Earl Poulett, who served as First Lord.

Opinion, whether out of Policy or Truth; upon all Occasions professing to stay until he speaks with Mr. *Harley*."[120] Following Godolphin's dismissal, "it was visible," said Burnet, "he [Harley] was the chief minister; and now it appeared, that a total change of the ministry, and the dissolution of the parliament were resolved on."[121]

It had, of course, been rumored from the beginning of the changes that Godolphin would go; but Harley had waited to act until he was reasonably sure of his ground.[122] He sought to avoid any precipitate action that would unite the Whig factions against him, to avert the situation of 1708 when the Whigs in the Cabinet refused to serve under his leadership. And he needed time to reassure the City that a reorganized ministry would not mean financial ruin. Evidently he judged the moment correctly. Godolphin's dismissal did not bring panic in the City. Before the end of August Harley was able to persuade the Bank to supply at least some of the funds it had earlier refused Godolphin, and through private bankers he "found ways to remit . . . subsistance for the whole army in Flanders till Christmas."[123] Though Harley was confronted by an extremely serious financial situation, a major crisis had been averted.

"Thus past this great affair," James Brydges wrote, reporting the news of Godolphin's dismissal, "& after this I presume nobody can question but Her Majesty is resolved to go thro' with the Scheme that is laid, & we are in daily expectation of the alterations being made, that are said to be intended in the several Commissions of Lieutenancy & Justices of Peace

[120] Swift to Archbishop King, 9 September 1710, *Swift Correspondence*, I, 174–5.
[121] Burnet, *History*, VI, 11.
[122] For the early rumors, see for example *Private Correspondence of Sarah, Duchess of Marlborough*, I, 309, 337.
[123] Harley to Newcastle, 26 August 1710, HMC, *Portland MSS*, II, 217–18. McInnes, *Robert Harley*, pp. 127–8; B. W. Hill, "The Career of Robert Harley, Earl of Oxford, from 1702–1714" (Cambridge University Ph.D. thesis, 1961), pp. 187–92.

throughout the kingdom, in order to influence the ensuying Elections, for which we expect every week the writs to bear teste."[124] But the dissolution had not yet been decided upon, and it now became the central issue for Harley as it was for both Whig and Tory leaders. Harley's purpose, as Defoe expressed it, was "to find out and improve those blessed mediums of the nation's happiness, which lie between the wild extremes of all parties,"[125] and to this end he hoped to persuade a number of Whigs to remain in office. He was particularly anxious that Cowper continue as Lord Chancellor, Somers as Lord President, Boyle as Secretary of State. Newcastle agreed to stay on as Lord Privy Seal, and he figured largely in Harley's efforts to enlist Whig support.[126] In these negotiations the essential point for the Whigs was the continuation of the old Parliament. The passions roused by the Sacheverell trial together with growing resentment of the war made it virtually certain that a new election would return a Tory majority. Whig ministers might be prepared to serve with Harley so long as they and their former policies would not be subject to direct attack; but from a Tory House of Commons they could expect no quarter. In their eyes, a new Parliament meant the end of any hope for coalition government. But while the Whigs, Newcastle among them, argued against a dissolution, they feared it was inevitable, the more so once the Treasurer had been dismissed. Godolphin himself, writing four days after his

124 Brydges to Mr. Drummond, 24 August 1710, Buck and Davies, "Letters on Godolphin's Dismissal in 1710," p. 236.

125 Defoe to Harley, 17 July 1710, HMC, *Portland MSS*, IV, 550.

126 Halifax and Somerset were also deeply involved in the negotiations. For Newcastle's part in these negotiations see HMC, *Portland MSS*, II, especially pp. 210–21. For letters to Harley from Newcastle, Halifax, and Somerset, see *ibid.*, IV, *passim*. For Harley's correspondence with Halifax, BM, Portland Loan, 29/151; and *ibid.*, 29/156, for a series of notes from Somerset arranging secret meetings with Harley and Shrewsbury. See also Brydges to Cadogan, 7 April 1710, Davies, "The Seamy Side of Marlborough's War," p. 43; Halifax to Marlborough, 25 August 1710, Blenheim, Marlborough Papers, BII, 4; Boyer, *Annals*, IX, 240; Burnet, *History*, VI, 13, Onslow's note.

removal, thought it was "impossible not to conclude that a
dissolution must soon follow the Stepps wch have been already
made."[127]

Nonetheless, now, as in the months before, the Whigs
urged Harley to reassure moderate men that he did not wish
to make them desperate; and they warned him that unless
he reached some accommodation with the Whigs, he would
become the victim of his own violent men. Newcastle "incul-
cated the danger it would be to himself [Harley] to be thrown
into the Tories, who were every day pushing him to render
himself desperate with every body else, and they would soon
make him feel their former resentments."[128] Robert Monckton, a client of Newcastle's, wrote to the same purpose, warning him against the "rigids" in his party, who "think of nothing
less than driving the pilots out of the steerage as soon as they
get the numbers to support them in it."[129] William Carstares,
the principal of the University of Edinburgh, spoke of "the
apprehensions that many have that yourself and your friends
who are concerned for the quiet of her Majesty's government
and the present settlement may be obliged to join with others
who being of other principles may at last overpower you, and
hinder you doing that public good which you would."[130] To
quiet such apprehensions, Defoe thought that "acquainting
some people they are not all to be devoured and eaten up will

---

[127] Godolphin to Cowper, 12 August 1710, Hertfordshire R.O., Pan-
shanger MSS, D/EP, F54. For fears of a dissolution, see Godolphin to
Marlborough, 16, 19 June 1710, Blenheim, Marlborough Papers, BII, 8;
Marlborough to the Duchess of Marlborough, June 1710, *Private Correspond-
ence of Sarah, Duchess of Marlborough*, I, 356. Also Newcastle to Halifax, 12
August 1710, HMC, *Portland MSS*, II, 215; and Newcastle to Cowper, 2
August 1710, Hertfordshire R.O., Panshanger MSS, D/EP, F55.

[128] Newcastle to Somers, August [1719], HMC, *Portland MSS*, II, 217.
The date is either a slip of the pen or a misprint. The content of the
letter places it in August 1710.

[129] R. Monckton to Harley, 21 August 1710, *ibid.*, IV, 571. See also Monckton to Harley, 26 August 1710: "All heads of that party say it is of
necessity that when you have done their business you must be removed."
Ibid., p. 577.

[130] Reverend W. Carstares to Harley, 15 August 1710, *ibid.*, X, 328.

have all the effect upon them could be wished for; assuring them that moderate counsels are at the bottom of all these things; that the old mad party are not coming in; . . . that toleration, succession or union are not struck at, and they may be easy as to the nation's liberties."[131]

But it was difficult for Harley to reassure honest Whigs they would not be devoured when Monckton reported "that the Tories tell us positively we are all to be out of her [the Queen's] service and that all will not be enough neither."[132] And in fact the majority of Harley's Tory constituents thirsted for revenge. In their view the ministerial changes heralded the end of Whig domination, the advent of Tory government. They looked to a repudiation of Whig ministers and Whig measures, and they saw no reasonable grounds for delaying their triumph or for diluting it by making the changes less than total. Harley's method of proceeding was at best incomprehensible, at worst too well understood. In June Harcourt urged him to make some gesture to the Tories to counter Whig assertions that they would remain in power: "I had much rather displease you, than not serve you, and therefore take the liberty of telling you, you are in my poor opinion more concerned than any man living, that something may ere long be done to show the Queen's favour towards the Church of England, if there be a real intention that way. . . . My endeavours have not been wanting that all distrust might be laid aside. But what I say goes but for little anywhere."[133] Sir Thomas Hanmer wrote to his friend Prior: "You see I might have lost the summer if I had stayed to see the fruits of the secret consultations which were to change the world. Methinks they ripen very slowly." He feared

that the time which has already been lost must make a new election more inconvenient (were it now to come never so soon), and delaying it much longer will make it impossible. The conclusion,

131 Defoe to Harley, 28 July 1710, *ibid*, IV, 557–3
132 Monckton to Harley, 12 August 1710, *ibid.*, p. 563.
133 Harcourt to Harley, 21 June 1710, HMC, *Portland MSS*, IV, 546.

therefore, the dullest of us may draw, that without that step nothing can go on, for a new ministry with an old Parliament will be worse than the Gospel absurdity of a piece of new cloth in an old garment, or new wine in old bottles.[134]

A new Parliament was as much sought by the Tories as it was feared by the Whigs. Brydges observed reasonably enough that "they who had credit enough with the Queen to persuade her into the measure she has taken, will hardly think themselves safe in a House of Commons, where the majority is against them, & where by a dissolution they think they shall have as considerable an one on their side."[135] "We hope now there will soon be a Dissolution," Orrery wrote at the beginning of August, "& that the Kingdom is so well Disposed, that Elections Cannot go wrong."[136] Sure of their strength in the countryside, the Tories looked forward to a safe majority in the House of Commons and long and profitable tenure of the seats of power.

With Godolphin's dismissal, Tory hopes rose higher still. "Now the greatest Difficulty is got over, I cannot beleive others will be able to stand long in the Way," Bromley wrote to his friend Dr. Charlett. "The year is so far advanced, we may soon expect a Dissolution. . . . I am sensible the dilatory Proceedings have given some Strength as well as Courage to our Enemies, & have wearied & disheartned our Freinds, but I hope the latter will now be worried & double their Diligence, & then I shall not fear their recovering any Ground they may have lost."[137] But when the passing weeks brought neither a dissolution nor further removals, even Harley's most extravagant

[134] Sir Thomas Hanmer to Prior, 15/26 June 1710, HMC, *Bath MSS*, III, 437.

[135] James Brydges to Lord Stair, 3 July 1710, Buck and Davies, "Letters on Godolphin's Dismissal in 1710," pp. 230–1.

[136] Orrery to Harley, 6 August 1710 [N.S.], Longleat, Portland MSS, X, f. 137.

[137] Bromley to Dr. Charlett, 12 August 1710, Bodleian Library, MS Ballard 38, ff. 150–1.

admirers expressed increasing concern. "You are so slow in your changes that we have not yet new healths enough to last for three bottles of wine amongst five," Dr. Stratford complained to Harley's son at the end of August.[138] Several days later his tone was more serious: "We are now alarmed with a coalition, we are told those who threatened to throw up are willing to keep their places and to join with those already in, and the visits your father is said to have paid of late to Lord Halifax have given no little disquiet to us."[139] Shortly thereafter he was "at a loss to account for the delay of that which must be done at last. No one but thinks they have gone too far to stop; and we fear we lose ground by deferring that which is designed."[140] Harley's son-in-law, Viscount Dupplin, wrote from Scotland that they would lose support there "unless the Queen go in to a thorough measure in strengthening the hands of her friends and discouraging her enemies. . . . Wherefore what you do, do it with all your might, and the sooner the better."[141] The government's followers, said Dupplin, were "like a brave, numerous, bold army without a commander to give them orders. Now some people attribute this to your slowness at London, and wish you would let your friends know here what way you would have them unite, and in what measure you would have them to join, that they might serve their Queen and country to the best advantage."[142]

Complaints poured in from particular friends and distant acquaintances, from the humble and the great. The Auditor was present at an interview between his brother and Dr. Atterbury, the High Church Dean of Christ Church, in which,

after some compliments, he [Atterbury] told Mr. Harley that he came from some of his particular friends to acquaint him how very

[138] Dr. Stratford to Edward Harley, 31 August 1710, HMC, *Portland MSS*, VII, 16.
[139] Dr. Stratford to Edward Harley, 5 September 1710, *ibid.*
[140] Dr. Stratford to Edward Harley, 9 September 1710, *ibid.*, p. 18.
[141] Viscount Dupplin to Harley, 8 August 1710, *ibid.*, IV, 558.
[142] Viscount Dupplin to Harley, 13 August 1710, *ibid.*, p. 564.

uneasy they were at his conduct, that the Parliament was not yet dissolved, nor so many of the Whigs turned out as was expected, and that they were wholly in the dark as to the measures he was taking, which had created a very great uneasiness, and that out of his friendship, he had acquainted him with it. This was the only time I ever saw Mr. Harley express any passion in public affairs. He told the Doctor he knew very well the persons from whom he delivered the message, and was so sensible of the difficulties he had to struggle with, that nothing but his duty and promise to the Queen could make him be concerned any further; and therefore desired he would let those persons know that if they expected he should communicate all the measures he thought were absolutely necessary for conducting the Queen's affairs over the difficulties he would let her Majesty know that it was impossible for him to be of any further service, and therefore would ask leave to retire into the country.[143]

This was bravely said, but it did not silence Harley's critics: nothing would silence them but a new Parliament and a clean sweep of Whig office-holders. Yet accession to these demands meant the end of his moderate scheme, and this he was not prepared to contemplate. Beset by Tory clamors for a swift and thorough purge of Whigs from government, he continued to resist, at the same time assuring honest Whigs that he had no wish to make them desperate. Swift reflected the general view when, early in September, he wrote from London that "there is such an universal Uncertainty among those who pretend to know most, that little can be depended on . . . for it is thought there are not three People in *England* entirely in the Secret, nor is it sure, whether even those three are agreed in what they intend to do."[144]

It was an impossible position. While the Tories attacked him for being the occasion of "ye present delayes," Whig propagandists noisily charged the new ministers with "favour-

---

[143] Edward Harley, "Memoirs," HMC, *Portland MSS*, V, 650–1.
[144] Swift to Archbishop King, 9 September 1710, *Swift Correspondence*, I, 175.

ing a French interest, and countenancing the Pretender, terrifying the poor ignorant people with notions of Popery and persecution."[145] Harley's "reserved mysterious way of acting," said Swift,

. . . was imputed to some hidden Design, which every Man conjectured to be the very Evil he was most afraid of. Those who professed the Height of what is called the Church Principle, suspected that a Comprehension was intended, wherein the moderate Men on both Sides might be equally employed. Others went further, and dreaded such a Correspondence, as directly tended to bring the old exploded Principles and Persons once more into play. Again, some affected to be uneasy about the Succession, and seemed to think there was a View of introducing that Person, whatever he is, who pretends to claim the Crown by Inheritance.[146]

But the explanation for Harley's actions lay in his dilemma. He knew as well as anyone the temper of the country and he feared the High Church majority that new' elections were likely to return to Parliament. Newcastle's warning that, without Whig support, he would be at the mercy of the Tories was real enough. An anonymous letter, undated but apparently written some time before the dissolution, asks: "Were it amiss for you to consider well whether you are safer in a Parliament of Tory's than of Whigs, . . . can you expect those men will stick to you when there shall be occasion who draw near you and serving their turn use your name with the utmost indignity. Is it prudent to carry things to the extremity against One Party, without being very well assured of the other."[147] Harley understood the danger. But by the end of the summer, harassed by the Tories and discouraged by the inconclusive negotiations with the Whigs, he concluded that the old Parliament must go. Informing Newcastle of the decision, he said the

---

[145] C. Lawton to Harley, 21 September 1710, BM, Portland Loan, 29/313. Defoe to Harley, 12 September 1710, HMC, *Portland MSS*, IV, 593.

[146] Swift, "Some free Thoughts," p. 86.

[147] Anonymous letter addressed to "The Right Honble Robert Harley at his House in Yorke Buildings London," BM, Portland Loan, 29/62.

Queen had resolved upon it "in her own breast," but that it was indeed "impossible to carry on [Parliament] without intolerable heats."[148]

The decision to dissolve Parliament marked the final collapse of Harley's attempt to keep a sizable number of Whigs in the ministry: by the end of September, Somers, Devonshire, Boyle, Cowper were out; Rochester, Buckingham, St. John, Harcourt, High Tories all, were in. The best efforts of Harley and Newcastle failed to persuade Cowper to remain in the Lord Chancellor's post. According to Cowper, Harley "used all Arguments possible to perswade me to stay in place:—All shod. be easy:—The Danger of going out: A Whig Game intended at bottom; enumerated wt. Whigs in; declind. (shuffling) to tell all the Removes intended, tho' asked." To which Cowper replied that before his dismissal he had spoken to Godolphin of his wish to retire, "being weary of my place; . . . that things were plainly put into Torys hands; a Whig Game, either in whole or part, impracticable; that to keep in, when all my Friends were out, wod. be infamous; that in a little time, when any Tory of Interest would press for my place, he must needs have it."[149] The day before he had told Harley's emissary that "things were too far gone towards the Tories, &c for me to think it prudent to keep my Place, if I might; and that in case of a Tory Parlt., Mr. Hy. would find himself born along into measures he might not like."[150] On September 23 he resigned. "Our friends have quite gone off the stage," Halifax wrote to Newcastle at the end of September, "and those who were most reasonable and most disposed to set things right

---

[148] Harley to Newcastle, 14 September 1710, HMC, *Portland MSS*, II, 219.

[149] Cowper, *Diary*, pp. 43–4.

[150] *Ibid.*, pp. 42–3. For Harley's and Newcastle's efforts to persuade Cowper to remain in office, see *ibid.*, pp. 42–7; also Newcastle to Cowper, 2 September, 5 November 1710, Hertfordshire R.O., Panshanger MSS, D/EP, F55; Cowper to Lady Cowper, 18 September 1710, "Fryd. morning," *ibid.*, F193; Cowper to Newcastle, 25 September 1710, HMC, *Portland MSS*, II, 221; Newcastle to Harley, 30 September 1710, *ibid.*, IV, 604.

on the other side are not so much the masters of the field that they were; the auxiliaries they have taken in, whether by choice or necessity I will not determine, will have a share in the command."[151]

Harley had concluded that the Crown's business could not be carried on by a deeply divided Parliament and that the Tories must to some extent be pacified. But he saw no reason to bolster the Tory position further by removing still more Whigs from office, or to lend widespread government support to Tory candidates in the forthcoming General Election. The greater the Tory majority, the more difficult his task would be; and, in any case, the Tories were strong enough to win on their own. "The true reason why the court did not interpose in matter of elections," Swift wrote later, "was because they thought themselves sure of a majority, and therefore could acquire reputation at a cheap rate."[152] But at the time he told Archbishop King that "people were surprised when the Court stopt its hand as to farther removalls; . . . The new Ministry are afraid of too great a Majority of their own side in the H. of C. and therefore stopt short in their changes."[153]

The Tories complained bitterly of the government's lack of support and pressed for the removal of all Whig justices of the peace and lords-lieutenant in the counties, local offices of considerable importance in the making of elections. According to the High Tory Duke of Beaufort, the "other side" had it "that the interest of her Majesty and her officers is to influence all that is possible against us. This we suffer and have no encouragement to contradict them." He could not help regretting "that so many honest gentlemen are to be suppressed when they are using the greatest endeavours to support her undoubted hereditary right to that Church she is so zealous in

---

[151] Halifax to Newcastle, 26 September 1710, HMC, *Portland MSS*, II, 221.
[152] Swift, "Memoirs," p. 126.
[153] Swift to Archbishop King, 10 October 1710, *Swift Correspondence*, I, 185–6. Lockhart and Boyer concurred. *The Lockhart Papers*, I, 319–20; Boyer, *Annals*, IX, 248.

inclination for."[154] Dr. Stratford had the same complaint: "We say here, that you who are at the helm are afraid of having too good a Parliament and take measures to cool the affection of the country."[155] In spite of such apprehensions, the elections returned an overwhelmingly Tory House of Commons, and one not particularly indebted to Harley.[156] "The Tories here are not a little pleased with the success of the elections," Dr. Stratford reported, "and the more because there was no previous change of the lieutenancies and commissions of the peace. That circumstance makes us think our obligation much less to you at Court for the Parliament we hope to have."[157]

When the new Parliament met, Harley's situation was anything but secure. The Tory majority in the Commons was suspicious, even hostile. The government's reluctance to support Tory candidates and the continuance of a number of Whigs in office cast doubt on his intentions. And while Tories had not spurned Dissenting votes, High Churchmen suspected —and deplored—an alliance between Harley and Dissent. "In a great many of the elections the no conformist have voted for the Torys," Peter Wentworth reported to his brother, "and 'tis thought it proceeds from the assurance Mr. Harley has given there preachers that there shall be nothing this P—— done against them, but their tolleration keep inviolable." Four days later he wrote: "I have been told that the Dean of Christ

154 Duke of Beaufort to Harley, 9 October 1710, HMC, *Portland MSS*, IV, 611. See also C. Lawton to Harley, n.d., BM, Portland Loan, 29/313, in which the writer urges alteration of the Commissions of the Peace. In August Harley horrified the Tories by appointing Cowper Lord Lieutenant of Hertfordshire, an action which Bromley found "unaccountable." Bromley to Harley, 12 August 1710, HMC, *Portland MSS*, IV, 563. See also Bromley to Dr. Charlett, 12 August 1710, Bodleian Library, MS Ballard 38, ff. 150–1.

155 Dr. Stratford to Edward Harley, 4 October 1710, HMC, *Portland MSS*, VII, 20.

156 The Whigs were outnumbered two to one. Trevelyan, *England under Queen Anne*, III, 73 and 348, note 78.

157 Dr. Stratford to Edward Harley, 15 October 1710, HMC, *Portland MSS*, VII, 22–3.

Church in Oxford have writ to a great man that they ought not to put any trust in that spaun of a presbiterian Harley."[158] Less volatile Tories might put the case less strongly, but the point is that the Tory gentlemen did not trust Harley. Their views were more extreme than his, yet they constituted the party's majority in the House of Commons and they accurately reflected Tory feeling in the country. They were, for the most part, uninterested in moderation, and it is hardly surprising that Harley could not command their support. As for the House of Lords, Harley pointed out in his "Plan" that "the Faction have most of their Strength there, and most of their able Men."[159] But he counted on a certain amount of Whig support for his moderate policies and he hoped to increase this by retaining a number of Whiggish peers in lesser offices at Court and in lieutenancies in the counties. By serving as a counterweight to the Tory House of Commons, a Whiggish House of Lords could in fact help Harley to pursue a middle course. Still, Swift wrote that "even after some Management, there was but a weak and crazy majority" in the upper House,[160] and Harley was to encounter a good deal of difficulty in holding it together.

So much for Parliament. Of the principal ministers in Harley's government, only Shrewsbury and Newcastle, both Whigs, and Dartmouth among the Tories could be described as true moderates. Rochester, Ormonde, and Buckingham were High Tories; Harcourt and Granville were more committed to Harley than to his moderate scheme. St. John's moderation was grounded in expediency; no longer a Harleyite, his differences with Harley can only have been exacerbated by Harley's reluctance to make him Secretary of State. There was no

---

[158] Peter Wentworth to Lord Raby, 27, 31 October 1710, *Wentworth Papers*, pp. 151-2. For Tory attention to Quaker votes, see Sir Thomas Hanmer to Prior, 11 September 1710, HMC, *Bath MSS*, III, 442; and C. Lawton to Harley, n.d., BM, Portland Loan, 29/313.

[159] "Mr. Harley's Plan," BM, Stowe MSS, 248.

[160] Swift, "An Enquiry," p. 149.

guarantee that these men would support moderate measures consistently or at all: Rochester's loyalty throughout the first session of the new Parliament was enormously important to Harley, and his death, in May 1711, a serious political loss. Overall, in reviewing Harley's position, one is struck by the fact that his strongest support was the Queen. Granted that the calling of a new Parliament was unavoidable, it had placed him in exactly the situation predicted by his Whig friends. The urgent need to deal with the nation's financial problems and to set in motion negotiations for the peace presented difficulties enough for any minister, but Harley had to deal with deep divisions within his own party as well. Swift reflected the general view when he wrote to Stella: "They think he will never carry through this undertaking. God knows what will come of it."[161]

[161] Swift, *Journal to Stella*, I, 76.

CHAPTER V

The Inconstancy of Court Friendships:

1710 – 1711

O n the great issues confronting the new ministry there was general agreement. Discussing Tory policy at the opening of the new Parliament, Bolingbroke wrote in the "Letter to Sir William Windham" that on the need for peace, he "saw no difference of opinion among all those who came to the head of affairs at this time." All

seemed equally convinced of the unreasonableness and even of the impossibility of continuing the war on the same disproportionate foot. Their universal sense was that we had taken, except the part of the States General, the whole burden of the war upon us, and even a proportion of this; while the entire advantage was to accrue to others. . . . that the ends proposed when we engaged in it might have been answered long before, and therefore that the first favorable occasion ought to be seized of making peace; which we thought to be the interest of our country and which appeared to all mankind, as well as to us, to be that of our party.[1]

But while the ministry was agreed on the necessity for peace, Harley and St. John at least were prepared to support the war

1 Bolingbroke, *Works*, I, 116–17.

wholeheartedly until a favorable agreement could be reached.[2] In the meantime, the financial situation required immediate attention. Auditor Harley wrote that when his brother came into the Treasury,

he found the Exchequer almost empty, nothing left for the subsistence of the Army, but some tallies upon the third general mortgage of the customs; the Queen's civil list near 700,000 *l.* in debt; the funds all exhausted, and a debt of 9,500,000 *l.*, without any provision of Parliament; which had brought all the credit of the Government to a vast discount. In this condition the nation had then in pay 255,689 men.[3]

Harley had been able to provide subsistence for the forces abroad until the end of December. He had now to deal with the current deficit and the problem of raising the coming year's supply; and he had also to find some means of securing the £9,000,000 unfunded debt. He acted decisively, and to good effect. Early in the new year he negotiated an agreement with the Bank to cash Exchequer bills—interest-bearing notes issued by the government—on demand and at face value, a step of enormous significance in restoring public credit. To raise funds for the year's supply, two lotteries were enacted in the first six months of 1711. The first, for £1,500,000, was oversubscribed by nearly £300,000 when the books were officially opened on March 13; a second was launched in June, producing another £2,000,000 in nine days' time.[4] Speaking of the phenomenal success of the first of the lotteries, Abel Boyer wrote that it was "a remarkable Instance of the Wealth of this Nation, and

---

[2] The Dutch agent in London reassured the States General that in spite of the Tory majority in the Commons, he was persuaded every effort would be made "*pour pousser vigoureusement la guerre.*" L'Hermitage to the States General, 17/28 October 1710, BM, Add. MSS, 17,677DDD.

[3] Edward Harley, "Memoirs," HMC, *Portland MSS*, V, 650.

[4] Edward Harley, "Memoirs," HMC, *Portland MSS*, V, 651-2; Boyer, *Annals*, IX, 324-5; Dickson, *The Financial Revolution in England*, pp. 61-74, 373-9.

at the same time, an undoubted Symptom of the Recovery of the Publick *Credit,* owing to the Care and Industry of the present Managers of Her Majesty's Treasury."[5]

But the most spectacular of Harley's financial measures dealt with the problem of the floating debt. In May of 1711 he proposed that a newly incorporated joint-stock company, invested with a monopoly of the South American trade, take over the unsecured £9,000,000.[6] The government's creditors would become shareholders in the South Sea Company; in return the government would pay the Company annual interest and management fees until 1716, thus allowing a small dividend to be returned to the stockholders. Beyond this the Company's profits would come from its trading monopoly. That this monopoly was then jealously guarded by Spain did not dampen Tory enthusiasm for the scheme. Presumably the Tories were satisfied that the peace they hoped for would secure those concessions necessary for the trade to go forward, which was certainly the impression the ministry sought to convey. And they were elated by the prospect of a financial enterprise launched under Tory auspices and guided by Tory hands. Harley, for his part, counted on the secret negotiations then in progress with France to provide English access to the South American trade. At the same time, he wanted to do something for the Tory interests in the City and to consolidate his support in the financial community. Thus the Queen, which in practice meant Harley, was to appoint the first Court of Directors of the new Company; and it was further stipulated that no governor or director of the Bank or the East India Company, both bastions of Whiggery, could serve on the

[5] Boyer, *Annals,* IX, 325.

[6] For the South Sea scheme, see Edward Harley, "Memoirs," HMC, *Portland MSS,* V, 652–3; Boyer, *Annals,* IX, 369–71, 379–80. J. G. Sperling, *The South Sea Company, An Historical Essay and Bibliographical Finding List* (Boston, Mass.: Baker Library, Harvard Graduate School of Business Administration, 1962); Carswell, *The South Sea Bubble,* pp. 53–9; Dickson, *The Financial Revolution in England,* pp. 64–71.

directorate of the South Sea Company.[7] In fact, Harley himself became the first governor and St. John was a director, one
of a number of purely political appointees.[8] The Bank and the
East India Company acquiesced in the scheme once their own
exclusive privileges were guaranteed, and the bill establishing
the Company passed its final reading in the Commons on May
25. The Tories were jubilant. "Mr. Harley's project for providing a fund of interest for the national debts, is agreed to
with great applause," St. John wrote; and Harley's daughter
reported that the proposal "caused great rejoicing, there were
bonfires and ringing of bells in the city last night; it is a
glorious thing."[9]

The Tories had found less cause for rejoicing in the months
preceding the introduction of the South Sea scheme. Following
their victory at the polls the previous autumn, they had pressed
still more insistently their claims to place and favor. Yet Harley
made no move to gratify their expectations. In his "Plan," he
said that in the House of Commons, "avoiding giving Jealousies, and the hopes of Places after will render that House
easy this Session."[10] Thus a number of Whigs remained in
minor offices, and the clean sweep of lieutenancies and Commissions of the Peace urged by the Tories did not take place.
In December the Duke of Leeds warned Harley that "if the
Queen do not lay hold of this time both openly to encourage
some of her friends and as openly to discourage some of her

[7] The only division on the South Sea Bill came over the question of
whether the Queen rather than the stockholders should appoint the first
governor and directors, and it was carried by a vote of 110 to 29. In April
Tory efforts to install their own candidates in the directorships of the Bank
and the East India Company had been largely unsuccessful. For the division,
see J. G. Sperling, "The Division of 25 May 1711, on an Amendment to the
South Sea Bill: A Note on the Reality of Parties in the Age of Anne,"
Historical Journal, IV (1961), 191–202.

[8] For the directors, see Carswell, *The South Sea Bubble*, pp. 57–8.

[9] St. John to Marlborough, 8 May 1711, *Bolingbroke Correspondence*,
I, 203; Lady Dupplin to her aunt Abigail Harley, 3 May 1711, HMC, *Portland
MSS*, IV, 683.

[10] "Mr. Harley's Plan," BM, Stowe MSS, 248.

enemies the last error will be worse than the first and past any possibility of remedy for the future."[11] Several months later "some great men" complained to Swift

of the suspicions entertained by many of our friends in relation to Mr. Harley. . . . The cause of their complaint was, That so great a number of the adverse party continued in employment; and some, particularly the Duke of Somerset and Earl of Cholmondely, in great stations at court. They could not believe Mr. Harley was in earnest; but, that he designed to constitute a motley comprehensive administration, which they said the kingdom would never endure.[12]

When Swift represented these complaints to him, Harley spoke of "the necessity of keeping men in hopes, the danger of disobliging those who must remain unprovided for, and the like usual topics among statesmen." But he assured Swift that "it was his opinion and desire, that no person should have the smallest employment, either civil or military, whose principles were not firm for the church and monarchy."[13] This was cold comfort for the Tories, who wanted only to be certain that no Whig should have the smallest employment, whatever his principles. Swift confessed that "this manner of proceeding in a prime Minister, . . . appeared to me wholly unaccountable, and without example."[14]

The complaints of the Tory majority were not restricted to the matter of employments: they were anxious also to punish the supposed evil-doers in the late ministry, a partisan proceeding in which they received little encouragement from Harley. "The country members are violent to have past faults enquired into, and they have reason," Swift wrote to Stella, "but I do not

[11] Duke of Leeds to Harley, 7 December 1710, HMC, *Portland MSS*, IV, 642.
[12] Swift, "Memoirs," pp. 124–5. Somerset, the Master of the Horse, was not dismissed until January 1712. Cholmondeley was Treasurer of the Household and remained in office until April 1713.
[13] *Ibid.*
[14] Swift, "An Enquiry," p. 143.

observe the ministry to be very fond of it."[15] Peter Wentworth told his brother that he believed Harley and Rochester
"will be both deceived if either of them thinks they can govern
this house of Commons, there being a great many country
Gentlemen that are resolved to proceed in methods of their
own. Some impeachments they say they are resolved to have,
to begin with Lord Godolphin, but some great men 'twas
thought had art enough to get that waved."[16]

Denied places and denied impeachments, in the winter of
1710–11 the country gentlemen made good their threat to
proceed in methods of their own and organized into the October Club as a means of putting pressure on the government.[17]
"We are plagued here with an October Club," Swift wrote in
February,

that is, a set of above a hundred parliament-men of the country,
who drink October beer at home, and meet every evening at a
tavern near the parliament, to consult affairs, and drive things on
to extreams against the Whigs, to call the old ministry to account,
and get off five or six heads. The ministry seem not to regard
them, yet one of them in confidence told me, that there must be
something thought on to settle things better.[18]

In the same month Wentworth reported that

this loyal country club is a great disturbance to Mr. Harley, who
finds they are past his governing; their Number is increased to a
150. They are most of them young gentlemen of estates that has
never been in Parliament before, and are not very close, but declare to every body what they designe, to have every Whig turn'd
out, and not to suffer that the new Ministry shou'd shake hands as
they see they do with old.

[15] Swift, *Journal to Stella*, I, 159.

[16] Peter Wentworth to Lord Raby, 8 December 1710, *Wentworth Papers*,
p. 161. See also Burnet, *History*, VI, 41–2, Dartmouth's note, for the ministry's
reluctance to initiate impeachment proceedings.

[17] For the October Club see H. T. Dickinson, "The October Club"
Huntington Library Quarterly, XXXIII (1969–70), 155–73.

[18] Swift, *Journal to Stella*, I, 194–5.

He added that several members had told him the ministry "begin to send the old Fellows among them, but damn they won't be bite so, and that neither their weadles nor threats shall bring them under government."[19] By Swift's account, the October men,

who professed in the greatest degree what was called the High-church principle, . . . held their meetings at certain times and places, and there concerted what measures they were to take in parliament. They professed their jealousy of the court and minis-try; declared, upon all occasions, their desire of a more general change, as well as of a strict enquiry into former mismanagements; and seemed to expect, that those in power should openly avow the old principles in church and state.[20]

The October Club's strength lay in its numbers and in its unity: "What has once been carried by the majority of their club they will stand to a man in the House."[21] Functioning as a caucus within the House of Commons, it harassed the gov-ernment at every turn, pushing for inquiries and impeachments and proposing bills the ministers were known to view with disfavor. With the assistance of the House of Lords, which threw out the most extreme of their proposals, Harley man-aged by persuasion and division to keep the October men in check. Nevertheless, they dramatized the split between Harley and the High Tories, and in the spring of 1711 they were strong enough to pose a real threat to his ministry. "I have complaints of you from the Tory side, who I fear want to drive things too suddenly and to extremities," John Drummond wrote from Amsterdam in March. "I hope you will agree amongst yourselves and then nothing can hurt you, if other-wise, everything will; and a watchful diligent enemy will make

[19] Peter Wentworth to Lord Raby, 20 February 1711, *Wentworth Papers*, p. 180. See also *The Lockhart Papers*, I, 324; Roberthon to Bernstorff, 21 March 1711, N.S., Klopp, *Der Fall des Hauses Stuart*, XIV, 673–4.

[20] Swift, "Memoirs," p. 125. See also Swift, *History*, pp. 99–100.

[21] Peter Wentworth to Lord Raby, 20 February 1711, *Wentworth Papers*, p. 180.

good use of your divisions for their advantage."[22] Swift was
more reassuring:

I am sometimes talked into frights, and told that all is ruined; but
am immediately cured when I see any of the Ministry: Not from
the satisfaction they give me in any one point, but because I see
them so perfectly easy, and I believe they could not be so if they
had any fear at heart. My comfort is, they are persons of great
abilities, and they are engaged in a good cause. And what is one
very good circumstance, as I told three of them the other day,
they seem heartily to love one another.[23]

The ministers may have seemed heartily to love one an-
other, but February 1711 is exactly the date Harley gave for
St. John's first attempt to form his own party in the House of
Commons. "To prevent this," Harley wrote in his "brief
Account of Public Affairs,"

lord Rochester and Harley desired to have a meeting, and to cool
such rash attempts; and it was contrived Mr. Secretary St. John
should invite us to dinner (which was the last time he ever invited
Robert Harley, being now about three years) where was the duke
of Shrewsbury, earl Poulet, lord Rochester, and others; and lord
Rochester took the pains to calm the spirit of division and ambition.[24]

The evidence for St. John's activities in the winter of 1710–11
is not conclusive, but his "Letter to Sir William Windham"
makes clear that he shared the High Tory view, which, as he
described it, was "to improve the queen's favor, to break the
body of the whigs, to render their supports useless to them, and
to fill the employments of the kingdom down to the meanest
with tories. We imagined that such measures, joined to the
advantages of our numbers and our property, would secure us

[22] Drummond to Harley, 28 February/10 March 1711, HMC, *Portland
MSS*, IV, 663.
[23] Swift to the Earl of Peterborough, [19] February 1711, *Swift Correspondence*, I, 211–12.
[24] Oxford, "A brief Account of Public Affairs," *Parliamentary History*
VI, ccxlv.

against all attempts during her reign."[25] He looked with favor upon the Commons' resolve to inquire into the conduct of the late ministry: "For my own part, I do not, I confess, see how those who are now in the administration, and who have taken such a broken shattered game into their hands, can be safe, and avoid bearing the load of other people's guilt, unless they make a plain and obvious discrimination between their own management, and the natural necessary consequences of that which went before."[26] This obviously pleased the Tory gentlemen. So did his sponsorship of the bill to impose a landed property qualification on members of Parliament. In a speech which Peter Wentworth described as "pretty remarkable," St. John

gave some touchs upon the late management, as that we might see a time when the mony'd men might bid fair to keep out of that house all the landed men, and he had heard of Societys of them that joint'd Stocks to bring in members, and such a thing might be as an Administration within an Administration, a juncto; and these mony'd men might arise to such a pitch of assurance as to oppose the Crown and advise in matters that did not belong to them.[27]

No doubt the House applauded St. John's oratory, but it is a mistake to make too much of his connection with the Qualifications Bill. The ministry approved it as a less troublesome alternative to the Place Bill, the latest in the series of backbench attempts to exclude from the House of Commons office-holders and pensioners of the Crown, a measure opposed by both Harley and St. John in the Commons and finally thrown out in the Lords. In supporting the Qualifications Bill St. John was speaking for the government; and at the next election neither he nor Harley hesitated to circumvent the law.[28] But his

25 Bolingbroke, *Works*, I, 115.

26 St. John to Drummond, 12 December 1710, *Bolingbroke Correspondence*, I, 40. See also to Drummond, 5 January 1711, *ibid.*, pp. 59–60.

27 Peter Wentworth to Lord Raby, 26 December 1710, *Wentworth Papers*, p. 167.

28 For the Qualifications Bill, see Burnet, *History*, VI, 40, and Onslow's note; paper headed "Remarkables in the Parliament begun the 25th of Nov:

denunciation of the moneyed men reflected his own deeply felt
principles, which were also the principles of the Tory gentlemen. This is the central point: St. John voiced the feelings of
the large number of Tories in the House of Commons who
were dissatisfied with Harley. The country gentlemen—within
and outside the October Club—looked to him for leadership
whether or not he solicited their support. He said as much in
the "Letter to Sir William Windham," when he remarked that
in the House of Commons Harley's "credit was low, and my
reputation very high. You know the nature of that assembly:
they grow, like hounds, fond of the man who shows them
game, and by whose halloo they are used to be encouraged."[29]
What steps he took to "list" a party for himself it is impossible
to say; but he had a constituency at hand, and given Harley's
refusal to take up the party leadership, it was predictable that
St. John would move to assume that role.[30]

There is on record one major clash between Harley and St.
John in the winter of 1710–11. St. John undertook to promote
and then to plan a military expedition to take Quebec, a scheme
originally proposed by Godolphin's ministry two years before.
His own project had taken shape by the end of 1710, and it
was from the outset opposed by Harley. "Pray do me the
justice to believe that I am not light nor whimsical in this
project," St. John wrote to Harley. "It will certainly succeed if
the secret is preserved, and if it succeeds you will have done
more service to Britain in half a year, than the ministers who
went before you did in all their administration. I hope you will
support me in it since I have gone so far."[31] Far from supporting him, Harley refused even to attend the meetings at which

---

1710," Staffordshire R.O., Dartmouth MSS, D1778, V, 200; Holmes, *British
Politics in the Age of Anne*, pp. 178–82.

[29] Bolingbroke, *Works*, I, 117.

[30] Dickinson believes that by early 1711 St. John "was not merely agreeing
with Harley's critics, but was positively inciting them to further action."
Bolingbroke, p. 81.

[31] St. John to Harley, 17 January 1711, HMC, *Portland MSS*, IV, 655.

the expedition was discussed. By his own account, he "avoided coming, and gave lord Rochester his reasons; and after he desired his lordship to be a means to the queen, to hinder that expedition, but it happened to be too late."[32] It was characteristic of Harley to withdraw rather than confront St. John face to face, and perhaps ill-judged as well. What success his tactics might have had cannot be known, for he was in the end defeated by misfortune: St. John took advantage of Harley's convalescence following the attempt on his life to gain the Queen's approval for the expedition. This was one of "the transactions during that time" that Harley later described as "too public, as well as too black . . . to remember or to mention."[33]

The Auditor reports that the day after the assassination attempt, his brother, "finding himself extremely ill, and in great pain, told me that the expedition which was then fitting out, he apprehended, might be of very ill consequence to the Queen's affairs at that time, and directed me to desire the Lord Poulett to acquaint the Lord Rochester, then President of the Council, that it was his dying request that he would advise the Queen that it might be laid aside."[34] Rochester supported Harley in his opposition to the project but they did not succeed in blocking it.[35] Whether Harley objected on grounds of principle is not known. What he and the Auditor specify is their belief that St. John intended to make a fat profit out of the contracts for supplying the expedition. In addition, the commander of the land forces was to be Jack Hill, Mrs. Masham's brother, an attempt on St. John's part to ingratiate himself at Court, which cannot have pleased Harley. Mrs. Masham's close connection with the expedition—she is also said to have been one of those

[32] Oxford, "A brief Account of Public Affairs," *Parliamentary History*, VI, ccxliv.

[33] *Ibid.*, p. ccxlv.

[34] Edward Harley, "Memoirs," HMC, *Portland MSS*, V, 654–5.

[35] For Rochester's opposition, see Rochester to Harley, 19 April 1711, HMC, *Portland MSS*, IV, 675–6.

who would profit from it—doubtless served St. John well in securing the Queen's approval; and she must have resented Harley's stand against an enterprise that would bring her brother fortune and renown. According to the Auditor, "Mr. Harley being now confined to his bed, Mr. Secretary St. John and others pushed on this matter with the utmost eagerness, having laid a scheme for securing themselves 20,000*l.* for buying clothes and other things for this Expedition."[36] Harley himself relates in his "brief Account" that he refused to authorize payment of funds until ordered to do so by the Queen; and he says flatly that "the public was cheated of above 20,000*l.*"[37] He also maintained that he had protected St. John by keeping the House of Commons from looking into the matter, an assertion that was used against him at the time of his impeachment. He answered then that there had not been sufficient grounds to bring charges against St. John and his associates, a view he thought the House of Commons shared. As Mallet wisely observes, this "rather proves his [Harley's] Mistake, than his Antagonist's Misbehaviour. You will likewise consider, that at the Time the Earl's Paper was sent to the Queen, these two noble persons were at open Variance, which Circumstance might very possibly give Things the Appearance of Conviction, that when more coolly considered, did not rise quite so high."[38] Even if St. John did take a commission on the supplies for the expedition, this did not necessarily make him guilty by the standards of the time. The significant point about the Quebec expedition is St. John's open and successful challenge to Harley. The expedition was St. John's peculiar property: "As that *whole design was form'd by* me, you will easily imagine that I have a sort of paternal concern for the Success of it," he wrote to Drummond.[39] As its success would have

---

[36] Edward Harley, "Memoirs," HMC, *Portland MSS*, V, 655.

[37] Oxford, "A brief Account of Public Affairs," *Parliamentary History*, VI, ccxlv.

[38] [Mallet], *Memoirs of the Life and Ministerial Conduct, . . . of the Late Lord Visc. Bolingbroke*, pp. 212–13.

[39] St. John to Drummond, 26 June 1711, BM, Portland Loan, 29/266.

strengthened his position in the ministry, its disastrous failure cannot have helped him, particularly as Parliament had never approved the project or voted it funds. St. John's insistence on the necessity for secrecy meant that even the Admiralty had not been consulted or informed of the squadron's destination. The expedition's failure resulted in large part from the ineptitude of its commanders, Sir Hovenden Walker and Jack Hill, and it is a curious reflection on St. John's judgment that he chose so ill.[40] The appointment of Hill was of course political; but why Walker was put in command of the squadron, given an unimpressive naval record, remains unexplained. But for the Harley–St. John relationship the expedition's failure was comparatively unimportant. From Harley's point of view, St. John's crime had been to push the project in the first place and, worse, to take unscrupulous advantage of Harley's illness to press his point with the Queen. Before the squadron ever left Spithead, the damage was already done.

I I

On March 4 Swift told Stella that Mr. Harley was "much out of order; pray God preserve his health, every thing depends upon it. The Parliament at present cannot go a step without him, nor the queen neither." And he continued gloomily:

The nearer I look upon things, the worse I like them. I believe the confederacy will soon break to pieces; and our factions at home increase. The ministry is upon a very narrow bottom, and stand like an Isthmus between the Whigs on one side, and violent Tories on the other. They are able seamen, but the tempest is too great, the ship too rotten, and the crew all against them.[41]

[40] [Mallet], *Memoirs of the Life and Ministerial Conduct, . . . of the Late Lord Visc. Bolingbroke*, pp. 208 11; W. T. Morgan, "Queen Anne's Canadian Expedition of 1711," *Queen's Quarterly*, XXXV (August 1927–October 1928), 460–89; Gerald S. Graham, ed., *The Walker Expedition to Quebec, 1711* (Toronto: The Champlain Society, 1953), especially the introduction.

[41] Swift, *Journal to Stella*, I, 205–6.

Four days later the Marquis de Guiscard tried to assassinate Harley and, as Burnet put it, "an odd accident, that had almost been fatal, proved happy to him."[42] The tempest subsided, though not entirely and not for long; and Guiscard's attack and the interlude following it had a number of significant political consequences.[43]

Guiscard, a profligate French nobleman whose adventuring had forced him to leave France, had once been employed by the late ministers. They had given him the command of a regiment of French deserters and for a time considered undertaking a project he proposed for invading the southern coast of France, there to join forces with the Protestant rebels in the Cevennes. But the English ministers apparently suspected both his trustworthiness and his competence to lead such an expedition, and the project was abandoned.[44] Guiscard subsequently lost his regiment, and at the same time his means of support. For the next few years he solicited the government for a pension, until the Queen at length ordered him five hundred

---

[42] Burnet, *History*, VI, 41–2.

[43] The principal accounts of the assassination attempt include several written on the day of the attack or one or two days after: Swift to Archbishop King, 8 March 1711, *Swift Correspondence*, I, 213–15; Swift, *Journal to Stella*, I, 210–12; Peter Wentworth to Lord Raby, 9 March 1711, *Wentworth Papers*, pp. 185–7; L'Hermitage to the States General, 9/20 March 1711, BM, Add. MSS, 16,677EEE; Lady Dupplin to her Aunt Abigail Harley, 8 March 1711, HMC, *Portland MSS*, IV, 667. One of Harley's sisters was staying with him in London at the time of the attack and remained there throughout his convalescence. Her account is dated 22 March 1711, *ibid.*, 669–70. For subsequent reports see Swift, "Memoirs," pp. 127–8; *The Examiner*, no. 32, written by Swift; and Mrs. Manley, *A True Narrative of What Passed at the Examination of the Marquis de Guiscard*, printed in *The Works of Jonathan Swift, D.D.*, ed. by Sir Walter Scott (Edinburgh, 1824), V, 331–61. Also, Abel Boyer, *The Political State of Great Britain* (London, 1711), I, 275–335. There is a copy of this in the BM, Portland Loan, 29/166, annotated by Harley, so that his account of the attack is on record. Auditor Harley's "Memoirs" were written at least six years later, but they are useful as a sympathetic account, as is the essentially unfriendly account in Burnet, *History*, VI, 41–5.

[44] Godolphin to Earl Rivers, 24 August 1706, speaks of the project being laid aside, HMC, *Bath MSS*, I, 93.

pounds a year.[45] On the change of ministry this was reduced to four hundred, enough to live on but not to support Guiscard's extravagant tastes. At this point, or perhaps before, angry and desperate about his financial circumstances, he set about restoring his credit with the Court of France by supplying it with British intelligence secrets. At the same time, he tried repeatedly to see the Queen in the hope that he could persuade her to restore his pension to the full amount. Guiscard did not lack connections with the new ministry. The Duke of Ormonde had obligations to his brother and had earlier used his influence on Guiscard's behalf.[46] Auditor Harley claimed that Guiscard was on intimate terms with St. John, "at whose office he was every day," and while the Auditor is a partial witness, Boyer concurred that the Marquis "had liv'd in great intimacy" with the Secretary of State.[47] But Guiscard's friends were not disposed to help him further. "It is not above ten Days ago, that I was interceding with the Secretary, in his Behalf, because I heard he was just starving," Swift wrote on the day of the assassination attempt; "but, the Secretary assured me had 400*l.* a Year Pension."[48]

At the end of the winter of 1710–11 Guiscard's treachery was discovered and on the eighth of March he was arrested on a charge of high treason. Swift passed him in the Mall in St. James's Park that day, "at two o'Clock, an Hour before he was

[45] In a note, Boyer corrects his earlier assertion that the pension was secured by St. John's intercession, saying he has been informed that Godolphin procured it for Guiscard. *Political State*, I, 329.

[46] "It is the opinion of the best men . . . that the Marquis de Guiscard may obtain a regiment, the Duke of Ormond employing his interest for him, in regard he has not forgot the favours he received from the Comte his brother." From a letter to M. Thelluson, banker at Amsterdam, 12 February 1706, HMC, *Portland MSS*, VIII, 214.

[47] Edward Harley, "Memoirs," HMC, *Portland MSS*, V, 654; Boyer, *Political State*, I, 299–300.

[48] Swift to Archbishop King, 8 March 1711, *Swift Correspondence*, I, 215–16. See also Boyer, *Political State*, I, 300, for the ministers' refusal to help Guiscard further.

taken up, and I wondered he did not speak to me."[49] He may already have had reason to fear he was found out. He was brought to St. John's office at the Cockpit where he was examined by the Committee of the Privy Council: all the principal ministers but Shrewsbury were present, and St. John presided over the interrogation. Confronted with the evidence of his guilt, refused his freedom and remanded into custody, Guiscard produced a penknife from his pocket and stabbed Harley in the chest. He struck two blows, but on the first the knife's blade broke against Harley's breastbone, blunting the force of the second blow and probably saving Harley's life. The other ministers present, led by St. John, Newcastle, and Ormonde, drew their swords and fell upon the assassin, who, "having gather'd still fresh Forces from his Frenzy," was striking wildly at all those who were near him.[50] He was finally subdued by the Queen's messengers and taken off to Newgate where he died nine days later from the injuries he had suffered. Thus far all accounts agree. But on the details of what happened before and after the attack they differ widely, in part because, as Boyer observed, "what pass'd during the Horror, Surprize, and Confusion occasion'd by this barbarous Attempt, can hardly be distinctly related; since no Spectator could be so unconcern'd as to observe every particular Circumstance of this Tragical Scene";[51] in part because Guiscard died without revealing what his motive had been, if indeed he had any motive other than his own desperation; and largely because the question of Guiscard's intention became an issue between St. John and Harley.

According to Harley's sister, St. John, whose sword had broken in the melee,

grappled with the Frenchman who stabbed at him (as they think not knowing the knife was broke). St. John then ran out called for

[49] Swift to Archbishop King, *Swift Correspondence*, I, 215.
[50] Boyer, *Political State*, I, 308.
[51] *Ibid.*, p. 307.

a surgeon and I think named Beoushair [Buissière], and without a sword in the utmost confusion ran away to St. James's, went to Mrs. Masham's lodging in the fright. . . . He, that is St. John, rested a little and then took the Queen's doctor that is a Scotchman [Arbuthnot] up and told the Queen, who did not believe they had told her truth, but that he was dead, till she had spoke with Beoushair after he had dressed him, when he came to the Secretary's office.[52]

Other accounts vary on particular points, but all convey the same impression of St. John's furious activity: breaking his sword, restrained by his colleagues from killing the assassin on the spot, running for the surgeon, running to St. James's Palace to tell the Queen. Harley's behavior was equally remarkable, in a totally opposite sense. "It is impossible to express to you the firmness and magnanimity which Mr. Harley showed upon this surprising occasion," St. John wrote to Drummond. "I, who have always admired him, never did it so much; the suddenness of the blow, the sharpness of the wound, the confusion which followed, could neither change his countenance, nor alter his voice."[53] Harley's sister heard from the Duchess of Ormonde "that her Ld tould her they ware all amazd to see our good Brother so unmovd shewing neither anger nor fear being ye only undisturbd person in ye compeny."[54] He was on his feet and walking about the room while he waited for a surgeon to be brought; he is said to have removed the knife blade from his wound himself and pocketed both blade and handle, saying, "They belong to me." He inquired of the surgeon whether his wound was mortal; and when the wound was dressed, directed the surgeon to attend to Guiscard. While confusion swelled around him, he "all the while appear'd the only Person uncon-

[52] —Harley to hir Sister [Abigail Harley], 22 March 1711, HMC, *Portland MSS*, IV, 669–70. Swift, in his letter to King, also says that St. John's sword was broken. *Swift Correspondence*, I, 214.

[53] St. John to Drummond, 13 March 1711, *Bolingbroke Correspondence*, I, 102–3.

[54] Mrs. Martha Hutchins to her sister, Abigail Harley, March 1711, BM, Portland Loan, 29/68.

cern'd at the Accident that had befallen him."[55] Two days
after the attack Harley's son, sending news to his aunt, thanked
God "for this his Wonderfull preservation of my Father,
Nothing but his power cou'd have saved him . . ., this shews
how excellent it is to trust in God, If you had but seen the
Tranquillity ye easiness of his mind after the vilanous Action,
His Religion, & in what he trusted plainly appeared:—I was
concerned least you shou'd be frighted, He spoke [of that?]
tho He was in exquisite pain."[56] Harley's concern for his
family was characteristic; so was his tranquillity and easiness of
mind. The assassination attempt called forth his greatest
strengths: he could not strike back, he had only to endure the
pain. His fate was in the hands of God and his extraordinary
courage flowed from his ready submission to God's will. The
first letter he wrote after the attack, addressed to his sister, is
worth quoting in full.

I resolved to make my first Essay with a Pen to be writing to my
Dearest Sister, & I am sure tho it be wrote by a trembling hand
you are Satisfyed it comes from my Heart, al my Dear Sisters
tender concerne expressed in your letters to my children flowd I
know from the same place, I read in my own heart the same
tenderness for your Dear Self, as yours is written in my heart: let
us joine in adoring & obeying our Good God for his undeserved
favor, to one less than the least of his mercies. & let it teach intire
dependance upon him, Submission to his wil, & faith in his direct-
ing & protecting us.[57]

But Harley's provident escape and his recovery were
clouded by his suspicions of St. John. "It is not here to be
omitted," the Auditor wrote, "with what industry Secretary
St. John took care to have it published that Guiscard's design

---

[55] Boyer, *Political State*, I, 310. All accounts follow the same lines, but
only Harley's sister and Mrs. Manley say that he removed the blade from
the wound himself.

[56] Edward Harley to his aunt Abigail Harley, 10 March 1711, BM, Portland Loan 29/67.

[57] Harley to his sister Abigail Harley, 17 April 1711, *ibid*.

was against himself; and if the intimacy of Guiscard with him be considered, there was a great deal of reason for his throwing out this amusement."[58] The Auditor's dark suggestion that St. John and Guiscard were co-conspirators is utterly unsubstantiated and deserves no further consideration; but the question of whether St. John or Harley was Guiscard's intended victim became a bitterly controversial issue. According to Swift,

Mr. St. John affected to say in several companies, that Guiscard intended the blow against him; which, if it were true, the consequence must be, that Mr. St. John had all the merit, while Mr. Harley remained with nothing but the danger and the pain. But I am apt to think Mr. St. John was either mistaken, or misinformed: However, the matter was thus represented in the weekly paper called the Examiner, which Mr. St. John perused before it was printed, but made no alteration in that passage.[59]

Now the author of the *Examiner* at that time was Swift himself, and in the number devoted to the assassination attempt he had written:

The Murderer confessed in *Newgate*, that his chief Design was against Mr. Secretary *St. John*, who happened to change Seats with Mr. *Harley*, for more Convenience of examining the Criminal: And being asked what provoked him to stab the Chancellor? He said, that not being able to come at the Secretary, as he intended, it was some Satisfaction to murder the Person whom he thought Mr. *St. John* loved best.[60]

The paragraph outraged Harley's family and friends,[61] so much so that Swift retreated and in the following week's *Examiner* protested that he had not expressed his own opinion

---

[58] Edward Harley, "Memoirs," HMC, *Portland MSS*, V, 654.

[59] Swift, "Memoirs," p. 128. See also Swift, "An Enquiry," p. 145.

[60] *The Examiner*, no. 32, 15 March 1710, Swift, *The EXAMINER and Other Pieces Written in 1710–11*, p. 109.

[61] Edward Harley to his aunt Abigail Harley, 27 March 1711, BM, Portland Loan, 29/66; Lady Dupplin to her aunt Abigail Harley, 22 March 1711, *ibid.*, 29/68; Swift, "An Enquiry," p. 145.

but was only quoting Guiscard. Wary of embroiling himself further in the controversy, he turned over to Mrs. Manley the materials he had collected to write a full account of the attack: "I was afraid of disobliging Mr. Harley or Mr. St. John in one critical point about it, and would not do it myself."[62]

But Swift had not invented Guiscard's supposed confession or the theory that he had intended to kill St. John. Peter Wentworth's account of the attack was written the next day, and he identified his informant as the Duke of Argyll, whom he had seen the evening before. Argyll had not been present at the examination of Guiscard but he was dining nearby, and "he and Lord Rivers came runing from Dinner. . . , as soon as they heard Mr. Harley was stabed at the Cock pit."[63] Argyll was standing at the door when Guiscard was brought out and heard him tell the Duke of Ormonde "he did not intend to have stabed Mr. Harley but he did intend to stab Mr. St. Johns, who had used him very ill, as had the Duke of Marlborough, who he had sent a challenge to but he had treated him like a foot man and wou'd not answere him, and if he had had an opportunity before he went he wou'd have stab'd him."[64] One cannot attach too much weight to Guiscard's declarations: emotionally overwrought, bruised and battered by the blows of his captors, he was not necessarily a reliable witness even as to his own original intentions. Still, if St. John had indeed been his "most familiar friend" and "lately his Best support at Court," it is plausible if not provable that Guiscard wished "to wreak his

---

[62] Swift, *Journal to Stella*, I, 245. Mrs. Manley's pamphlet, *A True Narrative of What Passed at the Examination of the Marquis de Guiscard*, appeared in April 1711. Swift told Stella: "It is worth your reading, for the circumstances are all true."

[63] Peter Wentworth to Lord Raby, 9 March 1711, *Wentworth Papers*, pp. 186–7.

[64] *Ibid.*, p. 186. Dartmouth, who was present, confirms Guiscard's remarks about Marlborough but not that he referred to St. John as his intended victim. Dartmouth later saw Guiscard in prison but says he confessed nothing and that he "rambled like a man who was lightheaded." However, Dartmouth recollected these events twenty years after they took place. Burnet, *History*, VI, 44, Dartmouth's note.

Furious Resentment" on the Secretary.[65] The theory is lent further substance by the report that, at the end of his examination, just before he was to be taken away, Guiscard asked to speak to St. John privately, a request that was refused. All the principal accounts mention the incident, including Harley's sister, though she quotes Harley as denying it: "Some report that he [Guiscard] desired to speak with St. John alone but my brother says that is not true."[66] But the weight of evidence is against Harley. Conceivably the shock of Guiscard's blows made him forget what had happened immediately before—he did not remember that there had been a second blow; conceivably he chose to forget. But assuming the incident did take place, it is not unreasonable to suppose that the assassin wanted to speak to St. John alone because St. John was his intended victim. In any case, it was widely believed that this was so, and St. John never denied it. Harley obviously believed that St. John was responsible for the story, and he regarded this as another example of St. John's treachery, a base attempt to deprive him of credit and undermine his position as first minister. The issue could never have become so important, the conflict over it so rancorous, had the relationship between the two ministers been reasonably sound; but trust had gone from it long since, and it was fast losing even the semblance of cordiality.

I I I

It seems probable that St. John had embarked on his own course well before Guiscard's attack, but it was not until the weeks afterward that his differences with Harley came to light. Swift later wrote, with due caution, that he was

[65] Boyer, *Political State*, I, 304.
[66] —Harley to hir Sister [Abigail Harley], 22 March 1711, HMC, *Portland MSS*, IV, 669–70. Swift does not mention it in his letter to King, but it is in Mrs. Manley's *True Narrative*.

not altogether sure, that Mr. St. John did not entertain some prospect of succeeding as first minister, in case of Mr. Harley's death; which, during his illness, was frequently apprehended. And, I remember very well, that, upon visiting Mr. Harley, as soon as he was in a condition to be seen, I found several of his nearest relations talk very freely of some proceedings of Mr. St. John; enough to make me apprehend, that their friendship would not be of any long continuance.[67]

In April St. John rose to defend his old friend James Brydges when he was among those implicated by a House of Commons inquiry into the supposed financial abuses of the late ministry. Brydges was Paymaster-General of the Forces Abroad and had been in that office since 1705. For the three years when St. John was Secretary-at-War they had worked in close association, so that St. John's action was motivated by something more than friendship. He had reason to fear too close an investigation of their transactions: in defending Brydges he was also defending himself.[68] But, as Swift observed, "Mr. secretary in his warmth of speech, and zeal for his friend Mr. Brydges, . . . said, he did not know that either Mr. Brydges or the late ministry were at all to blame in this matter; which was very desperately spoken, and giving up the whole cause: for the chief quarrel against the late ministry was the ill management of the treasure, and was more than all the rest together." Dining at Harley's, Swift "turned to Mr. Harley, and said, if the late ministry were not to blame in that article, he [Mr. Harley] ought to lose his head for putting the queen upon changing them. He made it a jest; but by some words dropt, I easily saw that they take things ill of Mr. St. John, and by some hints given me from another hand that I deal with, I am afraid the secretary will not stand long." He added: "I see

<hr>

[67] Swift, "Memoirs," p. 128.

[68] For evidence that St. John had reason to fear a full disclosure of Brydges's accounts, see Davies and Tinling, "Letters of Henry St. John to James Brydges," pp. 157–8, and "Letters from James Brydges, Created Duke of Chandos, to Henry St. John, Created Viscount Bolingbroke," pp. 130–1.

not how they can well want him neither, and he would make a troublesome enemy."[69] It is easy to see why St. John's conduct outraged the Tory House of Commons; Harley's displeasure is more difficult to explain, since he had not shown much enthusiasm for inquiring into past mismanagements and in fact, when consulted, advised Brydges not to resign his post.[70] But the fact that Harley's brother, the Auditor, delivered to the Commons the report on which the charges were based suggests that Harley approved of this particular investigation.[71] At the same time he may have hoped to conciliate the Tory gentlemen by letting the inquiry run its course without interference from the ministry. St. John acted as an individual but he represented the ministry: the Tories must have viewed his defense of Brydges as another indication of the government's unwillingness to support Tory measures. In Harley's view, St. John's action created further divisions within the party.

There were other reasons for Harley "to take things ill of Mr. St. John." Early in May Swift told Peterborough:

Our divisions run farther than perhaps your Lordship's intelligence hath yet informed you of, that is [to] a triumvirate of our friends whom I have mentioned to you: I have told them more than once, upon occasion, that all my hopes of their success depended on their union, that I saw they loved one another, and hoped they would continue it, to remove that scandal of inconstancy ascribed to Court-friendships. I am not now so secure.[72]

Some weeks later Dr. Stratford described to Harley's son a visit to the third member of the triumvirate, Harcourt, the Lord Keeper. Harcourt's son had told him "some dismal stories of my old friend Mr. St. John. . . . There is a coldness between that unhappy [man] and his father that has happened of late,

[69] Swift, *Journal to Stella*, I, 252–3.

[70] Harley to Brydges, 13 May 1711, Davies and Tinling, "Correspondence of James Brydges and Robert Harley, Created Earl of Oxford," p. 463. Harley answered Brydges's letter of 6 May 1711, *ibid.*, pp. 462–3.

[71] *Parliamentary History*, VI, 1016–19.

[72] Swift to Peterborough, 4 May 1711, *Swift Correspondence*, I, 226.

and though I know not the cause, I am convinced that the Lord Keeper is as much dissatisfied with him as your father has reason to be. This is new to me, for I thought there had been an intelligence there that could not have been broken."[73] The accuracy of the report is less important than that it existed at all: henceforth divisions within the ministry were not to be denied.

In speaking of St. John's ambitions in the weeks following the assassination attempt, Swift felt compelled to

do Justice to Mr. St. John by repeating what he said to me with great Appearance of Concern, (and he was but an ill Dissembler) that if Mr. Harley's Accident should prove fatal, it would be an irreparable Loss; that as Things then stood, his Life was absolutely necessary; that as to Himself, he was not Master of the Scheme by which they were to proceed, nor had Credit enough with the Queen; neither did he see how it would be possible for them in such a Case to wade through the Difficulties they were then under.[74]

St. John of course dissembled much more successfully than Swift knew, but he had good reason to be apprehensive about taking over the direction of affairs at that particular point. As Swift observed on the day of the attack, "nothing could happen so unluckily to *England*, at this Juncture, as Mr. *Harley's* Death, when he has all the Schemes for the greatest Part of the Supplies in his Head, and the Parliament cannot stir a Step without him."[75] Later in March St. John himself wrote Drummond: "Our friend recovers apace, and will, we hope, in a few days be able to return to the head of business; his short absence from which situation is, I do assure you, very sensibly felt."[76] At the end of the month the House adjourned for a week, "in a

---

[73] Dr. Stratford to Lord Harley, 25 June 1711, HMC, *Portland MSS*, VII, 35.

[74] Swift, "An Enquiry," p. 145.

[75] Swift to Archbishop King, 8 March 1711, *Swift Correspondence*, I, 215.

[76] St. John to Drummond, 20 March 1711, *Bolingbroke Correspondence*, I, 111.

complyment to their Speaker," said Peter Wentworth, "who they found by the greif he was in for the death of his son wou'd not be able to attend the business of the house; but 'tis believed that if Mr. Harley had not been still ill of his wound, and that they hop'd by that time he might be able to come abroad, that complyment would hardly have been paid."[77] L'Hermitage reported the slow progress of the war subsidy through the House in Harley's absence and hoped it would move more quickly on his return; and on April 16 Peter Wentworth had news that "Mr. Harley is gone to lye at Kingsenton for the Air, and 'tis hoped he'll come soon to town to enter upon business, for there's nothing to be done without him."[78]

Some things were done in Harley's absence, though not to the government's liking. The October Club rallied its forces to defeat a tax on leather proposed as part of the year's supply. According to Peter Wentworth,

when 'twas too late Mr. St. Johns made them a long speech of what a fatal consequence 'twas to the affairs of the nation to refuse so good a fund for a supply, and that our credit wch was just reviving to a great heighth this vote would throw it all down again. So that several Politians that cou'd not endure Mr. Harley say they see now there's no man the Court imploys has address enough to manage the House of Commons but him; if he had been well he wou'd either have had intelligence of what was intended and so have endeavour'd to have brought them to the house in a better temper, or at least when there he wou'd have seen how 'twou'd have gone and wou'd have put it off for a fitter opportunity.[79]

---

[77] Peter Wentworth to Lord Raby, 16 April 1711, *Wentworth Papers*, p. 189. Swift was of the same opinion: "I think it very handsomely done; but I believe one reason is, that they want Mr. Harley so much." *Journal to Stella*, I, 220–1.

[78] Peter Wentworth to Lord Raby, 16 April 1711, *Wentworth Papers*, p. 195. L'Hermitage to the States General, 23 March/ 3 April, 13/24 April, 27 April/ 8 May 1711, BM, Add. MSS, 17, 677EEE.

[79] Peter Wentworth to Lord Raby, 27 March 1711, *Wentworth Papers*, pp. 189–90.

Since parliamentary practice forbade the reconsideration of a rejected bill during that session, St. John introduced the same measure shortly thereafter as a duty on skins and hides, and in this form it passed, "some body" having "bestir'd them selves and . . . brought the house into the temper is desired."[80] There is no evidence that St. John encouraged the October men on this occasion: on the contrary, he was unable to control them. More generally, his inability to take over the management of affairs in Harley's absence was apparent, and not least of all to St. John himself. This accounts in part for the urgency with which he wrote the Earl of Orrery in May, three weeks after Harley's official return to the House:

Mr. Harley, since his recovery, has not appeared at the Council, or at the Treasury at all, and very seldom in the House of Commons. We, who are reputed to be in his intimacy, have few opportunities of seeing him, and none of talking freely with him. As he is the only true channel through which the Queen's pleasure is conveyed; so there is, and must be a perfect stagnation till he is pleased to open himself, and set the water flowing.[81]

No doubt Harley was avoiding St. John. But it must be remembered that he was still weak from his wound—"my right arme continues weak," he told his sister in July "& change of weather I have great paine in my breast"[82]—and his absence from business was partly a matter of health. Furthermore, St. John's letter is dated May 18: on May 23 Harley was created Earl of Oxford and six days later appointed Lord Treasurer.[83]

---

[80] *Ibid.*, p. 190. Burnet, *History*, VI, 31-2 and Onslow's note. Onslow said he had heard that the rejection of the leather duty "was carried against Harley by the private instigation of St. John, who had got the violent tories into his separate management." But there is no evidence to substantiate this view.

[81] St. John to Orrery, 18 May 1711, *Bolingbroke Correspondence*, I, 216-17.

[82] Harley to his sister Abigail Harley, 24 July 1711, BM, Portland Loan, 29/67.

[83] Harley was elevated to the peerage as Baron Harley of Wigmore Castle, Earl of Oxford and of Mortimer. There was some objection to the title on the grounds that Harley's claim to descent from the DeVeres and

Rochester died on May 2, so that for most of the month Harley was preoccupied with his promotions and with other changes in the ministry. St. John acknowledged this when, in the same letter, he compared the present stagnation to the situation the preceding summer, when the changes in the ministry seemed to have been halted. In the circumstances it is not surprising that Harley was inaccessible to his colleagues. St. John's correspondence reveals that by May 22 he was again in touch with Harley: this was the eve of Harley's elevation to the peerage and a number of crucial decisions had presumably been made.

Guiscard's attack raised Harley's popularity to heights it would never reach again. An admirer, congratulating him upon his escape, spoke of "that Attestation wch Providence has giv'n to the Sincerity of your intentions; not onely establishing you in the Esteem of Prince and People, but, as it were,—consecrating your Share in the Ministry, so as to make it Irreligion to doubt of a national Blessing, upon your Deliverance from that popish Rage, wch picked you out, as the Minister from whom it met with the chief obstruction."[84] On Harley's return to the House of Commons, Speaker Bromley congratulated him in the name of the House. They had reason to believe, he said

That your Fidelity to Her Majesty, and Zeal for Her Service, had drawn upon you *the Hatred of all the Abettors of Popery and Faction. . . .* If your *Fidelity to Her Majesty, and Zeal for Her Service,* could ever be doubted, and wanted any Testimonials to prove them, you have now the most Honourable, the most Ample, and the most Undeniable, that can be given; and after these, it would be an unpardonable Presumption in me, to imagine I could add to them, by saying any Thing of your Faithful Discharge of those great Trusts you have been honoured with: To which your

---

the Mortimers was not valid. He was also criticized for the pretentiousness of the preamble to the patent, and for having it published, which was unusual. Swift, *Journal to Stella*, I, 265; Burnet, *History*, VI, 68.

[84] W. Atwood to Harley, 19 March 1711, BM, Portland Loan, 29/125.

eminent Abilities at first recommended you, and your distinguishing Merits have since justified Her Majesty's wise Choice.

Harley's enemies had made attempts against his reputation and
his person, but, God be thanked, they had hitherto been
disappointed.

And may the same Providence, that has wonderfully preserved
you from some unparalleled Attempts; and that has raised you up
to be an Instrument of Great Good in a very critical Juncture,
when it was much wanted, continue still to preserve *so invaluable a
Life*, for the Perfecting of what is so happily begun; that we may
owe to your Counsels, and to your Conduct (under Her Majesty)
the Maintenance and Firm Establishment of our Constitution in
Church and State.[85]

Mallet said later that the address "was ridiculed by the Whigs,
as an egregious Testimony of the Meanness of party Spirit, as it
was very well known they were not Friends."[86] But it was a
great moment: the Commons had not spoken so handsomely
before, and they would not do so again.

Harley's promotions, signal marks of the Queen's favor,
were more tangible and more durable honors than the fine
phrases of the Speaker's address. Elevation to the peerage was
considered a political as well as a social advancement, and the
Lord Treasurership gave formal recognition to Harley's preeminent position in the ministry. In a practical sense, as Dr.
Stratford put it, "the Businesse will be lighter to your Lordship, now you have the Sole Authority of that Place, of which
before you had the Trouble."[87] Oxford's new titles strengthened his position; in addition he appeared to have gained the
full support of Bromley and Sir Thomas Hanmer, two of the
ablest and most influential High Tory leaders in the House of
Commons. In June Hanmer turned down an offer of place in

---

[85] Boyer, *Political State*, I, 331–2.
[86] [Mallet], *Memoirs of the Life and Ministerial Conduct, . . . of the
Late Lord Visc. Bolingbroke*, p. 199.
[87] Dr. Stratford to Oxford, 29 May 1711, BM, Portland Loan, 29/158.

the ministry—not for the first or last time—but he assured Bromley that he refused only because "his own private Affairs be so distracted and dispersed," and Bromley believed he was sincere. "In the mean time," Bromley reported, "he expresses an entire Satisfaction in the measures that are taken, and in those employed under her Majesty, & assures me he will on all Occasions contribute his utmost Endeavors to serve and support them."[88]

Unfortunately Hanmer's satisfaction was not shared by the Tory gentlemen. Not long after the adverse vote on the leather tax, Peter Wentworth heard that "the house of Commons begins to be out of humour again, and talks of going into the examination of the male-administration of the late Ministry."[89] "The October Club grumbles still, and wants a thorough change," Swift wrote in the middle of April;[90] and several weeks later he told Peterborough: "We believe Mr. Harley will soon be Treasurer, and be of the House of Peers; and then we imagine the Court will begin to deal out employments, for which every October-member is a candidate; and consequently nine in ten must be disappointed: the Effect of which we may find in the next session."[91] But while the October Club clamored for places, Lord Poulett advised Harley against naming the High Tory Earl of Nottingham to replace Rochester as Lord President. There was no need to do so in order to secure Rochester's following: "The credit of Rochester's confidence and friendship remains alive in you, and every friend he had will be yours to a man." And Nottingham was "direct the contrary to your management or interest, for he is party sense in person without respect to the reasons of things."[92] At the

---

[88] William Bromley to Oxford, June 1711, *ibid.*, 29/128.

[89] Peter Wentworth to Lord Raby, 6 April 1711, *Wentworth Papers*, p. 192.

[90] Swift to the Duke of Argyle, 16 April 1711, *Swift Correspondence*, I, 223.

[91] Swift to Peterborough, 4 May 1711, *ibid.*, I, 226.

[92] Earl Poulett to Harley, 4 May 1711, HMC, *Portland MSS*, IV, 684.

same time, Halifax renewed his approaches from the Whig side, offering cooperation and support.

I think there is no medium between a vigorous asserting the Queen, and her government, or being lost for ever. Men's eyes are turned towards you, expecting their safety from your interest and prudent management under the present difficulties. The danger is great, the trouble infinite, you have courage to undertake and you may have what assistance you please to carry you through so great and glorious a work and may depend upon the good wishes and weak endeavours of myself.[93]

Poulett reported to Harley that Halifax "said he had power to assure you might command him, Somers, and every Whig in England." He continued:

Anglesey and old Leeds [High Tories] say there will be no government if you do not resolve. . . . In short I think you and all with you sink without any chance, if you do not answer the telling call of Heaven upon you. . . . You may now secure your own undertaking by showing your charge is to reconcile all upon a national foot and thereby complete your own power, that all will adore it and none oppose or dare to injure you where all are sensibly interested for your support.[94]

Whatever Harley chose to do, he could not please all his critics; though all were agreed that he must act speedily and decisively to "complete" his power and place his ministry upon a strong foot. But the changes, when they came, showed that Harley was not to be deflected from his moderate scheme. Promotions went for the most part to moderates and loyal supporters. The High Tory Duke of Buckingham replaced Rochester as Lord President, but Poulett suggested him "because you may always turn him out without offence to any party."[95] When Newcastle died in July, another High Tory,

93 Halifax to Harley, 18 April 1711, *ibid.*, p. 675.
94 Poulett to Harley, 18 April 1711, *ibid.*, pp. 674-5.
95 Poulett to Harley, 4 May 1711, *ibid.*, p. 684. Poulett was promoted to Lord Steward, and three Treasury Commissioners moved up: William

the Earl of Jersey, was appointed to succeed him; but Jersey died on the day of his appointment and the place was filled by John Robinson, Bishop of Bristol, an experienced diplomat without strong party connections. Those who had looked for a decisive move in favor of the High Church group were as disappointed as the advocates of a new alliance with the Whigs.

On June 5 Swift wrote: "I past by the treasury to-day, and saw vast crowds waiting to give lord treasurer petitions as he passes by. He is now at the top of power and favor."[96] The day before, at the close of the first session of Parliament, the House of Commons drew up and sent to the Queen a representation "concerning Mismanagements and Abuses" of the late ministry. The paper concluded with a denunciation of those ministers who "framed to themselves wild and unwarrantable schemes of balancing parties, and under a false pretense of temper and moderation, did really encourage faction by discountenancing and depressing persons zealously affected to your majesty and to the church." It continued:

. . . we cannot forbear with all humility and earnestness to beseech your majesty that you would avoid, as the greatest enemies to your royal dignity, and to your people's safety, all persons who shall endeavour to engage you in such pernicious measures, and that you would employ, in places of authority and trust, such only as have given good testimonies of their duty to your majesty, and of their affection to the true interest of the Kingdom.[97]

Oxford was not named but there was no doubt that he was intended. His "wild and unwarrantable schemes of balancing parties" were as displeasing as ever to the Tory gentlemen, and while the present Parliament sat, his position would not improve unless he changed his policy. Furthermore, so long as the

---

Benson replaced Harley as Chancellor of the Exchequer, Henry Paget was given a peerage and made First Lord of the Admiralty, and Sir Thomas Mansell became Comptroller of the Queen's Household.

[96] Swift, *Journal to Stella*, I, 285.
[97] *Parliamentary History*, VI, 1030–1.

majority in the House of Commons remained dissatisfied, St. John's opportunity remained: left alone in the Lower House, he was free to make good use of it. Even should he eschew a disruptive role, the government would be hard-pressed to keep the Tory forces in check. Oxford's illness had demonstrated the difficulty of managing the Commons: "If he be made a peer," Swift had written of Oxford's promotion, "they will want him prodigiously in the House of Commons, of which he is the great mover, and after him the secretary, and hardly any else of weight."[98] It seems obvious that Oxford's interests would have been better served had he remained in the lower House, but the power and prestige of the peerage were then thought to outweigh any political advantage a seat in the Commons could provide: refusal of his promotion for political reasons did not present itself as an alternative.[99]

Thus, while it was true that Oxford was "at the top of power and favour," the political situation was fundamentally unchanged. His position remained precarious, and the loss of Rochester and Newcastle removed from him two of his strongest supports. As before, much depended on the role St. John chose to play.

[98] Swift, *Journal to Stella*, I, 249.

[99] Harley's only reservation was financial: "I believe Mr. Harley must be lord treasurer; yet he makes one difficulty which is hard to answer: he must be made a lord, and his estate is not large enough, and he is too generous to make it larger; and if the ministry should change soon by any accident, he will be left in the suds." Swift, *Journal to Stella*, I, 249. According to the Auditor and to Dr. Stratford, he was reassured by the prospect of his son's marriage to the daughter of the Duke of Newcastle. Edward Harley, "Memoirs," HMC, *Portland MSS*, V, 655; Dr. Stratford to Lord Harley, 16 June 1711, *ibid.*, VII, 32.

CHAPTER VI

"The Divisions Between These Two Great Men":

1711–1713

HE great task before the ministry was making peace, and to this end secret negotiations with France had been under way since the change of ministry the preceding summer.[1] The ministers hoped by prior agreement with France to secure particular advantages for England which would then become part of a general settlement. And while they insisted that the Queen had declared "she would enter into no separate Treaty" and "was resolved not to act without Her Allys, and particularly the States [the Dutch Republic],"[2] they were convinced that England had too long been engaged in a war, "the great load of which has fallen on Britain, as the great

[1] For the peace negotiations, I follow A. D. MacLachlan, "The Great Peace: Negotiations for the Treaty of Utrecht, 1710–1713" (Cambridge University Ph.D. thesis, 1965) and his article "The Road to Peace 1710–13," in Holmes, ed., *Britain after the Glorious Revolution*. For the early stages of the negotiations and the preliminary articles, see also G. M. Trevelyan, "The 'Jersey' Period of the Negotiations Leading to the Peace of Utrecht," *English Historical Review*, XLIX (1934), 100–5, and his *England under Queen Anne*, III, 89–94, 176–91.

[2] Oxford to Marlborough, 28 August/8 September 1711, Longleat, Portland MSS, V, f. 245. The States-General was the representative assembly of the seven provinces which composed the Dutch Republic. In the eighteenth century the Republic itself was often referred to as "the States-General," or simply "the States."

advantage of it is proposed to redound to the House of Austria, and to the States General."[3] Peace was a necessity for all parties. The Queen would "support the confederates in all their just demands, and consent to no treaty, wherein they shall not find their reasonable satisfaction." If she stipulated particularly advantageous terms for Great Britain, "it is no more than what the share she has had in the war may justly entitle her to."[4]

But while England's interests were to be thus secured, the confederates regarded the secret and separate negotiations with France as a violation of the Treaty of Grand Alliance, and when in the autumn of 1711 the Preliminary Articles agreed on by France and England were announced to the world, they responded with cries of outrage. The Dutch had been informed of the secret talks the previous spring; the other allies, while they suspected much, had been told nothing. All objected to the vagueness of the general terms relating to the settlement of their claims; and when the details of the concessions made to England were disclosed, their indignation turned to anger. The Dutch resented most bitterly England's monopoly of the trading privileges in the Spanish Empire she had, by the Barrier Treaty of 1709, agreed to share with them; and they were apprehensive that their barrier—those border towns and fortresses they were by the same treaty permitted to garrison as protection against France—was not guaranteed. The German allies deplored the abandonment of the Austrian claim to the Spanish throne: they viewed with dismay the prospect of a Bourbon king of Spain and the Indies, though this was permitted by the terms of the Treaty of Grand Alliance, provided the crowns of France and Spain should never be united, a condition which the French now guaranteed.

St. John told the Queen that "this agreement contains more advantages for your Majesty's kingdoms, than were ever, perhaps, stipulated for any nation at one time,"[5] but Shrewsbury

[3] St. John to Lord Raby, 6 May 1711, *Bolingbroke Correspondence*, I, 192.

[4] St. John to Harrison, 9 October 1711, *ibid.*, pp. 389–90.

[5] St. John to the Queen, 25 September 1711, *ibid.*, p. 372.

at least, on the government side, was uneasy about their method of proceeding, which "looks so like bargaining for yourselves apart, and leaving your friends to shift at a general treaty."[6] The Whigs, partly on the same grounds and certainly from political motives, as a party strongly opposed the Preliminary Articles as a basis for the peace. They revived the cry of "no peace without Spain," though since the death of the Emperor Joseph in April 1711, few can have meant it seriously: the new emperor was the Archduke Charles of Austria, whose pretensions to the Spanish crown the allies had supported. Continued advocacy of his claim implied acceptance of an Austrian prince uniting in his person Spain and the Hapsburg territories, and from the English point of view Hapsburg predominance in Europe was no more desirable than Bourbon. Still, the Whigs belabored the ministers with the slogan, at the same time accusing them of conspiring with France at the expense of the allies and, following from this, of secretly planning to bring in the Pretender at the Queen's death, this last in spite of the fact that the Preliminary Articles included French recognition of the Protestant succession. "This declaration in the very beginning of the negotiation," Strafford wrote to Oxford, "that they mean the protestant succession, and will make no difficulty about the Pretender, will stop the mouths of those who called us Jacobites."[7] Strafford was far too sanguine: the Whigs came to equate the peace with "the French interest" and the French interest with the Pretender; and their outright opposition to the peace threw them into an increasingly close relationship with Hanover. Convinced that they would never find favor with the Tory Queen, they made common cause with the heirs apparent, who, for their part, were glad to find allies in opposition to the peace.

For the next two years political conflict centered on the peace, and in the bitterly partisan struggle both sides came to believe that ultimately peace, or at any rate this peace, de-

---

[6] Shrewsbury to St. John, 27 August 1711, *ibid.* p. 337.
[7] Strafford to Oxford, 26/15 January 1712, HMC, *Portland MSS*, IX, 322.

pended on the life of the Queen. If the Queen lived, so the argument ran, her ministers could probably bring the negotiations to a successful conclusion. But if she died and the Electress Sophia or her son, George Louis, succeeded to the throne of England, the Tories would be out, the Whigs returned to favor, and the Preliminary Articles dropped in favor of terms more acceptable to the allies. Because both parties believed so firmly in the inevitability of these alternatives, the Queen's health became a matter of urgent concern. Her frequent illnesses, real or rumored, had always been cause for alarm— "Bank stock is fallen three or four *per cent.* by the whispers about the town of the queen's being ill, who is however very well," Swift reported in July 1711[8]—but the battle for the peace was waged to the continuous accompaniment of Tory reassurances that the Queen was well and Whig reports that she was dangerously ill or dead.

The conduct of the peace negotiations further divided Oxford and St. John. Until the spring of 1711, in addition to Harley only Shrewsbury, Dartmouth, and Rochester knew of the secret talks with France; St. John was "deliberately excluded" until the end of April, when, at Shrewsbury's insistence, the preliminary French proposals were laid before the whole Cabinet. Even so, it was autumn before St. John was fully informed of the details of his colleagues' diplomacy.[9] Harley's wish to exclude him stemmed from fundamental differences in policy. Harley wanted to maintain, insofar as this was possible, at least the semblance of cooperation with the allies, in particular with the Dutch, whom he regarded as "the essential prop of English policy," both because of their inveterate Protestantism and because Dutch investment was vital to English credit.[10] At the same time he wanted to reassure his Whig supporters that the ministry did not intend to abandon

[8] Swift, *Journal to Stella*, I, 313.
[9] MacLachlan, "The Great Peace," pp. 19–23. Shrewsbury to Harley, 26 April 1711, HMC, *Bath MSS*, I, 201–2.
[10] MacLachlan, "The Great Peace," pp. 11–12.

its allies. To accomplish these ends, he did his best to keep all options open. His methods were of necessity devious: they leaned to deception, evasion, and obfuscation. He did not wish, by precipitate action, to further antagonize the allied governments or alienate parliamentary opinion at home.[11]

St. John was ill-disposed both by temperament and conviction to acquiesce in Harley's policies. Recognizing that special privileges could be purchased only at a price, he was prepared to gain advantages for England at the expense of the allies, even if their opposition ultimately drove the Queen to make a separate peace. He missed no opportunity to denounce the selfishness of the confederate powers, attacking with particular ferocity the Dutch and the Barrier Treaty: there were, he declared repeatedly, no compelling reasons why the military and commercial advantages conceded to Holland by the folly of the late ministry should be safeguarded by a new settlement.[12] These were sound Tory views: they represented a policy the Tories were prepared to support. The gentlemen in the House of Commons applauded St. John's inflammatory rhetoric, and he in turn drew strength from his role as their spokesman. Most probably it was his effectiveness as an advocate for the Tory position that induced Harley to exclude him from the early phases of the negotiations. The entire thrust of Harley's policy of waiting and delaying, of preserving alternatives, would have been threatened by St. John's intervention. Harley had good reason to keep the secret from his Secretary of State.[13]

St. John later accused Oxford of incompetence and neglect in his handling of the negotiations, at the same time claiming that "the whole negotiation of the peace and of the trouble-

[11] For Harley's policy, see *ibid.,* pp. 684–5, and MacLachlan, "The Road to Peace, 1710–13," *Britain after the Glorious Revolution,* esp. pp. 204–13.

[12] *Bolingbroke Correspondence,* I, II, *passim.*

[13] For St. John's attitude to the peace, see MacLachlan, "The Great Peace," pp. 18–19, 682–3, and "The Road to Peace, 1710–13," *Britain after the Glorious Revolution,* esp. pp. 207–13.

some invidious steps preliminary to it, as far as they could be transacted at home, were thrown upon me."[14] Historians have been inclined to accept St. John's judgment at face value. But recent research has made it clear that, while St. John exercised some influence on the course of the negotiations and, in his capacity as Secretary of State, conducted the formal diplomatic correspondence, the direction of affairs remained in Oxford's hands. It is a measure of Oxford's control—and of something less than total trust in his Secretary—that he received copies of St. John's letters to Torcy, the French foreign minister, and maintained his own private correspondence with Torcy as well.[15] St. John's exclusion from the first phase of the negotiations and Oxford's subsequent refusal to allow him a major role exacerbated the split between the two men, and their differences in policy reflected St. John's alignment with the Tory right against Oxford's more moderate position.

By Oxford's account, through the summer of 1711 and on into the autumn " 'the Treasurer's hands were full of negociating the peace in all courts abroad;' and besides the ordinary and necessary duty of his office at home, he had frequent occasions of calming the quarrels and grudges Mr. Secretary had sometimes against lord Dartmouth, sometimes against lady Masham, and sometimes against the treasurer himself."[16] In August St. John refused to sit in the Cabinet Council when, after a long absence, the Whig Duke of Somerset returned to resume his place. Somerset, the Master of the Horse, infuriated by the dissolution of Parliament in September 1710, had opposed the new ministry in the elections; but he had kept his place, though he would not come to council, largely because of the Queen's attachment to his wife, who had replaced the Duchess of

---

[14] Bolingbroke, "A Letter to Sir William Windham," *Works*, I, 117. See *ibid.*, pp. 117-20, and "Letters on the Study and Use of History," *ibid.*, II, 325-6, for the accusations against Oxford.

[15] MacLachlan, "The Great Peace," pp. 23-4, 684, and "The Road to Peace, 1710-13," *Britain after the Glorious Revolution*, pp. 207-8, 213; McInnes, *Robert Harley*, pp. 131-6.

[16] Oxford, "A brief Account of Public Affairs," *Parliamentary History*, VI, ccxlvi.

Marlborough as Groom of the Stole.[17] According to Swift, St. John declared "that He would never sit in Council, with a Man who had so often betrayed them; and was openly engaged with a Faction, which endeavoured to obstruct all Her Majesty's Measures."[18] Following the incident, Swift reported that "the Whigs whisper, that our new ministry differ among themselves, and they begin to talk out Mr. Secretary: they have some reasons for their whispers, although I thought it was a greater secret. I do not much like the posture of things; I always apprehended, that any falling out would ruin them."[19] In September Dr. Stratford told Lord Harley he was "very sorry for Mr. St. John's sake, that his behaviour to your father is so much known. Should this end, as it must at least if it continues, in dismissing him from his post, he is undone. . . . But this is the consequence of that which was instilled into him last winter, by some who took that way to make their court to him, that he was of capacity enough to stand upon his own legs."[20] Somerset did not try to take his place again; but "upon this Incident, He declared open War against the Ministry."[21] And from this point on, the Tories, led by St. John, called more loudly than ever for his dismissal. But partly on the Queen's account, partly because his presence in the ministry served Oxford's moderate design, Somerset stayed on another six months, and Oxford labored unsuccessfully to win his support for the peace.[22]

In the entry for October 20, 1711, Swift noted in the *Journal to Stella:*

[17] Peter Wentworth to Lord Raby, 5 September 1710, *Wentworth Papers*, pp. 143-4; Cowper, *Diary*, p. 50; Burnet, *History*, VI, 14, and Dartmouth's note.

[18] Swift, *History*, p. 14. Swift to Archbishop King, 26 August 1711, *Swift Correspondence*, I, 248; *Journal to Stella*, I, 332.

[19] Swift, *Journal to Stella*, I, 346.

[20] Dr. Stratford to Lord Harley, 8 September 1711, HMC, *Portland MSS*, VII, 55.

[21] Swift, *History*, pp. 14-15.

[22] Somerset to Oxford, 25 September 1711, BM, Portland Loan, 29/156; 29 November 1711, HMC, *Portland MSS*, V, 118; and Oxford to Somerset, 1 December 1711, *ibid.*, p. 119.

The secretary told me last night, that he had found the reason why the queen was cold to him for some months past; that a friend had told it him yesterday; and it was, that they suspected he was at the bottom with the duke of Marlborough. . . . He was in a rage to be thus suspected; swears he will be upon a better foot, or none at all: and I do not see, how they can well want him in this juncture.[23]

It has been suggested that St. John was in fact attempting to form some sort of an alliance with Marlborough in the late summer and autumn of 1711[24] but there is no evidence to substantiate the claim. In the first eighteen months of the new ministry St. John's attitude toward Marlborough seems to have been if anything harsher than Oxford's. There was no apparent difference between them on the central issue: both felt it was necessary to keep Marlborough as Captain-General at least until the peace preliminaries were signed; but at the same time he must continue on their terms and subject to their authority. Their approach to him was therefore a combination of persuasion and threat, with the emphasis changing according to Marlborough's declarations and his conduct. Through the course of these negotiations, carried on directly and through a number of intermediaries, Oxford seems to have been consistently more cordial and, predictably, more restrained than the Secretary. Oxford secured Treasury funds to proceed with the building of Blenheim, suspended since the change of ministry; and many months after Marlborough's dismissal at the end of December 1711, his secretary conveyed the Duke's thanks to the Lord Treasurer for some favor: "He [Marlborough] is very much obliged to your Lordship for your continued kindness to him, of which he has commanded me to assure you that he will retain a lasting sense."[25] All this, of course, does not

---

[23] Swift, *Journal to Stella*, II, 388–9.

[24] Feiling, *A History of the Tory Party*, pp. 428–9. According to "Mr. Carte's Memorandum-book," Oxford told Lord Lansdowne "that Bolingbroke was betraying all their counsels to lord Marlborough." But Lansdowne was remembering in 1725, long after the event. Macpherson, *Original Papers*, II, 532.

[25] Arthur Maynwaring to Oxford, 18 October 1712, HMC, *Portland MSS*, V, 238. For the ministers' attitudes to Marlborough, see Coxe, *Marlborough*,

exclude the possibility that St. John had some hopes of securing
Marlborough's support for his own designs. Certainly he
would have welcomed it. But there is no evidence to suggest
that he ever approached the Duke.

"We are so weary with expecting farther Removals, that
we begin to drop the Discourse," Swift wrote to Archbishop
King in July 1711. "Neither am I sure, whether those in Power
may not differ a little in Opinion as to the Matter. However, it
seemth generally agreed, that there will be many Changes
before next Session, and that it is necessary there should be
so."[26] But as Oxford's ministry moved into its second year and
prepared to do battle for the peace, the expected removals were
not forthcoming. In September Swift was still wearily waiting,
and in November he reported to Stella: "I am told they design
giving away several employments before the parliament sits,
which will be the thirteenth instant. I either do not like, or do
not understand this policy."[27] At the end of the summer
Shrewsbury wrote to express his concern about the government's situation in the House of Lords: "So many of our
friends in the Lords' House being dead, and many more soured
or at least become luke-warm by disappointments in their
expectations, I apprehend matters in that House at least will
meet with difficulties."[28] Bromley worried about the Commons, not "that the enemies to peace can give any trouble," but
he feared

uneasiness of another kind there, gentlemen being very desirous to
answer the expectations of those that sent them thither, and to act

---

VI, 6–10, 44–51. For St. John's in particular, see *Bolingbroke Correspondence*,
I, *passim;* Blenheim, Marlborough Papers, BII, 1. For Oxford's in particular,
see HMC, *Portland MSS*, IV, 577–655, *passim;* HMC, *Bath MSS*, I, 202–12;
Longleat, Portland MSS, IV, ff. 122, 132–3, 160–1 and V, ff. 237, 255.

[26] Swift to Archbishop King, 12 July 1711, *Swift Correspondence*, I, 237.

[27] Swift, *Journal to Stella*, II, 400. Swift to Charles Ford, 8 September
1711, *Swift Correspondence*, I, 258: "We are weary of expecting Removals
in the Excise, Customs, etc. yet they say something must be done before
the Sessions."

[28] Shrewsbury to Oxford, 27 August 1711, HMC, *Bath MSS*, I, 207.

as becomes a House of Commons chosen by a spirit raised from an opinion of great corruption in the late administration, that it would now be detected and punished, and that something would be done to secure our constitution in church and state against the vile principles and practices that had been countenanced to the endangering of both.

He warned Oxford that no one could tell "how far their well meant zeal may carry them." Bromley would do his best to "keep them within those bounds which it is truly my concern they should not exceed . . . but all I can do will be ineffectual without your assistance."[29]

In the face of these warnings, Oxford, while he would not countenance further removals, was actively engaged in recruiting Whig support for the peace.[30] But he did not meet with much success, and as the opening of Parliament approached, there were persistent reports that the Whig lords intended to address the Queen against the peace.[31] In part to give the government time to rally its forces, in part because both Oxford and the Queen had been ill, Parliament was prorogued until December 7. The Queen was "very ill of the gout," Lady Strafford reported to her husband; "and Lord Oxford 'tis also said is ill, but for reasons of State, and for the same reason the Parliament is adjourn'd."[32]

The delay did not prove particularly useful. Swift's *Conduct of the Allies*, a forcefully argued presentation of the ministers' case for the peace, appeared on November 27 and had an immediate success.[33] But the signs were ominous none-

---

[29] Bromley to Oxford, 25 November 1711, HMC, *Portland MSS*, V, 116.

[30] He remained in close touch with Halifax and through him approached Somers. See HMC, *Portland MSS*, V, 79–133, *passim;* and BM, Portland Loan, 29/151. See also Burnet, *History*, VI, 76-7, and Boyer, *Annals*, X, 281, for the government's efforts to win support for the peace.

[31] Harcourt to Oxford, 12 November 1711, HMC, *Portland MSS*, V, 108-9; Sir Robert Davers to Oxford, 1 November 1711, *ibid.*, p. 106.

[32] Lady Strafford to Strafford, 15 November 1711, *Wentworth Papers*, p. 207.

[33] According to Swift, the pamphlet went through two editions in less than a week and a thousand copies were sold in the first two days after

theless. "I saw such an Appearance on Tuesday in the H. of Lords, that it seems necessary to me to have all our Friends in Town," Bromley wrote; Shrewsbury concurred, urging the Treasurer "to take the requisite care that our friends come to town in time."[34] But at the end of November Peter Wentworth reported that "all the Whigs are in town, but the Torys that think they have been neglected delay coming"; and Oxford's son-in-law complained that the Treasurer had delayed so long in summoning the Scottish peers they could not get down in time for the opening of the session.[35] Their threatened absence was a matter of some consequence, since the sixteen Scots lords could, as a rule, be counted on to vote with the Court.[36] To add to the ministry's difficulties, in the middle of November Marlborough returned to England and lent his strength to the opposition forces.[37] Opinion on the peace

---

its publication. *Journal to Stella*, II, 423, 427-8. Five editions appeared before the end of 1711 and three more subsequently.

[34] Bromley to Oxford, 15 November 1711, BM, Portland Loan, 29/128. Shrewsbury to Oxford, 23 November 1711, HMC, *Bath MSS*, I, 217.

[35] Peter Wentworth to Strafford, 27 November 1711, *Wentworth Papers*, p. 215. Viscount Dupplin to Oxford, 25 November 1711, HMC, *Portland MSS*, V, 115. See also Kinnoull to Dupplin, 3 December 1711, *ibid.*, p. 121.

[36] By the terms of the Act of Union (1707), the Scottish peers elected sixteen of their number to represent them in the House of Lords. The Scots were in no hurry to make the journey to London. Dissatisfied with what they considered to be the ministry's neglect of their interests, they were further incensed by reports that a considerable number of English lords opposed the grant of an English peerage to the Scottish Duke of Hamilton. The Whig lords, and a number of Tories as well, feared the grant would be the first of several and that the government intended to pack the House of Lords with men dependent on the Court. In the event, only five of the sixteen Scottish peers were on hand for the opening of the session; and on December 20 the Lords refused by a vote of 57 to 52 to allow the Duke of Hamilton to take his seat in the upper House. Hamilton to Oxford, 13 November 1711, HMC, *Portland MSS*, V, 109; Kinnoull to Oxford, 16 November 1711, *ibid.*, 112. For the dispute over Hamilton's English peerage, see G. S. Holmes, "The Hamilton Affair of 1711-1712: A Crisis in Anglo-Scottish Relations," *English Historical Review*, LXXVII (1962), 257-82.

[37] According to St. John's report, "in his [Marlborough's] conversation with the Queen, he has spoken against what we are doing." St. John to

divided on party lines, but Whig and Tory agreed that the government's future depended upon its success in getting the Preliminary Articles through Parliament. "The Torys cry, if we shrink now and don't go thro' with the Peace they are undone, the Whigs will get up again," Peter Wentworth wrote, "and these latter seem to be in some hopes this will be the case."[38] Swift thought the ministry "to stand very unsteady: if they can carry a Peace, they May hold; I believe not else."[39]

On December 1, Swift wrote: "The parliament will certainly meet on Friday next, the Whigs will have a great majority in the house of lords; no care is taken to prevent it; there is too much neglect; they are warned of it, and that signifies nothing: it was feared there would be some peevish address from the lords against a Peace."[40] Four days later he reported with more certainty: "The Whig lords are doing their utmost for a majority against Friday, and design, if they can, to address the queen against the Peace. Lord Nottingham, a famous Tory and speech-maker, is gone over to the Whig side."[41] Nottingham's defection was motivated by pique as well as principle: consistently denied office under the new ministry, he had in recent months been passed over both for the Lord Presidency and the Privy Seal. Now, in return for Whig support of a new bill against occasional conformity, he agreed to join them in opposition to the peace. Thus when the Parliament met on December 7, Nottingham moved as an amendment to the address of thanks for the Queen's speech that "no Peace could be safe or honourable to Great-Britain, or Europe, if Spain and the West-Indies were allotted to any

---

Strafford, 21 November 1711, *Bolingbroke Correspondence*, I, 480. See also Burnet, *History*, VI, 76–7, and Dartmouth's note.

[38] Peter Wentworth to Strafford, 4 December 1711, *Wentworth Papers*, p. 217.

[39] Swift, *Journal to Stella*, II, 429.

[40] *Ibid.*, II, 426.

[41] *Ibid.*, p. 430. For Nottingham's role on this occasion, see Henry Horwitz, *Revolution Politicks: The Career of Daniel Finch Second Earl of Nottingham, 1647–1730* (Cambridge University Press, 1968), pp. 228–34.

branch of the House of Bourbon."[42] The motion, saved from
defeat by a single vote when the ministry moved the previous
question, carried by eight votes—a comparable amendment in
the Commons was defeated 232 to 106—and while only one
other Tory joined Nottingham in opposition, a number of
Whig placemen, including Somerset and Marlborough, voted
against the Crown.[43] The defeat threatened the ministry as
well as the peace. "It is a mighty blow and loss of reputation to
lord treasurer, and may end in his ruin," Swift wrote.[44] And
Lord Wharton, "coming out of the House after the vote of the
address," was said to have "clapped his hand upon the Lord
Treasurer's shoulder, and said, by God, my lord, if you can
bear this you are the strongest man in England."[45]

The defeat in the Lords was variously blamed on Oxford's
failure to move against the Whigs and to shore up the government's strength in advance—"Delay, and tenderness to an
inveterate party, have been very instrumental to this ill state of
affairs," Swift observed;[46] on the defection of several peers
who had earlier promised to vote with the government; and on
the Queen, who by countenancing open opposition in the
ranks of her servants, made it impossible for the government to
marshal its forces behind the peace.[47] When Arbuthnot asked

[42] *Parliamentary History*, VI, 1036.

[43] Burnet, *History*, VI, 79–86; Coxe, *Marlborough*, VI, 139–41. See also
G. S. Holmes, "The Commons' Division on 'No Peace without Spain,' 7
December 1711," *Bulletin of the Institute of Historical Research*, XXXIII
(1960), 223–34. Holmes points out that eleven Tories opposed the government in the Commons. Of these only one (his son) belonged to Nottingham's connection, indicating that there were already in 1711 some Tories who
objected to the conduct of the peace negotiations and thus foreshadowing
the later split in the party.

[44] Swift, *Journal to Stella*, II, 432.

[45] R. Palmer to R. Verney, 11 December 1711, HMC, *Verney MSS*, p.
507.

[46] Swift to Deane Stearne, 29 December 1711, *Swift Correspondence*, I
282.

[47] Peter Wentworth to Strafford, 7, 11, 14 December 1711, *Wentworth
Papers*, pp. 220–5; Swift, *Journal to Stella*, II, 432–7; Oxford to Strafford, 8
December 1711, *Bolingbroke Correspondence*, II, 48–50.

him "How he came not to secure a majority," Oxford "could answer nothing, but that he could not help it if people would lie and forswear. A poor answer for a great minister. There fell from him a scripture expression, that *the hearts of kings are unsearchable.*"[48] Swift was convinced that the Queen was false, and he said St. John agreed; Erasmus Lewis, Dartmouth's Under-Secretary of State, gave him reason to believe "the whole matter is settled between the queen and the Whigs."[49] But Oxford did not despair. "You had better keep company with me," he told Swift, "than with such a fellow as Lewis, who has not the soul of a chicken, nor the heart of a mite." And Swift reported that "he seemed to talk confidently, as if he reckoned that all this would turn to advantage." When Swift observed "that those scoundrel, starving lords would never have dared to vote against the Court, if Somerset had not assured them that it would please the queen. He said, That was true, and Somerset did so."[50]

Oxford had reason to be confident. In the crisis he acted with decision and, for once, like a thorough Tory. He was said to have assured the Tories "there shou'd not be a Whig in place by Lady-day,"[51] and he wrote Strafford that "this proceeding will oblige the Queen, without reserve, to use the gentlemen of England, and those who are for her prerogative, it will draw marks of displeasure upon those who have barefaced set up a standard against her."[52] More predictably, St. John wrote in the same sense on the same day: "If she [the Queen] has vigour and firmness enough to assert her own dignity, she will unite the bulk of the nation in her interest, and leave the faction nothing but impotent malice, wherewith to torment them-

---

[48] Swift, *Journal to Stella*, II, 434.

[49] *Ibid.*, p. 435.

[50] *Ibid.*, p. 436.

[51] Peter Wentworth to Strafford, 18 December 1711, *Wentworth Papers*, p. 226.

[52] Oxford to Strafford, 8 December 1711, *Bolingbroke Correspondence*, II, 50. The letter is printed in a note.

selves, but not to hurt her or those who serve her. . . . The success of the Whigs in the House of Lords will be their ruin and her salvation."[53]

Within the next weeks first Marlborough, then Somerset was dismissed, though the Queen refused to part with Somerset's Duchess. And to ensure a favorable majority in the House of Lords, the Queen created twelve new Tory peers, an expedient viewed with some suspicion by Tories as well as Whigs, but one that served its purpose very well.[54] Swift, who did not "like the expedient, if we could have found any other," said later he did not see "how the Treasurer can justly be blamed for preserving His Cause, his Friends and himself from unavoidable Ruin. . . . Perhaps he was brought under that Necessity by the Want of proper Management; but when that Necessity appeared, he could not act otherwise without unravelling whatever had been done."[55] Peter Wentworth agreed. Reporting the new creations and Marlborough's dismissal, he wrote: "The tories say this is something like, the Treasurer is now in earness; if he had begun this with him and the Duke of Somerset, he wou'd never have lost so matterial a vote as he did in the house of lords, nor have been at the trouble to have desired the Queen to make use of her prerogative in so large an extent to bring above twelve lords into the house at once."[56]

Though it was rumored he would become Lord Bolingbroke, St. John was not among the new peers: "Mr. Secretary will be a lord at the end of the session," Swift wrote; "but they want him still in parliament."[57] In his "Letter to Sir William

[53] St. John to Strafford, 8 December 1711, *ibid.*, p. 53.

[54] Burnet, *History*, VI, 94–5, and Dartmouth's note; Hertfordshire R.O., Panshanger MSS, Sir David Hamilton's Diary, ff. 37–8; *The Lockhart Papers*, I, 369.

[55] Swift, *Journal to Stella*, II, 452; Swift, "An Enquiry," p. 150.

[56] Peter Wentworth to Strafford, 1 January 1712, *Wentworth Papers*, p. 236.

[57] Swift, *Journal to Stella*, II, 451; Peter Wentworth to Strafford, 18 December 1711, *Wentworth Papers*, p. 225.

Windham," St. John spoke of the twelve creations as "an unprecedented and invidious measure, to be excused by nothing but the necessity, and hardly by that."[58] His judgment might have been less harsh had he been among the twelve; but it is reasonable to suppose that he held Oxford responsible for allowing the Court's position to deteriorate so far that an adverse vote in the Lords was possible. In any case, the actions taken in December and January were in line with the policy he had urged from the first days of the ministry. Faced with a Whig challenge to the government's conduct of the peace negotiations, the Treasurer was forced to concede something to Tory demands on the matter of places and at the same time openly to acquiesce in a harder approach to the peace.

When Parliament reconvened in the new year, St. John took charge of the government's business in the House of Commons. Charges of peculation were brought against Marlborough and also against Walpole, Whig Secretary-at-War from 1708 to 1710, who was sent to the Tower and expelled from the House. The evidence suggests that neither Oxford nor St. John wanted to pursue Marlborough with any particular vindictiveness. For them the important point was his dismissal, once he had declared himself an enemy to the peace; and the charges brought by the Commissioners of Public Accounts made this easier to accomplish. "It was rightly conjectured by all Observers of Publick Affairs," Abel Boyer wrote, "That the Duke of *Marlborough* would not escape without a Censure; which seemed necessary to justifie his being removed from all his Employments." According to Swift, "the ministers' design is, that the duke of Marlborough shall be censured as gently as possible, provided his friends will not make head to defend him; but if they do, it may end in some severer votes." And St. John told Strafford that, while Marlborough would be "rendered accountable for great sums, and be left to the Queen's mercy," "our people have too much sense to give into a parlia-

58 Bolingbroke, *Works*, I, 117.

mentary persecution of him."[59] In the event, the Commons sustained the charges against the Duke by a majority of more than a hundred votes: "so the ministry is mighty well satisfied, and the duke will now be able to do no hurt."[60]

The Commons moved on from the censure of Marlborough to inquire into Britain's foreign alliances and the conduct of the war, and in these proceedings St. John played a leading part.

The great Trust of managing the Affairs of the Administration in Parliament during this Sessions, was committed to Mr. Secretary *St. John*, who, to influence the Nation in their Sentiments of the long Continuance of the War, and to excite the most earnest Desire of Peace, employed himself with indefatigable Diligence, in drawing up the most accurate Computations, as to the Number of our own Troops, the Number of Foreigners, and the Sums paid by Way of Subsidies during the Course of the War; which was certainly as dextrous and as efficacious a Piece of Management as had, perhaps, till then been attempted in Parliament.[61]

Swift wrote that the Secretary, "by the force of an extraordinary Genius, and Application to Publick Affairs, joined with an invincible Eloquence; laid open the Scene of Miscarriages and Corruptions through the whole Course of the War in so evident a manner, that the House of Commons seemed principally directed in their Resolutions upon this Enquiry by his Information and Advice."[62] St. John's particular target was the Dutch Barrier Treaty, which the Commons in due course declared "dishonourable and injurious to England," while "all who had advised and ratified that treaty, were public enemies to the kingdom."[63] He hoped the parliamentary attack would

[59] Boyer, *Annals*, X, 327. Swift, *Journal to Stella*, II, 470. St. John to Strafford, 18 January 1712, *Bolingbroke Correspondence*, II, 166. See also Coxe, *Marlborough*, VI, 149–60; *The Lockhart Papers*, I, 352–63, 375–6; Dickinson, *Bolingbroke*, p. 94.

[60] Swift, *Journal to Stella*, II, 471.

[61] [Mallet], *Memoirs of the Life and Ministerial Conduct, . . . of the Late Lord Visc. Bolingbroke*, p. 217.

[62] Swift, *History*, p. 98.

[63] Burnet, *History*, VI, 111–12.

pressure the Dutch to come into the peace, but whatever its effect in this respect, the denunciation of the allies and the late ministry was immensely pleasing to the Tories.[64]

The events of the winter did much to placate the Tory gentlemen, but to the extent that they looked for a definitive change in the ministry's policy, they remained unsatisfied. Swift wrote Archbishop King that the Treasurer's friends "and the Tories in general, are discontented at his Slowness in the changing of Commissions and Employments, to which the Weakness of the Court Interest in the House of Lords is wholly imputed: Neither do I find that those in the greatest Stations, or most in the Confidence of my Lord Treasurer, are able to account for this Proceeding or seem satisfied with it."[65] A correspondent informed Oxford that "there is a great deal of grumbling that several ill men are continued in employments. It is not fit for me to say that you have told me that when there is a peace all other things will follow. . . . Yet I think myself that you have been too long in putting some men in, and turning some men out."[66] Bromley repeatedly expressed his confidence in Oxford, but he was uneasy about his followers:

There wants no inclination in the members of this House of Commons to come into everything that may support you and render your Ministry easy and glorious; there only wants a confidence which will unavoidably increase, the longer the making those thorough changes are delayed, which I am persuaded your Lordship really intends to make, because you have been pleased so often to tell me you would make, and which I think your interest and safety, as well as theirs, require to be made.[67]

[64] MacLachlan feels St. John's bullying approach was not very effective, but, on the contrary, may have stiffened Dutch resistance. "The Great Peace," pp. 332–4.

[65] Swift to Archbishop King, 29 March 1712, Swift Correspondence, I, 294–5.

[66] C. Lawton to Oxford, 14 April 1712, HMC, Portland MSS, V, 163.

[67] Bromley to Oxford, 29 April 1712, ibid., p. 168. See also Bromley to Oxford, 28 February 1712, BM, Portland Loan, 29/313.

A group of October men, impatient with Oxford's delaying and disgusted by what they considered to be the October Club's surrender to the ministry, seceded to form the March Club. A considerable number of Tories, George Lockhart wrote, "being weari'd with expecting what they thought they deserv'd and had been often promis'd, sett up a club which they call'd the March Club, in contradistinction to the October Club, whom they termd creatures and slaves to the Ministry." "They call themselves the Primative October men," Peter Wentworth reported, "and are resolved to take no places, and are provoked that the October admitted Mr. St. Johns for their president."[68] St. John presided for only one meeting, but in the eyes of these uncompromising Tories his presence symbolized the odious domination of the Court. The March men's influence was never great but they constituted one more dissident group to add to the ministers' difficulties, St. John's as well as Oxford's. St. John in fact suffered a personal defeat at their hands when a resolution he proposed on behalf of his friend Arthur Moore, sued in the Commons for settlement of a private claim, was rejected by the votes of the March men added to those of the Whigs.[69] In principle independent and hostile to the Court, they resolutely refused to be controlled or led.

While the parliamentary session moved forward at home, the peace congress had been in progress at Utrecht since January 1712. The ministers continued to negotiate behind the scenes; and Oxford and St. John continued to differ as to how they should proceed. As before, St. John took a harder approach to the allies and was inclined to favor a separate peace:

[68] *The Lockhart Papers*, I, 366. Peter Wentworth to Strafford, 8 April 1712, *Wentworth Papers*, pp. 283–4. See also Swift, *History*, p. 100; and Robert Wodrow, *Analecta: or, Materials for a History of Remarkable Providences; Mostly Relating to Scotch Ministers and Christians* (The Maitland Club, 1842–3), II, 36. Also Dickinson, "The October Club," pp. 167–70.

[69] Peter Wentworth to Strafford, 8 April 1712, *Wentworth Papers*, p. 284; Dickinson, *Bolingbroke*, p. 96.

he went so far as to confess he wished the Dutch would continue to hold out so that England could negotiate with a free hand.[70] And Oxford, while he refused to give ground on the trading concessions secured in the preliminaries, still hoped to settle in concert with the Dutch and the other allies.[71] When in March the last of a series of deaths in the French royal family left only a child between Philip of Anjou, then ruling in Spain, and the throne of France, Oxford proposed that Spain go to the Duke of Savoy. He assumed that Philip would choose to give up Spain rather than renounce his French inheritance: the two crowns would thus be effectively separated, satisfying the allies and the parliamentary opposition at home. St. John seems not to have known the details of Oxford's scheme, and to the extent that he did, to have been unsympathetic to it. In any event, the negotiation collapsed when in May 1712, Philip elected to renounce his claim to the French throne and remain in Spain.[72] The question now was the means by which Philip's renunciation could be guaranteed to the satisfaction of England and her allies. Once again, Oxford's options had been narrowed by events. While he still insisted upon a general settlement, he was forced to move closer to St. John's position; and St. John took the opportunity to advance the negotiations for a separate peace.[73]

The ministers' differences did not prevent them from acting together to win parliamentary support for the peace, and in this they met with considerable success. At the end of 'May, when it became known that the Duke of Ormonde, commanding the British forces in Flanders, had been secretly ordered to

[70] St. John to Thomas Harley, 10 May 1712, *Bolingbroke Correspondence*, II, 323–8. MacLachlan, "The Great Peace," pp. 402–3, 435–40.

[71] MacLachlan, "The Road to Peace, 1710–13," *Britain after the Glorious Revolution*, pp. 211–12.

[72] St. John to Strafford, 29 April 1712, *Bolingbroke Correspondence*, II, 299–301; MacLachlan, "The Great Peace," pp. 414–15.

[73] MacLachlan, "The Great Peace," pp. 442–6, 496. *Memoirs of the Marquis of Torcy, Secretary of State to Lewis XIV* (London, 1757), II, 347–8.

refrain from offensive action pending the signing of the peace, the Whigs in both Houses failed to carry a motion of protest. In the Commons the government's margin was over one hundred; in the Lords it was twenty-eight. Both Oxford and St. John later disclaimed responsibility for initiating the orders, St. John blaming Oxford and Oxford blaming the Queen. But whoever was responsible, it appears that the ministers concurred in the decision. The significant point is the size of the parliamentary vote, particularly in the Commons, on an issue amounting to outright desertion of the allies.[74] In June Parliament again expressed its support of the ministry when the Queen presented the terms on which peace could be secured. Both Houses moved addresses of thanks and desired the Queen to finish the work.[75]

The session of Parliament ended, St. John moved to claim his reward. The earldom of Bolingbroke, in the elder branch of the St. John family since 1624, had lapsed the preceding October when the third Earl died without issue. In June St. John asked that the Queen revive the title in him. In a letter to Oxford fairly exuding humility and submission, he declared that if the request was "more than what I ought to expect, or if the consequence of it can be disobliging to anyone who is of moment in the service, burn my letter, forget that I asked it, and I promise you I will forget that I was refused it."[76] But when in fact the Queen did refuse him the earldom, making him a viscount instead, he was angry and distraught. "I would

[74] Sir Thomas Cave to Lord Fermanagh, 27 May 1712, *Verney Letters of the Eighteenth Century from the MSS, at Claydon House*, ed. by. Margaret Maria Lady Verney (London: Ernest Benn, 1930), I, 311. For the text of the orders, see St. John to Ormonde, 10 May 1712, *Bolingbroke Correspondence*, II, 320–1. For Bolingbroke's denial, see his "Letters on the Study and Use of History," *Works*, II, 320–1, and Burnet, *History*, VI, 128, Hardwicke's note. For Oxford's, *Parliamentary History*, VII, 175. See also Hill, "The Career of Robert Harley, Earl of Oxford," pp. 296–8, and MacLachlan, "The Great Peace," pp. 432–4.

[75] Burnet, *History*, VI, 131–3.

[76] St. John to Oxford, 28? June 1712, HMC, *Portland MSS*, V, 194.

forfeit anything in my power to recall the letter I wrote to your Lordship upon which you spoke to the Queen," he wrote to Oxford, "but it is impossible."

Let me therefore be punished for my indiscretion, and since I asked too much let the Queen be so good as to give me nothing.

It might disoblige some to do what I desired; it will certainly disoblige several to do what the Queen intends. To do nothing for me will to be sure disoblige nobody, since I can be answerable it shall not me.

I am perfectly satisfied to continue in the House of Commons, and if I did some little service in the last session I will endeavour to do more in the next.[77]

But St. John's second thoughts came too late. It is not clear whether, on reflection, he decided to accept the viscounty as better than no title, or whether custom made its rejection, once granted, virtually impossible. But his resentment was deep, and it was directed against Oxford, whom he blamed for what he considered his disgrace. "I was dragged into the house of Lords in such a manner, as to make my promotion a punishment, not a reward," he wrote later.[78] At the time he confessed to Strafford that his promotion was a mortification to him.

In the House of Commons, I may say, that I was at the head of business, and I must have continued so, whether I had been in court or out of court. . . . To make me a peer was no great compliment, when so many others were forced to be made to gain a strength in Parliament; and since the Queen wanted me below stairs in the last session, she could do no less than make me a Viscount, or I must have come in the rear of several whom I was not born to follow.

Though nothing had yet been done for him as a particular mark of favor, the Queen would go no farther: "I own to you

---

[77] St. John to Oxford, 3 July 1712, *ibid.*, p. 198. See also Swift, *Journal to Stella*, II, 545, 549–50.

[78] Bolingbroke, "A Letter to Sir William Windham," *Works*, I, 117. See also Oxford, "A brief Account of Public Affairs," *Parliamentary History*, VI, ccxlvi.

that I felt more indignation than ever in my life I had done." He had restrained himself from running to extremities and banished thoughts of resigning because he knew "that any appearance of breach between myself and the Lord Treasurer, would give our common enemies spirit. . . . To friendship therefore, and the public good, if I may be pardoned for so vain an expression, I sacrificed my private resentment, and remain clothed with as little of the Queen's favour as she could contrive to bestow."[79] By Oxford's account, St. John's rage "caused him to say and swear he would not take the title. After he had it he gave out it was only to take him out of the House of Commons, where his interest was too great."[80] Oxford protested his innocence to Swift, who thought the Queen was responsible: St. John "was not much at that time in her good Graces; some Women about the Court, having infused an Opinion into her that he was not so regular in his Life as He ought to be."[81] But Whether the Queen or Oxford was to blame, there is no denying that St. John wanted a peerage. He asked for the earldom in the first place; and he knew that whatever title the Queen conferred on him, he would leave the House of Commons. It was all very well for St. John to say after the fact that to make him a peer was no great compliment and that, rather than move up to the Lords as a viscount, he would have preferred to remain in the Commons; but in asking for the earldom he risked refusal. Ultimately he was himself to blame for his miscalculation. Impulsive as always, he failed to anticipate the consequences of his action. Too late he realized the advantages of staying in the Commons, where he dominated affairs and commanded strong support. It is hardly surprising that his resentment was extreme. "The Secretary laid the whole Blame of this Disappointment upon the Earl of

79 Bolingbroke to Strafford, 23 July 1712, *Bolingbroke Correspondence,* II, 483–4.
80 Oxford, "Account of Public Affairs," HMC, *Portland MSS,* V, 467.
81 Swift, "An Enquiry," pp. 151–2.

Oxford," Swift wrote, "and freely told me, that he would never depend upon the Earl's Friendship as long as he lived."[82]

For the remaining two years of the ministry—and of the reign—the relationship between Oxford and Bolingbroke was precarious in the extreme. Bolingbroke told Swift he would have no further commerce with the Treasurer other than "what was necessary for carrying on the publick Service,"[83] and sometimes even this was lacking. In August the Secretary went to Paris to confer with Torcy on matters pertaining to the peace. Oxford later claimed there was not much occasion for the trip but that "Lord Bolingbroke was permitted to go to please him";[84] and while Oxford discounted the value of the mission, it is true that Bolingbroke had wanted to go to France for some time.[85] Oxford evidently hoped to soften Bolingbroke's resentment over the peerage, but what exactly the visit was intended to accomplish is unclear. Oxford seems to have assumed that the trip would be short and that Bolingbroke would deal only with the interests of the Duke of Savoy: in any case, the Secretary's formal instructions made no mention of a separate peace. Once in France, Bolingbroke disposed of those points he was directed to cover within a few days; but he stayed on in Paris for another week, during which time he did his best to move the negotiations toward a separate settlement. He led the French to believe that once Philip had formally renounced his right to the throne of France, the Queen would sign a peace with France and Savoy, leaving the other allies to

---

[82] *Ibid.*

[83] *Ibid.*, p. 152.

[84] Oxford, "Account of Public Affairs," HMC, *Portland MSS*, V, 465.

[85] St. John to Strafford, 19 February 1712, *Bolingbroke Correspondence*, II, 183–4; St. John to the Lords Plenipotentiaries, 23 February 1712: "I cannot help thinking that the Queen might have contributed extremely to smooth your way at Utrecht, if she had, in this critical point of time, sent some man to the Court of France, who might have been thought in the full secret of his own; I offered the Queen to go, but I believe the measure is thought a little too bold." Gaultier went instead. *Ibid.*, pp. 192–3.

make what terms they could.[86] In this he was, of course, exceeding his instructions. However that may have been, his visit was a personal triumph. Swift wrote that the Secretary "was received at Court with particular Marks of Distinction and Respect"; and it was reported that when he went to the theater in Paris, the audience rose in his honor.[87] He attended a performance at the opera when the Pretender was also present, a circumstance that gave rise to persistent rumors that the two conferred in secret. But there is no conclusive evidence that a meeting ever took place.[88]

Oxford later observed with some annoyance that Bolingbroke's success "added new fuel to his vanity"; but he was sufficiently alarmed by the Secretary's activities to shift the negotiations out of his hands to Dartmouth's Southern Department, where technically they belonged.[89] Torcy and Prior, who was handling the British side of the negotiations in Paris, were greatly distressed, Torcy for reasons of policy as well as practicality: he was uncertain what direction the discussions might take under Dartmouth's management. "I thought Ld Bolingbroke who knows every step of the Negociation was to have carried it on," Prior complained to the Treasurer, "but I see it is transferred to the other office, and apprehend new difficulties will dayly arise from this Change."[90] To Bolingbroke he wrote: "I am sure Monsieur de Torcy presses you to resume your correspondence with us; it is little for me to say after him, how much the service must suffer, and how many

---

[86] Oxford to Ormonde, 5/16 August 1712. HMC, *Hodgkin MSS*, p. 213; Bolingbroke to Dartmouth, 21 August 1712, N.S., *Bolingbroke Correspondence*, III, 1–23. Bolingbroke's instructions are printed in a note, pp. 2–6. MacLachlan, "The Great Peace," pp. 536–7, 575–6.

[87] Swift, *History*, p. 149. Thomas MacKnight, *The Life of Henry St. John, Viscount Bolingbroke* (London, 1863), p. 304.

[88] Newsletter, 2 September 1712, HMC, *Various Collections*, VIII, 89; Swift to Archbishop King, 16 December 1716, *Swift Correspondence*, II, 238; Arthur Hassall, *Bolingbroke* (Oxford, 1915), p. 63.

[89] Oxford, "Account of Public Affairs," HMC, *Portland MSS*, V, 467.

[90] Prior to Oxford, 12/1 September 1712, BM, Portland Loan, 29/154.

incidents must needs arise from its being either put into a new channel, or divided into two; but—*Ich dien*."[91] Bolingbroke had no intention of abandoning the negotiations and he continued to correspond with both Prior and Torcy in spite of the official change. But Oxford had succeeded in checking, at least temporarily, the design for a separate peace.

Bolingbroke did not accept this new humiliation quietly. In mid-September Swift was "again endeavouring . . . to keep People from breaking to pieces, upon a hundred misunderstandings." He could not conceive "how Affairs can last as they are."[92] At the end of the month the dispute between the ministers erupted in a major Cabinet clash.[93] What appears to have been the crucial meeting took place September 28. The central issue was the signing of the peace, but the related question of whether Parliament should be dissolved was also a matter of contention. Bolingbroke evidently attacked Oxford and Dartmouth for their mismanagement of the negotiations, and made the case for an immediate—and separate—peace. If the Cabinet could not agree, he said, the dissolution of Parliament and new elections would resolve the question; and Harcourt, Shrewsbury, and Buckingham supported his position.[94] Oxford replied by denouncing Bolingbroke's conduct in France: the Secretary had, on his own initiative and without prior authority, made promises to the French that hindered the conclusion of a general peace. In addition, the Treasurer apparently accused Bolingbroke of meeting with the Pretender.

[91] Prior to Bolingbroke, 17/28 September 1712, *Bolingbroke Correspondence*, III, 98. See also Prior's letter of 1/12 September, *ibid.*, pp. 57–60; also Bolingbroke to Torcy, 10 September 1712, *ibid.*, p. 45; and Torcy to Bolingbroke, 16/27 September 1712, *ibid.*, pp. 82–3.

[92] Swift, *Journal to Stella*, II, 556.

[93] There are no firsthand reports of the clash. Again, I follow MacLachlan, who seems to have consulted all the available sources, including the dispatches of the Austrian, Hanoverian, and Dutch envoys in London. "The Great Peace," pp. 586–93.

[94] L'Hermitage to the States-General, 26 September/7 October 1712, BM, Add. MSS, 17, 677FFF, f. 361.

From Bolingbroke's point of view, the confrontation came too late, for by this time the Dutch had indicated their willingness to come to terms, provided they could keep the town of Tournai as part of their barrier. And while Bolingbroke was prepared to cede Tournai to France, Oxford not only accepted that it was essential to Dutch security but he knew that the French would ultimately give it up. In these circumstances, Oxford could argue persuasively that to make peace without the allies at the moment when they were ready to settle would put the worst possible face on the ministry's conduct both at home and abroad. Harcourt swung over to Oxford's side, Shrewsbury and Buckingham probably did the same; and Bolingbroke's proposal for an immediate settlement was dropped.

The encounter must have been a stormy one. Following the meeting, the Queen is said to have wept all night. Oxford took sick with "an ugly fit of the Rheumatism." Bolingbroke withdrew to the country, presumably to ponder his defeat, and it was variously reported that he would be dismissed.[95] In Bath, Dr. Stratford heard a report given out by the Whigs "that there is a great breach betwixt my Lord Treasurer and Lord Bolingbroke. I hear Lord Bolingbroke is at Ashden Park with Sir William Wyndham to hunt for some days. It is not a proper season for diversion, if he has acted a part that must be fatal to him, but I hope it is only given out by those who wish it."[96] Dartmouth, now officially in charge of the correspondence with France and smarting under Bolingbroke's open contempt, found his position intolerable and offered to resign. Erasmus Lewis informed Oxford that Dartmouth conceived it "impossible for him to live with Lord B, and as impossible for you to be without him during the negotiation. My Lord Dartmouth is

[95] L'Hermitage to the States-General, 3/14, 7/18 October 1712, *ibid.*, ff. 371, 374; Swift, *Journal to Stella*, II, 561, 565; Boyer, *History*, p. 605; Robethon to Baron de Grote, 15/26 November 1712, Macpherson, *Original Papers*, II, 358–9.
[96] Dr. Stratford to Lord Harley, 6 October 1712, HMC, *Portland MSS*, VII, 93.

therefore free and willing to retire, and says you may depend upon his readiness to serve you, as much as if he continued in employment."[97] The Queen persuaded Dartmouth to stay on;[98] but within a few months Bolingbroke recovered his ascendancy in the negotiations, and the elaborate efforts of Prior and later of Shrewsbury to show Dartmouth due deference in their official dispatches only confirm the insignificance of his role.[99] Bolingbroke's treatment of Dartmouth must have been particularly offensive to Oxford. Dartmouth was a moderate, and a loyal supporter of the Treasurer, and his resignation would have weakened Oxford's hold on the ministry.

Though Bolingbroke had been forced to retreat, he was still able to exert some influence on the making of the peace and his differences with Oxford remained unresolved. Bolingbroke urged haste while Oxford tarried; and the new barrier treaty proposed to the Dutch bore the hard stamp of the Secretary's hand.[100] The ill feeling between them was still further exacerbated when, that same autumn, Oxford and several others were awarded the Garter. According to Oxford, the Secretary "fell into the utmost rage about not being one."[101] Bolingbroke presumably thought this was an opportunity for the Queen to bestow upon him that mark of favor he had earlier been denied.[102] Once again he was passed over, and it is likely that, as he had blamed Oxford in the matter of his peerage, he held him responsible for this slight as well. His appointment as Lord Lieutenant of Essex cannot have gone very far to assuage his wounded pride.[103] Bolingbroke after-

[97] Lewis to Oxford, 14 October 1712, HMC, *Portland MSS*, V, 234–5. See also Lewis to Oxford, 6, 13 October 1712, *ibid.*, pp. 231–2, 234, for Bolingbroke's "rough" treatment of Dartmouth.

[98] Queen Anne to Oxford, 21 October 1712. HMC, *Bath MSS*, I, 222.

[99] *Bolingbroke Correspondence*, III and IV, *passim*.

[100] Bolingbroke to Oxford, October 1712, HMC, *Portland MSS*, V, 241–2. MacLachlan, "The Great Peace," pp. 604–13.

[101] Oxford, "Account of Public Affairs," HMC, *Portland MSS*, V, 467.

[102] [Mallet], *Memoirs of the Life and Ministerial Conduct, . . . of the Late Lord Visc. Bolingbroke*, pp. 270–1.

[103] L'Hermitage to the States-General, 7/18 October 1712, BM, Add. MSS, 17,677FFF, f. 375.

wards wrote that in those stormy months he thought of quitting the ministry. He did not resign: "I thought my mistress treated me ill, but the sense of that duty which I owed her came in aid of other considerations, and prevailed over my resentment."[104] But neither did he cease to build his own following: "The Divisions between these two great Men, began to split the Court into Parties," Swift later observed.[105] Through the autumn Swift tried repeatedly to bring the ministers together but in December he wrote despondently to Stella: "Tis impossible to save People against their own will; and I have been too much engaged in Patch-work already."[106]

Parliament was repeatedly prorogued through the early months of 1713 while the government awaited the conclusion of the peace. A number of points relating to trading privileges in North America were still in negotiation with the French; and the allies daily found new obstacles to signing. The ministers reasoned that the session would be easier if they could present to Parliament the final argeement with France at least; and Oxford was still inclined to wait on the allies on the grounds that a general settlement would command wider parliamentary support.[107] But as the winter dragged on, the ministers' patience wore thin. Bolingbroke represented to the French that if the negotiations were not speedily concluded, the Queen would ask Parliament for supplies to continue the war; and toward the end of March Oxford finally instructed the British Plenipotentiaries at Utrecht to sign with or without the Dutch.[108] The French at length gave in, and early in April the Dutch agreed to sign. But the delays inflamed the party debate: the Tories grew impatient, the Whigs stepped up their propaganda and continued to plot their parliamentary cam-

104 Bolingbroke, "A Letter to Sir William Windham," *Works*, I, 118.
105 Swift, "An Enquiry," p. 152.
106 Swift, *Journal to Stella*, II, 580. See *ibid.*, pp. 556, 568–9 for Swift's efforts to patch up the quarrel.
107 MacLachlan, "The Great Peace," pp. 619–20.
108 Bolingbroke to Shrewsbury, 17 February 1713, *Bolingbroke Correspondence*, III, 422–3; Oxford to Strafford, 20/31 March 1713, BM, Add. MSS, 31149, f. 221, quoted in MacLachlan, "The Great Peace," pp. 632–3.

paign. Bolingbroke, while he thought both Houses favorably disposed toward the peace, feared the effects of the expected Whig attack and urged that more be done to strengthen the government's position. "The long suspence of the treaty gives hopes to this faction, and consequently increases their clamour, and whets their rage," he complained to Strafford; "whilst those who wish well to their country, and who, thanks be to God! are a vast majority in every part of the kingdom, grow tired with expectation, and uneasy under the delay."[109] He called again for the removal of those Whigs remaining in office and assured a group of October men "he would use his utmost efforts to bring . . . [Oxford] to pursue more resolute and steady measures."[110] And he told Shrewsbury, with fulsome apologies for his indiscretion, that given the present, essentially favorable, political situation, "if we do not establish ourselves, and the true interest of our country, it is the Queen's and Treasurer's fault."[111]

Oxford did in fact take some steps to consolidate Tory support. General Cadogan, a Whig and a close associate of Marlborough, had been dismissed from all his appointments in January; and immediately before the opening of Parliament Lord Cholmondeley, the Treasurer of the Household, and Lord Chief Justice Parker, both Whigs, were dismissed from their places after they had spoken against the peace. Early in April Harcourt was promoted to the Lord Chancellorship and two months later Atterbury, the High Church Dean of Carlisle, was made Bishop of Rochester at Harcourt's insistent request.[112] To the Scottish Jacobite George Lockhart the Treasurer held out the hope that some new Justices of the

[109] Bolingbroke to Strafford, 19 March 1713, *Bolingbroke Correspondence*, III, 493-4.
[110] *The Lockhart Papers*, I, 412-13. See also Swift, *Journal to Stella*, II, 656.
[111] Bolingbroke to Shrewsbury, 3 March 1713, *Bolingbroke Correspondence*, IV, 489.
[112] Bolingbroke to Shrewsbury, 8 April 1713, *ibid.*, 29-30; Swift, *Journal to Stella*, II, 656; Burnet, *History*, VI, 176, and Dartmouth's note.

Peace might be appointed when he urged him to "hasten up" his friends against the opening of Parliament.[113] But at the same time he was actively—and secretly—seeking Whig support; and there were rumors that once the peace was signed, he would throw in his lot with the Whigs.[114]

Oxford's behavior, ambiguous and indecisive in part for reasons of policy, was nonetheless a matter of some concern to his friends. His illnesses were frequent, and he seems to have become more dilatory than ever in attending to business. In January the Queen, no doubt mindful of the crisis the year before, reminded him to send off the proxies for the Scottish peers.[115] From Paris both Prior and Torcy complained of his silence.[116] Swift wrote that all the Treasurer's friends "repine, & shrug their shoulders, but will not deel with him so freely as they ought."[117] And his brother begged him to take "a timely care" against the difficulties of the forthcoming session: "As your lordship is the Spring of Every thing so it is not possible they should move a right Without your continual direction in order to Which, the appointment of some time when your lordship would be attended by such in Whom you will confide Would lend very much to your own Ease and dispatch of Business."[118] Oxford later referred to a confederation formed against him at the beginning of the parliamentary session, and in a letter written in March 1714, he remarked that he had "been long endeavoring for more than a twelve month,

113 Oxford to Lockhart, 9 February 1713, BM, Portland Loan, 29/150.

114 See Halifax's letters to Oxford in BM, Portland Loan, 29/151, and HMC, *Portland MSS*, V, 254-93, *passim*. Swift, *Journal to Stella*, II, 643-4; *Wentworth Papers*, pp. 324-5.

115 Queen Anne to Oxford, 3 January 1713, HMC, *Bath MSS*, I, 225. The previous August she had reminded him of the proxies of the Scottish peers serving in Flanders. *Ibid.*, p. 219.

116 Prior to Oxford, 26/15 February, 16/5 April 1713, BM, Portland Loan, 29/154.

117 Swift, *Journal to Stella*, II, 607.

118 Auditor Harley to Oxford, 9 February 1713, BM, Portland Loan, 29/143.

to find a fair day to make a retreat in."[119] Whether or not he had thoughts of resigning in the winter of 1712–13, the quarrel with Bolingbroke had not been laid to rest; on the contrary, it threatened to split the ministry. Outwardly at least, Oxford responded by continuing as before; but his withdrawal from business foreshadowed a pattern that would increasingly characterize his political conduct.

Parliament finally met at the beginning of April, and in the first few weeks it seemed as if Bolingbroke's fears would prove groundless. The government withstood the Whig attack in both Houses, and its majorities seemed secure. A motion proposed by the Scottish lords to bring in a bill to dissolve the Union received widespread Whig support, by which, the Whig Arthur Onslow later observed, "I believe they meant only the distressing of the ministry." But the motion was defeated in the Lords and never introduced in the Commons.[120] Then in May it appeared that the opposition would concentrate its fire on the commercial articles of the treaty with France. The objection to the commercial treaty, which provided for a much freer trade between the two countries, was based in part on the genuine fear that its economic consequences would be harmful, in part on a general suspicion that no good could come from a closer relationship with France. The ministry's foes viewed the commercial treaty as one more manifestation of the pro-French policy they deplored.[121] The Whigs, said Bolingbroke, were endeavoring "to raise a ferment among the people, by scanning, straining, and misrepresenting every article, nay, every syllable in it; and propagating with wonderful industry, that all trade whatever with France is prejudicial to Britain."[122] Petitions flowed in from merchants

[119] Oxford to [?], 21 March 1714, BM, Portland Loan, 29/12.

[120] Burnet, *History*, VI, 159–61, and Onslow's notes. *The Lockhart Papers*, I, 414–37.

[121] For the commercial treaty, see Trevelyan, *England under Queen Anne*, III, 254–8.

[122] Bolingbroke to Prior, 31 May 1713, *Bolingbroke Correspondence*, IV, 152–3.

and manufacturers, deputations appeared before both Houses of Parliament to present evidence of the hardships their trade would suffer. And while all this was going on, "we act as if we had nothing to do, but get this Session over any how," Bolingbroke complained to Shrewsbury. "No principal of government established and avowed, nobody but my Lord Treasurer, and he cannot be in every place and speak to every man, able to hold out hopes and fears, or give a positive answer to any one question."[123] The Whigs' efforts, combined with the representations of the trading community, were in the end successful. According to Burnet, the treaty was "very feebly maintained by those who argued for it"; and at the third reading the House of Commons threw out by nine votes the bill that would have made the commercial articles effective.[124] The defeat in the lower House was unexpected—the government had anticipated that its principal difficulties would come in the Lords—and it was accomplished by the defection of a number of Tories, led by Sir Thomas Hanmer, who joined the Whigs in opposition. These "Whimsicals," or Hanoverian Tories, bound together by their fear that the ministry's pro-French policy threatened the Hanoverian succession, emerged as a group of considerable power. In this instance they were apprehensive about the economic effects of the treaty as well, but in all matters that touched on the succession, they would in future be a force to reckon with.[125]

Oxford was widely blamed for the defeat. "Lord T——— did not labour in it heartily saying he left it intirely to them, if they did not think it for the advantage of England," Peter

[123] Bolingbroke to Shrewsbury, 29 May 1713, *ibid.*, 139.

[124] Burnet, *History*, VI, 163-4.

[125] Somewhere between seventy and eighty Tories joined Hanmer in opposition. Dickinson, *Bolingbroke*, p. 108; McInnes, *Robert Harley*, p. 156 and note 22. For the Hanoverian Tories, see Holmes, *British Politics in the Age of Anne*, pp. 280-4. He emphasizes that there was a number of different elements within the group and that their vote was a "variable and unpredictable factor" (p. 283).

Wentworth wrote.[126] By other accounts, he had been advised to let the matter drop until the next session but had refused, confident the government interest would prevail.[127] But according to Swift, "Ld T—— said both to others and my self, that he did not care whether this Parlmt passt the Commerce or no, and that the next should have the Honor of it."[128] Whatever Oxford's attitude, he cannot have been pleased by the defeat; but Bolingbroke's chagrin was unconcealed.[129] He was deeply committed to the commercial treaty and its rejection was for him a personal rebuff. "Indeed, my Lord, we make a despicable figure in the world," he wrote the Treasurer. "You have retrieved many a bad game in your time; for God's sake make one push for government."[130] To Prior and to Shrewsbury he deplored the defeat, and, without naming Oxford, made it clear that he felt the Treasurer's indifference and mismanagement were to blame. He would not, he said, have minded so much defeat at the hands of "an insolent enemy's superior force," but

our enemies are in themselves contemptible, and our friends are well inclined. The former have no strength but what we might have taken from them, and the latter no dissatisfaction, but what we might have prevented. Let the game which we have, be wrested out of our hands; this I can bear: but to play, like children, with it, till it slips between our fingers to the ground, and sharpers have but to stoop and take it up; this consideration distracts a man of spirit, and not to be vexed in this case, is not to be sensible.[131]

126 Peter Wentworth to Strafford, 23 June 1713, *Wentworth Papers*, p. 338.

127 Esther Vanhomrigh to Swift, 23 June 1713, *Swift Correspondence*, I, 368; *Wentworth Papers*, pp. 337-8.

128 Swift to Charles Ford, 9 July 1713, *Swift Correspondence*, I, 375.

129 Dr. Stratford to Lord Harley, 18, 23, 25 June 1713, HMC, *Portland MSS*, VII, 143-6.

130 Bolingbroke to Oxford, June 1713, *ibid.*, pp. 299-300.

131 Bolingbroke to Prior, 25 July 1713, *Bolingbroke Correspondence*, IV, 201.

In Bolingbroke's view Oxford had not done enough to cut into Whig strength or to allay Tory dissatisfactions: he had in effect watched while the Whigs organized the government's defeat. That the Secretary had himself misjudged the temper of the Commons, that he failed to recognize the depth of feeling against the treaty among Tories as well as Whigs, did not enter his reckoning. Significantly in terms of his own future, he failed to appreciate the seriousness of the deepening divisions among the Tories.

Auditor Harley relates that

about this time Lord Bolingbroke, Lord Harcourt, and the now Bishop of Rochester fell into a strict alliance, and endeavoured to raise a great prejudice in the Church party against the Treasurer, upbraiding him for not being a sincere Churchman as they called it; and to make this pass had got lists out of every office of the names of such persons as they called Whigs, who were continued in their employments. The Lord Bolingbroke told me, if your brother will not set himself at the head of the Church party, somebody must.[132]

This was an open challenge. Oxford was hardly prepared to set himself at the head of the Church party, but on July 25 he wrote Bolingbroke a letter intended to reestablish his authority and at the same time to provide a basis for strengthening the ministry. Oxford summarized this letter, which he notes Mrs. Masham had seen and approved, in his "brief Account": he outlined a number of ministerial changes, including Bromley's appointment as Secretary of State in Dartmouth's place, and he professed "his desire to consult with him (lord Bolingbroke) how to unite the rest of our friends"; but much of the rest of the letter was devoted to a detailed criticism of Bolingbroke's negligence in the affairs of his department.[133] In reply, Bolingbroke assured the Treasurer that he would "never engage in

---

[132] Edward Harley, "Memoirs," HMC, *Portland MSS*, V, 660.
[133] Oxford, "A brief Account of Public Affairs," *Parliamentary History*, VI, ccxlviii.

any other interest, . . . but yours, and that of those friends with whom I now serve." Presumably because Bromley's promotion would strengthen Oxford's position, he questioned whether it was wise to remove Bromley as Speaker: "Can Mr. Bromley be in any post so useful as in the chair?" And he recapitulated the Tory diagnosis of the government's ills: the best use was not drawn from those who served the Queen, "either from want of encouragement to some, or want of using authority over others"; something must be done about "those who make use of the Queen's favour against her service and against her servants." Oxford was overburdened with work, and could not therefore supervise: "You are pulling at the beam when you should be in the box whipping and reining in, as the journey you have to go or the ways you pass through require. Separate, in the name of God, the chaff from the wheat," Bolingbroke implored the Treasurer, "and consider who you have left to employ; assign them their parts; trust them as far as it is necessary for the execution each of his part; let the forms of business be regularly carried on in Cabinet, and the secret of it in your own closet. Your Lordship would soon find those excellent principles, laid down in the Queen's Speech, pursued with vigour and success."[134]

This was, of course, a plea for party government, and it was a bold attempt on Bolingbroke's part to assert his own authority. "I am amazed at Lord Bolingbroke's demands," Dr. Stratford wrote to Lord Harley, "but . . . perhaps he may succeed. He will not be the only example where impudence has been of more use than merit, but the love I have for your father makes me wish he would think a little, whether it can be for his service to let the world see that he can be overborne."[135] But Oxford held his ground. Bromley, his staunch ally, was made Secretary of State, but Dartmouth remained in the ministry as Lord Privy Seal; and Sir Thomas Hanmer agreed to

---

[134] Bolingbroke to Oxford, 27 July 1713, HMC, *Portland MSS*, V, 311–12.
[135] Dr. Stratford to Lord Harley, 2 August 1713, HMC, *Portland MSS*, VII, 161.

stand for Speaker in the new Parliament. Bolingbroke became senior Secretary of State and his friend Sir William Wyndham moved up from Secretary-at-War to Chancellor of the Exchequer; but at the same time the Earl of Mar took office as Secretary of State for Scotland and the Earl of Findlater as Chancellor in Scotland, appointments that cut into the administrative provinces and the influence of Bolingbroke and Harcourt. The Scottish appointments "made Lord Bol——— stare," Erasmus Lewis reported.[136] And Oxford recorded with great satisfaction "the rage this [the changes] caused, as perfectly defeating their scheme."[137]

Oxford's new scheme was a conscious attempt to undercut Bolingbroke's position, and temporarily at least, it accomplished its purpose. There were rumors that Bolingbroke would resign and, alternatively, that he was to be dismissed; he told Strafford that the necessity for unity made him "pass over mortifications, which I would have been crucified rather than have endured."[138] Curiously, Oxford told Swift the following year that he had had no power since July 25, 1713, the date of his letter to Bolingbroke.[139] Thus he placed his loss of power at precisely the moment when he was moving to save himself. Conceivably he thought then that his position was hopeless; conceivably his interview with Lady Masham convinced him that she had turned against him, though he said that she approved the substance of his letter. There seems no reasonable explanation for his choosing July 25; but shortly thereafter an incident occurred that seriously damaged his standing with the Queen.

At the end of August Oxford went down to Cambridge-

---

[136] Newsletter to Dartmouth, unsigned but written by Lewis, 8 September 1713, HMC, *Dartmouth MSS*, I, 318.

[137] Oxford, "A brief Account of Public Affairs," *Parliamentary History*, VI, ccxlvii.

[138] Bolingbroke to Strafford, 2 September 1713, *Bolingbroke Correspondence*, IV, 261-2. See also Dr. Stratford to Lord Harley, 16 August 1713, HMC, *Portland MSS*, VII, 164.

[139] Oxford to Swift, 27 July 1714, *Swift Correspondence*, II, 85.

shire to celebrate his son's marriage to the daughter of the late
Duke of Newcastle. By Oxford's own account, on his return
"the Treasurer was so unfortunate as to ask a favour of the
Queen which was not agreeable to her Majesty to grant." He
spoke also of his "never enough to be lamented folly in mentioning to her Majesty the titles."[140] In the "Letter to Sir
William Windham," Bolingbroke wrote that he had heard,
"and I believe truly, that when he [Oxford] returned to
Windsor in the autumn of seventeen hundred and thirteen,
after the marriage of his son, he pressed extremely to have him
created Duke of Newcastle or Earl of Clare."[141] These, then,
were the titles the Queen had refused to grant. Whatever
Oxford's motivation in asking—and the wishes of the dowager
Duchess of Newcastle played some part[142]—he miscalculated
badly. Whether, in the Queen's view, he overstepped the
bounds of propriety in asking for the titles, or whether she
thought the request itself presumptuous, the result was the
same. Though he had raised the question only with Lady
Masham and the Queen, and had kept his promise "never to
speak of it since directly or indirectly, not to the nearest relation I had," still, he wrote, "this was made my crime."[143]

The knowledge that he had offended his royal mistress
seems to have shaken Oxford's confidence. Whatever strength
he had gained at the end of the summer, whatever resolution he
had demonstrated, was dissipated in the course of the autumn.
He began drinking heavily; and in November he was pro-
foundly shaken by the death of his eldest daughter. He was ill
much of the time and for weeks on end unable to attend to
public business. His complaints were real enough—chronic
inflammation of the eyes, fits of the gravel, rheumatism, gout—
but he seemed to court them. The old admonitions to "take
more care of yourself" grew more urgent and more frequent.

[140] Oxford, "Account of Public Affairs," HMC, *Portland MSS*, V, 466, 468.
[141] Bolingbroke, *Works*, I, 122.
[142] Edward Harley, "Memoirs," HMC, *Portland MSS*, V, 658.
[143] Oxford, "Account of Public Affairs," HMC, *Portland MSS*, V, 466.

"I am truly sorry, my Lord," Shrewsbury wrote in October, when Oxford's indisposition had continued intermittently for three months,

to hear the pain hangs so long upon you, and uneasy to give you any trouble at this time; yet I cannot forbear being impertinent out of my way, and telling you I heartily wish you would bring yourself into a method of keeping better hours. I know by experience that nothing is more prejudicial to a strong constitution, and more destructive to a weak one, than late hours of eating and sleeping.[144]

When he was well, he was negligent in the conduct of affairs, and the Queen complained of his obscurity: "I can not help desireing you againe when you com next, to speake plainly, lay everything open and hide nothing from me, or els how is it possible I can judg of anything. I spoke very freely and sincerely to you yesterday, and I expect you should do the same to her that is sincerly your affectionate friend."[145]

Bolingbroke made the most of the Lord Treasurer's incapacity. He was, of necessity, in more frequent communication with the Queen and he sought by conscientious attendance to insinuate himself into the royal favor.[146] At the same time, he seems to have succeeded in gaining Lady Masham. There had been rumors of jealousy between Lady Masham and the Treasurer the year before, and the fact that in July he had consulted her about his new scheme suggests that he feared losing her support. Swift spoke of "a Coldness between this Lady and the first Minister," which he ascribed to Oxford's neglect of her.[147] By the Auditor's account, "the Lady Masham, following the example of the Duchess of Marlborough, thought nothing ought to be done without her privity and consent, and finding

[144] Shrewsbury to Oxford, 9 October 1713, HMC, *Bath MSS*, I, 240–1.
[145] Queen Anne to Oxford, 8 December 1713, *ibid.*, p. 243.
[146] See for example Bolingbroke to Queen Anne, 17 December 1713, *Bolingbroke Correspondence*, IV, 394. Schutz to Roberthon, 4/15 December 1713, BM, Stowe MSS, 225, ff. 321–2.
[147] Swift, "An Enquiry," p. 153.

the Treasurer could not be brought into those corrupt measures that might fully gratify her avarice, she set herself against the Treasurer."[148] The Auditor relates that Bolingbroke bribed Lady Masham with promises of shares in the trade falling to Britain as a consequence of the Utrecht Treaty; and while this was never established, it was widely believed and may well have been true. In any case, it seems certain that by the end of 1713 she had shifted her allegiance to Bolingbroke.

In November Dr. Stratford wrote Lord Harley that he had heard Bolingbroke "broke out into these expressions against your father, 'I and *Lady Masham* have bore him upon our shoulders, and have made him what he is, and he now leaves *us* where *we* were.' "[149] Lady Masham's feelings are understandable at least to some extent without reference to imputations of bribery and corruption. Loyal to the Queen and aware of her failing health, Lady Masham daily saw the strain Oxford's conduct imposed upon her royal mistress. Furthermore, she did, apparently, believe with Bolingbroke that a direct commitment to party government would quiet the storms in the ministry. These considerations, together with whatever financial inducements he may have held out to her, led Lady Masham to align herself with Bolingbroke. And while her role was in no sense decisive in the final struggle, her defection weakened Oxford's position: at the moment when he was, by all accounts, losing favor with the Queen, he could ill afford to lose the good offices of the royal favorite.

"While the Queen's Favour to the Earl was thus gradually lessening," Swift wrote,

the Breaches between Him and his Friends grew every day wider, which he looked on with great Indifference, and seemed to have his Thoughts only turned upon finding out some proper Opportunity for delivering up his Staff; But this Her Majesty would not

[148] Edward Harley, "Memoirs," HMC, *Portland MSS*, V, 661.
[149] Dr. Stratford to Lord Harley, 26 November 1713, HMC, *Portland MSS*, VII, 174.

then admit, because indeed it was not easy to determine who should succeed him.[150]

Swift's final comment points to the difficulty of Bolingbroke's position. While he and Harcourt now headed their own growing following, it was questionable how much added strength they could command. The Hanoverian Tories were more suspicious of Bolingbroke's intentions than Oxford's, and Bromley's influence among the High Tories was thrown to Oxford's side. Discontent with Oxford was not equivalent to support of Bolingbroke. Thus through the autumn of 1713 Bolingbroke waited, urging Oxford to more decisive action, sending him extravagant compliments on the marriage of his son and condolences on the death of his daughter. "No person, even in your own family and among those who are nearest to you, can take a more sincere part in all the good and bad fortune which happens to you than I do," he wrote the Treasurer in November.[151] But Oxford was not deceived. In December, in answer to an accusing letter from the Treasurer, Bolingbroke protested:

I can truly say I am ready to contribute all the little in my sphere whenever your commands direct me. The only reason why I did not attend you this week was the belief that you intended to be here to-day, and therefore, pray my Lord, do not once entertain a thought that I give myself airs, or have the least luke-warmness. I see a man here every night that does the former with a witness. The pigmy stretches and struts, and fancies himself a giant.[152]

Oxford noted that the pigmy who fancied himself a giant was Dartmouth. Two weeks later the Secretary wrote again to Oxford:

I see an opportunity of giving new strength, new spirit to your administration, and of cementing a firmer union between us, and

[150] Swift, "An Enquiry," p. 154.

[151] Bolingbroke to Oxford, 19 November 1713, HMC, *Portland MSS*, V, 360.

[152] Bolingbroke to Oxford, 3 December 1713, *ibid.*, pp. 369–70.

between us and those who must support us. If you go to Windsor alone on Saturday, I'll talk to you on the subject. If I am wrong you will not lose much time in a coach on the road. Believe me for once, what I always am, and have been to you, sincere, however I may have been too warm and your Lordship, allow the expression, too jealous.[153]

Bolingbroke probably was this time sincere. In the "Letter to Sir William Windham" he pauses in the midst of a lengthy diatribe against Oxford to remark that as late as the winter before the Queen's death, Oxford might still have restored his credit and "acquired the confidence of the whole party."

I say he might have done all this; because I am persuaded that none of those I have named were so convinced of his perfidy, so jaded with his yoke, or so much piqued personally against him as I was: and yet if he would have exerted himself in concert with us, to improve the few advantages which were left us, and to ward off the visible danger which threatened our persons and our party, I would have stifled my private animosity, and would have acted under him with as much zeal as ever.[154]

However little zeal Bolingbroke had shown for serving under Oxford, his future, and the future of the party, depended upon a government safe in Tory hands. He hoped the hands would ultimately be his own but he knew that in the present circumstances he was not strong enough to act, alone. Had Oxford been prepared to alter his policy, there is every reason to believe that Bolingbroke would have joined with him. But Oxford had no intention of altering his course. He was, as Bolingbroke said, "incapable of taking such a turn."[155] Unless Oxford resigned, the battle would be fought to the finish. "A Country Vicar must quote Texts," Swift wrote. "Two men shall be in the Field, the one shall be taken, and the other left; but how soon, or which shall be taken, and which left, is a shuddering question."[156]

[153] Bolingbroke to Oxford, 17 December 1713, *ibid.*, p. 373.
[154] Bolingbroke, *Works*, I, 123.
[155] *Ibid.*
[156] Swift to Charles Ford, 9 July 1713, *Swift Correspondence*, I, 375.

CHAPTER VII

Oxford's Dismissal, Bolingbroke's Defeat

No people were ever in such a condition as ours continued to be from the autumn of one thousand seven hundred and thirteen, to the summer following," Bolingbroke wrote in the "Letter to Sir William Windham."[1] David Mallett thought "there never was a Juncture, within the Memory of any who are now living, when the Rage of Parties ran higher than at this Time."[2] The General Election of August and September 1713 returned another, possibly even larger, Tory majority to the House of Commons, but one in which Hanoverian and Jacobite groups emerged more clearly than in the previous Parliament.[3] The electoral campaign turned on the peace and the succession; and the Whigs, in an effort to detach the Hanoverian Tories from their party allegiance, proclaimed more loudly than ever the ministry's intention to restore the Pretender. "I find by all the pamphlets they give up the distinction of Whig and Tory," Erasmus Lewis wrote,

[1] Bolingbroke, *Works*, I, 126.
[2] [Mallet], *Memoirs of the Life and Ministerial Conduct, . . . of the Late Lord Visc. Bolingbroke*, p. 280.
[3] Holmes calculates the number of committed Jacobites in the House of Commons after the election of 1713 as not less than eighty and "probably in the region of 100." He puts the number of Hanoverian Tories at "an absolute maximum of 75." *British Politics in the Age of Anne*, pp. 279, 283. The Tory majority probably increased in England and Wales but the Whigs gained in Scotland. W. A. Speck, *Tory & Whig: The Struggle in the Constituencies, 1701–1715* (London: Macmillan, 1970), pp. 110, 123.

"and bend all their thoughts to make new distinction between the Tories themselves, as Hanover Tory and Pretender's Tory, English Tory and French Tory, for trade or against it."[4]

The succession was the overriding political issue from the autumn of 1713 until the Queen's death. Between Bolingbroke and Oxford it was an issue of major importance in their struggle for predominance within the ministry. It is generally agreed, with some differences in emphasis, that, while both Oxford and Bolingbroke were in touch with the Pretender and for a time at least prepared to contemplate his restoration on the death of the Queen, Oxford was at bottom for Hanover, while Bolingbroke was more sympathetic to the Stuart cause.[5] Both were attempting to provide against all eventualities, leaving all doors open as long as possible in order to insure their future security. The ministers agreed that a restoration was dependent on the Pretender's changing his religion; James's refusal, early in 1713, to abandon his Roman Catholicism seems to have ruled out the possibility of his succession for Oxford, and probably for Bolingbroke as well.[6] Certainly Bolingbroke

[4] Newsletter, 1 October 1713, HMC, *Dartmouth MSS*, I, 319.

[5] Feiling, *A History of the Tory Party*, pp. 454–60; Trevelyan, *England under Queen Anne*, III, 248–50, 266–9; F. Salomon, *Geschichte des letzten Ministeriums Königin Annas* (Gotha, 1894); H. N. Fieldhouse, "Bolingbroke's Share in the Jacobite Intrigue of 1710–14," *English Historical Review*, LII (1937), 44–59. For the ministers' correspondence with James and his agents, see HMC, *Stuart Papers*, I, *passim*, and the letters printed as an appendix to Salomon, *Geschichte des letzten Ministeriums Königin Annas*. For the correspondence with Hanover see Macpherson, *Original Papers*, II, *passim;* and BM, Stowe MSS, 225–7. Dickinson, *Bolingbroke*, pp. 117–18; McInnes, *Robert Harley*, pp. 168–70.

[6] See his letters to Oxford and to Bolingbroke, 3 March 1714, N.S., printed in the appendix to Salomon, *Geschichte des letzten Ministeriums Königin Annas*, pp. 339–41. Feiling and particularly Trevelyan emphasize Bolingbroke's close connection with the Jacobite Tories and suggest that he never ruled out the possibility of a restoration. But the most recent study of the question states flatly that from the time of James's refusal to renounce his religion, "Oxford and Bolingbroke dismissed the Jacobite cause." J. H. and Margaret Shennan, "The Protestant Succession in English Politics, April 1713–September 1715," in *William III and Louis XIV. Essays,*

rejected any thought of bringing James over while the Queen lived. But it is nonetheless true that in the last years of Anne's reign, while the Whigs and Hanoverian Tories accused the ministry as a whole of being in the Pretender's interest, Bolingbroke was particularly suspect. He courted the Jacobite interest in Parliament, and while he never seems to have gone beyond "hints and innuendos," he led at least some of the Jacobite leaders to believe "he really design'd the King's [James's] restauration," but that Oxford stood in the way.[7] Rumors that he had been in touch with James on his visit to France in 1712 persisted, and in the spring of 1714 it was widely believed that the disputes in the ministry turned around the question of the succession. "It has been thought proper to insinuate to the world, that I leaned to another interest, and that the disputes which have lately happened at Court were occasioned by the favour of some men to the Pretender's cause," Bolingbroke wrote to Strafford in May 1714. He wished well to the Protestant succession, he declared, but "my duty and allegiance are to the Queen, during her time, and my respect shall be paid the successor in no manner which is inconsistent with the first obligation. After the Queen, if I live after her, I will be true to my principle, and to my call, at the expence of all I have."[8] This is probably an honest statement, and in its emphasis and phrasing it does not preclude the possibility that he might be called to serve a Stuart king.

The ministers were, of course, officially committed to Hanover, and so was the Queen. But while there is no indication that the Queen made any move in the direction of her half-brother—"Oh fye . . . there is no such thing wt do they think I'm a Child, and to be imposed upon," she said to Sir

---

1680–1720, by and for Mark A. Thomson, ed. by R. Hatton and J. S. Bromley (Liverpool University Press, 1968), pp. 252–70.

7 *The Lockhart Papers*, I, 460, 413. See also *ibid.*, pp. 412–13, 441–4.

8 Bolingbroke to Strafford, 18 May 1714, *Bolingbroke Correspondence*, IV, 530–1.

David Hamilton when he mentioned his fear of the Pretender's coming in[9]—she was known to dislike the family of Hanover and she would not tolerate in her servants what she viewed as excessive solicitude for her successors. Her attitude made the position of the ministers extremely difficult. To combat Whig propaganda and regain Whimsical support they needed to make some strong gesture in favor of Hanover, but to do this would antagonize the Queen. Thus through the last six months of the reign, Bolingbroke, in attempting to win the Queen's support, tended to represent Oxford as placing the interests of Hanover ahead of the interests of the Queen. And Oxford, for his part, did little to quiet the rumors that Bolingbroke was for the Pretender. Archbishop King was right when he observed to Swift that "all your contests so farr as I understand them have no other foundation, but who shall have the ministry and employments the gaining these has no connexion with the Pretender, you may have them without him or under him."[10]

In this turbulent political atmosphere, the fate of the nation seemed more than ever tied to the life of the Queen. The consternation was therefore great when, in December 1713, she fell seriously ill at Windsor. Bolingbroke was at Windsor: Oxford was not. "I arrive here at this moment and find our good mistress extremely ill," Bolingbroke informed the Treasurer on December 24. "Her case you will have particularly from Dr. Arbuthnot. Her symptoms are the same as in her last ague, but stronger and more severe. God in his mercy preserve

[9] Hertfordshire R.O., Panshanger MSS, Sir David Hamilton's Diary, f. 46. Trevelyan, *England under Queen Anne*, III, 277. In a letter to the Duchess of Marlborough, the Queen wrote that the Jacobites "are as much my enemies as the papists, and I am very sensible that these people will always have designs against me." Sarah later endorsed the letter: "I think in this letter it is plain she does not intend to put herself into the hands of the Jacobites, and I never could observe that she had any scruples about wearing the crown, nor any inclination to those that were in that interest." Queen Anne to the Duchess of Marlborough, n.d., HMC, *Eighth Report, Appendix, Part I*, 52a.

[10] Archbishop King to Swift, 13 January 1714, *Swift Correspondence*, II, 3.

her. Let us see you here without delay."[11] Oxford did not come. On Christmas Day Bolingbroke wrote still more urgently: "We expected your Lordship here this morning with the utmost impatience. . . . I am now with most of your friends of the Council, who most heartily wish you here, and I suppose Dr. Arbuthnot sent you word yesterday that the Queen expressed a desire to see you. Your Lordship is the best judge what measure to take, but surely in all events and in all respects you should be here."[12] Bromley regretted that "we have not the satisfaction and support your Lordship's company would give us here," and added that he found "the Lords impatiently wish for you here, and hope they shall see you before to-morrow at noon."[13] Lewis was more direct: " 'Tis with the utmost concern that I tell you that besides the pain everybody suffers from the Queen's illness, we have the additional uneasiness of your not being here, which is the second topic of discourse, and I take the liberty to tell you everybody stands amazed at it."[14]

Oxford did in due course go down to Windsor, but by the time he arrived the crisis was over and the Queen well on the way to recovery.[15] His conduct seems as extraordinary now as it did then. Swift offered one explanation when he said that, in order to stop the report of the Queen's death, the Treasurer "appeared next day abroad in his Chariot with a pair of Horses, and did not go down to Windsor till his usuall Time."[16] Swift records an earlier occasion when the Treasurer had done the

[11] Bolingbroke to Oxford, 24 December 1713, HMC, *Portland MSS*, V, 374.

[12] Bolingbroke to Oxford, 25 December 1713, *ibid.*, p. 374.

[13] Bromley to Oxford, 25 December 1713, *ibid.*, p. 375.

[14] Lewis to Oxford, 25 December 1713, *ibid.*, p. 375.

[15] Oxford probably went to Windsor on December 26 or 27. L'Hermitage reported on 29 December/9 January 1713–14 that the Treasurer was returning to London the following day. BM, Add. MSS, 17,677HHH. Swift writes in "An Enquiry," p. 154: "Upon his Arrivall there, the Danger was over."

[16] Swift, "An Enquiry," p. 154.

same,[17] but the situations were hardly comparable. In December 1713 the urgent summons first from Bolingbroke, then from Lewis and Bromley, left no doubt of the emergency. It is simply not possible to believe that Oxford delayed in order to stop rumors of the Queen's death: for all he knew, they might be true. Rather, it seems most reasonable to view his behavior in the context of his withdrawal from affairs through the course of the autumn. Unsure of his position, reluctant to face either the Queen or his colleagues, unprepared to take hold if the Queen should die, he simply avoided the crisis. He seems to have persuaded himself there was no real emergency: his comment to Prior several weeks later was matter-of-fact, almost casual: "The Queen's gout is going off, she came out into the rooms on Thursday. The alarm arose from her being at Windsor, which I could not dissuade her from staying so long where she likes and found herself so well. You know she has every year an access of an ague."[18]

Oxford's conduct cannot have helped his dwindling credit with the Queen. Swift wrote that during that winter "the Queen's Countenance was wholly changed towards Him, She complained of his Silence and Sullenness, and in return gave him every Day fresh Instances of Neglect or Displeasure."[19] In March Auditor Harley admonished his brother severely.

Permit me to hint that in the present situation the chief thing to be intended is the obtaining an entire confidence with the Queen by an insidious and punctual attendance, and often expressing a resolution to do or hazard anything for her service.

Frequent meetings with some of the Lords and Commons would be of great service. In order to these it is necessary that you should appropriate more time for the despatch of business, by getting out earlier, and being freed from those who are only the

---

[17] In September 1712, Swift wrote: "Yesterday we were allarmed with the Queen's being ill. . . . Lord Treasurer would not come hear from London because it would make a Noise, if he came before his usuall time." *Journal to Stella,* II, 557.

[18] Oxford to Prior, 16/27 January 1714, HMC, *Bath MSS,* III, 444.

[19] Swift, "An Enquiry," pp. 157–8.

leeches of time. The leak that is sprung cannot be stopped without pumping.[20]

At the Treasury Oxford seems to have remained active, and very much in control of the affairs of the department.[21] And on several occasions throughout the spring he exerted himself effectively on other fronts. But he no longer had the will to save himself. Apart from these scattered bursts of activity, he sat out the remaining months of his ministry, until, at the end, he was unable to avert the impending disaster.

If the Queen was displeased with Oxford's conduct during her illness, she was infinitely more so with the behavior of the Whigs, who did not conceal their pleasure at the prospect of her death.[22] It was Bolingbroke's hope that her disgust at these proceedings would persuade her to take strong measures against the Whigs. "None can complain," he wrote, "if, after such attacks, she asserts the honour of her government with vigour, and some degree of severity."[23] He told Strafford he hoped that in the new Parliament "we shall hang more closely together, than we did the last year, and that a number of us shall constantly and warmly debate every point, that, day by day, the Whigs interpose in."[24] To Anglesey, a Whimsical leader, he observed "that unless we are, as Tories, wanting to ourselves, unless we abandon the rules of common prudence, the Church interest, and the Court interest will, for the future during her Majesty's reign, be synonymous terms."[25] But when Parliament met in February the divisions carried over

[20] Auditor Edward Harley to Oxford, 29 March 1714, HMC, *Portland MSS*, V, 405.

[21] McInnes, *Robert Harley*, pp. 159–60; Hill, "The Career of Robert Harley, Earl of Oxford," pp. 350–1.

[22] Swift to Archdeacon Walls, 2 February 1714, *Swift Correspondence*, II, 10; Bolingbroke to Queen Anne, 3 February 1714, *Bolingbroke Correspondence*, IV, 453–4.

[23] Bolingbroke to Shrewsbury, 19 January 1714, *Bolingbroke Correspondence*, IV, 428.

[24] Bolingbroke to Strafford, 13 February 1714, *Bolingbroke Correspondence*, IV, 470.

[25] Bolingbroke to Anglesey, 25 January 1714, *ibid.*, p. 441.

from the old Parliament quickly shattered Bolingbroke's dream of party unity. Sir Thomas Hanmer was duly chosen Speaker. But neither his election nor the dispatch of Oxford's cousin, Thomas Harley, to Hanover with assurances of the ministry's good intentions quieted Whimsical anxieties: fear for the succession continued to outweigh party loyalty for many of them. And while the government fought for its life against a formidable opposition, the struggle between Oxford and Bolingbroke all but paralyzed the ministry. "For God's sake, my Lord, how do you all do, and what do you all do, in your enchanted island?" Prior wrote from Paris. "For the stories we have here, of your irresolutions and misunderstandings, are monstrous."[26]

In March there was an open breach between Bolingbroke and the Treasurer. On March 17 Oxford introduced into the House of Lords a bill declaring it high treason to summon or bring foreign troops into the country. His intention remains mysterious. Some observers, including the Dutch agent in London, assumed the bill was designed to prevent the landing of forces in the Pretender's service and thus to provide for the greater security of the succession in the House of Hanover. If this was so, it represented an attempt on Oxford's part to win Whimsical support. But as Nottingham observed, the bill would also prohibit the summoning of troops to assure the accession of the Hanoverians, thus canceling the clause of the Barrier Treaty by which the Dutch agreed to send forces, if requested, at the Queen's death. Some thought this was Oxford's purpose.[27] The bill was thrown out, but not before Bolingbroke had pointed out that if it was directed against forces raised to restore the Pretender, it was unnecessary: such

---

[26] Prior to Bolingbroke, 9 February 1714, N.S., *ibid.*, pp. 463-4.

[27] Hill suggests that Oxford, alarmed by the effect of rumors that at the time of the Queen's recent illness the Elector was gathering troops to send into England, directed his measure against the landing of all foreign troops, whether in the service of the Elector or the Pretender. Hill, "The Career of Robert Harley, Earl of Oxford," pp. 353-4. Hill cites Oxford to Thomas Harley, 14 March 1714, BM, Add. MSS, 40,621, f. 176, in which Oxford speaks of these rumors, which he terms a "malicious invention."

action was already treasonable under existing law. And to this there was no answer. Clearly the measure was Oxford's own: he had not acted in concert with Bolingbroke. And it is plausible to suppose that it was intended to provide more secure guarantees to Hanover. Bolingbroke's open challenge was then aimed at undercutting the Treasurer's move by showing it to be unnecessary[28] and, by implication, a reflection of his hostility to Hanover.

Bolingbroke's challenge precipitated a crisis in the ministry. On March 22 Lady Masham wrote the Treasurer: "I am surprised at your Lordship desiring me to name what I know will be so disagreeable to her Majesty. I did not expect you ever would send me of such a message; you must excuse me, for I never will carry it, and I hope your Lordship will consider better of it both for the Queen's sake and for your own."[29] The point at issue can only have been Oxford's threatened resignation. His desire to lay down the staff was, of course, not new, but early in March, even before the vote on the foreign forces bill, he seems to have reached a decision. In a memorandum dated March 10 he put the case for resigning. Listing the complaints against him, "he is indolent—unacting, . . . he wil not be head of the Torys," he concluded: "Now is the time to retire. . . . He is not forc'd out by his enemies. . . . He is ready to Answer for his past Conduct—& quitting the stage without any Gross mischance, he can make the residue of his life easier to him self. Having been too long a Prophetic looker on."[30] Harcourt, informed of the Treasurer's intention, begged him to reconsider: "Should your Lordship give way to your resentment, consider how the Queen will be affected by it, what confusion in every part of the public service must

---

[28] L'Hermitage to the States General, 19/30 March 1714, BM, Add. MSS, 17,677HHH, ff. 127-8; News Letter, 18 March 1714, HMC, *Portland MSS*, V, 401.

[29] Lady Masham to Oxford, 22 March 1714, HMC, *Portland MSS*, V, 403.

[30] Memorandum in Oxford's hand, 10 March 1714, BM, Portland Loan, 29/10.

inevitably follow. . . . All I would ask from you is, that you would not come to any resolution till I have an opportunity of speaking fully to you."[31] He would satisfy Oxford that he was "as much at your command now as on the 11th February 1707[-8]," the day he resigned out of loyalty to Oxford following his dismissal from the Godolphin–Marlborough ministry. Oxford replied that he had found himself

A Burden to my Frends and to the only Party, I ever have or wil . . . for many months I have withdrawne myself from every thing but where neglect would be in excusable. When a Retreat happens to be desirable to ones frends, & agreeable to onesonne inclination & Interest it must . . . be right. I think the opportunity very neare and as I desire to have your approbation so I shall desire to have the advantage of your advice when I may the most decently withdraw myself.[32]

The interesting point is that Harcourt would not lend his approbation, nor would Lady Masham, nor would the Queen. It was the Queen who persuaded Oxford to stay on: "There was some talk of laying down, but the Queen overruled the start of passion," Bolingbroke wrote.[33] But Harcourt, and doubtless Bolingbroke, feared that the ministry could not survive Oxford's resignation, at least while Parliament was in session.[34] Negligent, despondent as he was, he still commanded a broader following than they could among the Whigs and

[31] Harcourt to Oxford, 17 March 1714, HMC, *Portland MSS*, V, 400. See also Harcourt to Oxford, 16 March 1714, BM, Portland Loan, 29/138.

[32] Oxford to Harcourt, draft letter, 19 March 1714, BM, Portland Loan, 29/138. For Oxford's desire to resign, see also a draft letter to an unknown correspondent, 21 March 1714, and a memorandum in Oxford's hand, 21 March 1714, *ibid.*, 29/12, 29/10.

[33] Bolingbroke to Strafford, 23 April 1714, *Bolingbroke Correspondence*, IV, 514.

[34] In August 1714 Swift wrote that before he left town at the end of May he had told Oxford he should resign at the end of the parliamentary session but that Bolingbroke "seemed to think otherwise." There was much greater reason to want him to stay on through the session. Swift to Bolingbroke, 7 August 1714, *Swift Correspondence*, II, 109.

those Tories who were strong for Hanover. At the beginning of a parliamentary session in which the succession over-shadowed all other issues, the Tory leadership, surveying the divisions within the party, saw that a decisive split within the ministry would end in their destruction. Bolingbroke's letter, written after Oxford had agreed to stay on, was a nice blend of sincerity and deceit, but it represented a wish to carry on.

I most sincerely desire to see your Lordship, as long as I live, at the head of the Queen's affairs, and of the Church of England party; to see the administration flourish under your direction, the quiet of the Queen's reign secured, and effectual measures taken to put those of our friends who may outlive the Queen beyond the reach of Whig resentment. These, my Lord, are the only views I have, and the only designs I am engaged in.[35]

Yet Bolingbroke despaired that effectual measures would be taken. "The Whigs pursue their plan, with good order, and in concert," he wrote to Strafford. "The Tories stand at gaze, expect the Court should regulate their conduct, and lead them on, and the Court seems in a lethargy. . . . All that can be done is doing, to prevail on our friend, my Lord Treasurer, to alter his measures, to renew a confidence with the Tories, and a spirit in them, and to give a regular motion to all the wheels of government. I am sanguine enough to hope we shall prevail."[36] His optimism did not carry much conviction. Still, in response to Bolingbroke's urgings a number of Whig army officers were dismissed from their posts and ordered to sell their regiments.[37] And at a meeting of ministers and Tory members of the House of Commons early in April, the ministers declared "that the Queen was determined to proceed in the interest of the Church, etc., and my Lord Bolingbroke farther added after-

---

[35] Bolingbroke to Oxford, 27 March 1714, HMC, *Portland MSS*, V, 404. See also Bromley to Oxford, 21 March 1714, *ibid.*, p. 403, for Bromley's efforts to heal Tory divisions.

[36] Bolingbroke to Strafford, 23 March 1714, *Bolingbroke Correspondence*, IV, 494.

[37] Dickinson, *Bolingbroke*, pp. 120–1.

wards that she would not leave a Whig in employ."[38] Some concessions had been made. At the same time, Oxford continued to correspond with his Whig friends.

In the next weeks the ministers, standing together, successfully withstood the Whig attack. Both Houses voted "that the Succession in the House of Hanover was not in danger under her Majesty's government," though the margin in the Lords was extremely narrow, and the Hanoverian Tories joined the Whigs in voting against the government.[39] The Lords addressed the Queen to offer a reward for the apprehension of the Pretender should he attempt to land in Britain or Ireland, but the ministry succeeded in amending the motion to enable her to do so at her discretion. The Treasurer was called upon to account for subsidies paid to certain Highland chieftains who were said to be Jacobites, and, in a rare show of unity, Bolingbroke commended his colleague's defense of government policy.[40] Thus far the ministry had avoided defeat, but it had not regained the support of the Hanoverian Tories. Even though "some of us were empowered to give from the Queen, the utmost assurances, that an honest Tory heart could wish to receive," Bolingbroke wrote, "it happened that this made no impression, and as long as the succession remained in danger, nothing else was, it seemed, to be regarded."[41] This was an admission that in the present circumstances Bolingbroke's High Church scheme was not sufficient to unite the Tories.

[38] A. N. Newman, ed., "Proceedings in the House of Commons, March–June 1714," *Bulletin of the Institute of Historical Research*, XXXIV (1961), 213. This is a fragment from the diary of Sir Edward Knatchbull. See also Bolingbroke to Oxford, 21 April 1714, HMC, *Portland MSS*, V, 425.

[39] The margin in the Lords was only fourteen. Bathurst to Strafford, Peter Wentworth to Strafford, 6 April 1714, *Wentworth Papers*, pp. 362–6. The vote in the Commons was 259 to 208. News Letter, 15 April 1714, *ibid.*, pp. 370–1; Holmes, *British Politics in the Age of Anne*, pp. 282–3.

[40] Oxford admitted the money had been paid to buy off the Highlanders, but he said the subsidy was much less than in King William's time. Bathurst to Strafford, 20 April 1714, *Wentworth Papers*, pp. 373–4.

[41] Bolingbroke to the Lord Chancellor of Ireland, 20 May 1714, *Bolingbroke Correspondence*, IV, 550.

Within the ministry, nothing had changed. "We are disjointed to a degree that nothing could preserve the appearances of our being together," Lewis observed, "if our enemies were wise enough to sit still and see us tear one another to pieces."[42] There were persistent rumors of changes in the ministry and of Oxford's impending dismissal.[43] A memorandum of Oxford's dated May 14, and almost certainly the basis for a conversation with Lady Masham, confirmed her continuing hostility to him.

> You disable a sure friend to serve you.
> And thereby you help nobody.
> *you* can not set any one up
> *you* can pull anyone down. . . .
> What is your scheme?
> The first point is to support the Qu——— in order to yet encorage her . . . do not terrify her with dissent of her fast friends. . . .
> The enemy make their advantage of your Coldness or Anger to L. T. What view can you have in it? . . .
> Has it not done hurt enough to ye Queen already?
> If you hate him however Counterfeit indifference for ye Queens Service.[44]

Lady Masham was in fact rapidly coming to hate the Treasurer, if she had not done so before, and by the beginning of the summer she thought he should resign.

Through the balance of the parliamentary session Oxford and Bolingbroke maneuvered against each other, the last illusions of unity gone. There was a curious unreality about the combat: Oxford wanted only to resign, Bolingbroke loathed him but wanted him to stay. Ultimately it was the Queen who would resolve the issue, but Bolingbroke seems to have thought

[42] E. Lewis to Thomas Harley, 9 April 1714, HMC, *Portland MSS*, V, 413.
[43] *Wentworth Papers*, pp. 375–6; L'Hermitage to the States General, 21 May/1 June 1714, BM, Add. MSS, 17,677 HHH; from Mr. Gatke, 21 May/1 June 1714, BM, Stowe MSS, 227.
[44] Memorandum in Oxford's hand, 14 May 1714, BM, Portland Loan, 29/10.

that if the government survived the session, he could then persuade her to part with Oxford. Bolingbroke presumably felt that he would then have time to rebuild the ministry before the next meeting of Parliament.[45] He looked, eventually, to Oxford's dismissal; but he did not want the Queen to act until he felt himself strong enough to take over the government. In the meantime, he did all he could to improve his credit with the Queen.

In April Baron Schütz, the Hanoverian minister, threw the Queen and the ministry into turmoil by requesting a writ of summons to Parliament for the young Duke of Cambridge, the Electress Sophia's grandson. The scheme, approved by the Electress and encouraged by the Whigs, meant, of course, that the Electoral Prince would come to England: this was its purpose.[46] But the Queen, apart from her known antipathy to the family of Hanover, had steadfastly refused to receive any of its members in England. The prospect of confronting her successor may have stirred whatever feelings of guilt or regret she harbored about her deposed father and her exiled half-brother; certainly it was an unnecessary reminder of her mortality. The Queen was present at the Cabinet meeting in which the request was discussed—"I never saw her Majesty so much moved in my life," Oxford reported[47]—and Bolingbroke, in an obvious move to gain favor, joined with her in declaring that the writ should be refused. He was overruled: legally there were no grounds for refusal, and he must have known

[45] Swift's claim that Bolingbroke did not agree that the Treasurer should resign at the end of the session is puzzling, since Bolingbroke clearly wanted him out by the end of July. But Swift left London at the end of May, and his remark could have referred to Bolingbroke's attitude earlier in the spring. Swift to Bolingbroke, 7 August 1714, *Swift Correspondence*, II, 109.

[46] W. Michael, *England Under George I*, Vol. I: *The Beginnings of the Hanoverian Dynasty* (London: Macmillan, 1936), pp. 28–33.

[47] Oxford to Thomas Harley, 13/24 April 1714, HMC, *Portland MSS*, V, 418. On 7 April Sir David Hamilton reported the Queen "extreamly grievd abt ye Talk of some of ye Family of Hanover's coming over." Hertfordshire R.O., Panshanger MSS, Sir David Hamilton's Diary, f. 61.

this. Oxford represented in the strongest possible terms to Hanover the inadvisability of the Prince's coming to England; Schütz was disgraced, the Prince remained at home.[48] But according to Auditor Harley, "Lord Bolingbroke and Lady Masham took this occasion to insinuate that this was a contrivance of the Treasurer's," and the Auditor thought "that the insinuations used with the Queen on this subject were what chiefly induced her Majesty to part with the Treasurer."[49]

The ministers clashed in May over the payment of arrears due the Hanoverian troops who had refused to follow Ormonde's orders when he withdrew from the field in 1712. Again the Queen's favor seemed to be at issue. Oxford supported the resolution to order payment, Bolingbroke opposed it, explaining to Strafford that it had been "silently introduced" in a select committee of the Commons as part of the year's supply and that "the Queen was entirely ignorant of it." He thought this method of proceeding "inexcusable to the Queen, and not very honourable to the House of Hanover." If the Queen had altered her earlier resolution, she should signify her pleasure to have the arrears paid, and they should be voted "with the unanimous consent of the House."[50] Dr. Stratford passed on to Lord Harley an account of a dinner at the Speaker's house at which Lord Anglesey

said that your father had spoken to him to desire him to speak to all his friends to be for giving the arrears to the Hanover troops, and told him that it was the Queen's desire they should be given. Lord Anglesey said he spoke to Lord Bolingbroke upon it, that Lord Bolingbroke told him it was not the Queen's desire. Lord Anglesey asked him who he must believe, your father or him.

[48] Oxford to Thomas Harley, 13/24 April 1714, HMC, *Portland MSS*, V, 417–19.

[49] Edward Harley, "Memoirs," HMC, *Portland MSS*, V, 622.

[50] Bolingbroke to Strafford, 18 May 1714, *Bolingbroke Correspondence*, IV, 532–3. See also Oxford to Thomas Harley, 13/24 April 1714, HMC, *Portland MSS*, V, 419; L'Hermitage to the States General, 14/25 May 1714, BM, Add. MSS, 17,677HHH, f. 221; *The Lockhart Papers*, I, 467–70; [Defoe], *The Secret History of the White-Staff*, pp. 34–5.

Lord Bolingbroke said if he would go along with him to the Queen he should hear it from herself, that it was not her desire.[51]

Bolingbroke's Tory friends joined with him in opposing payment, Oxford's following apparently was split. The motion was not passed, the arrears not paid.

His stand on these issues, and his introduction of the foreign forces bill earlier in the spring, suggest that in the last months of his ministry Oxford aligned himself more decisively with the Hanoverians, choosing to strengthen his support among Whigs and Whimsicals, though at the same time he sought to avoid further antagonizing the Queen. Writing to Cowper early in May, he said he had spoken to Lord Halifax and thought they were "agreed in almost every point." He deplored the agitation about the Duke of Cambridge, which "wil drive every body to the wall," that "things are to be precipitated, & that a very little time wil not be allow'd to establish that real & effectual Friendship between the Queen and the Elector, wch is so necessary for the Common Peace." He appealed to Cowper and Halifax to save the country from ruin: he was ready to do his part.[52] Cowper replied that had Schütz consulted him about the writ for the Duke of Cambridge, "I flatter myself I should have had presence of mind to have endeavoured the preventing a step, which must now prove inconvenient, whatever is done upon it." But he could not see "any way left to do good, but by your Lordship exerting yourself speedily, so far as to get those out of power who will not so much as profess themselves to be for the true interest of their country."[53] Rumors that Oxford would declare for the Whigs continued to circulate; and while Whig reports

[51] Dr. Stratford to Lord Harley, 3 June 1714, HMC, *Portland MSS*, VII, 185.

[52] Oxford to Cowper, 12 May 1714, Hertfordshire R.O., Panshanger MSS, D/EP, F60.

[53] Cowper to Oxford, 14 May 1714, HMC, *Portland MSS*, V, 440. See also Halifax to Oxford, 8 May, 29 May 1714, HMC, *Portland MSS*, V, 437, 451, and 27 February 1714, BM, Portland Loan, 29/151.

that he would in fact not be sorry to have the Electoral Prince come over seem, in the light of his letter to Cowper, clearly to have been untrue, it was certainly among the Whigs and Whimsicals that he would find allies against Bolingbroke.[54]

In May Bolingbroke, supported by Harcourt and Atterbury, launched a major offensive against both Oxford and the Whigs. Sir William Wyndham introduced into the House of Commons a bill designed to suppress the Dissenting schools and academies which had, since the Restoration, educated the children of Dissenters, and, incidentally, the sons of a number of members of the Established Church as well, including Oxford himself. Its intent was "to prevent the growth of schism and for the security of the Church of England as by law established," but according to the Auditor, "they brought in the Bill against Schism, with no other design than to embarrass the Treasurer."[55] The bill in fact served a number of purposes. Any measure for the greater security of the Established Church was irresistible to the Tories, and Bolingbroke calculated, correctly, that on this issue he could bring the Whimsicals back to their Tory allegiance. He could count on the Queen's support, for the bill appealed to her High Church principles. And he had indeed put Oxford in a difficult position. If Oxford opposed the bill he would alienate the Tories, and, more significantly, invoke the Queen's displeasure. If he voted for it, he would seriously damage his reputation among Whigs and Dissenters. The bill "will alarm the Sectaries, and my humble opinion is that noe body should be made uneasy if it can be avoided," Lord Berkeley of Stratton wrote, "but I doubt it is design'd to inflame the high church against those of the ministry who doe not appear zealous for this bill."[56]

[54] Cadogan to Robethon, 15/26 May 1714, BM, Stowe MSS, 227. "Memorial" in Oxford's hand, 31 March 1714, BM, Portland Loan, 29/12. *The Lockhart Papers*, I, 461–2.

[55] Newsletter, 13 May 1714, HMC, *Portland MSS*, V, 439; Edward Harley, "Memoirs," HMC, *Portland MSS*, V, 661.

[56] Lord Berkeley of Stratton to Strafford, 25 May 1714, *Wentworth Papers*, p. 383.

The Schism Bill passed in the House of Commons by a majority of more than one hundred votes. Auditor Harley was one of the very few Tories opposed.[57] Bolingbroke moved the bill in the Lords, "shewing the advantages it would be of in uniting the Nation, and stifling for the future the divisions amongst us." Oxford spoke toward the end of the debate: "For his part he was of opinion the Bill would be of very good consequence, and as for those little hardships which some of the Lords had complained of, they could be amended by the Committee."[58] Its harsher provisions somewhat softened by amendment, the bill passed the Lords by less than ten votes; but it was a tactical victory for Bolingbroke, and while there was some talk of his dismissal, more generally he was thought finally to have triumphed over Oxford. "I must tell you the vogue is against you, as far as I can learn it," Dr. Stratford wrote gloomily to Lord Harley. "It is thought you cannot keep your ground, though no one thinks others can hold it longer than the next session, nor even to the end of this, as near as it is, if the alteration be before it is up."[59] The Hanoverian Resident in London reported that Bolingbroke had entirely gained the Queen and that the Treasurer would resign in a few days.[60] Swift, despairing of reconciling his friends, had by this time withdrawn to the country to await the final catastrophe.

Through the end of May and the beginning of June, the weeks when the Schism Bill was before Parliament, Oxford continued to talk of resigning. In a series of notes, apparently for an interview with Bolingbroke, he wrote: "You promised me to act in Concert. Is there any thing I have done or brought in but in Concert. . . . On ye other hand has not every thing

[57] L'Hermitage to the States General, 1/12 June 1714, BM, Add. MSS, 17,677HHH, f. 238.

[58] Newsletter, 1 June 1714, *Wentworth Papers*, pp. 385-6. *The Lockhart Papers*, I, 462. [Defoe], *The Secret History of the White-Staff*, pp. 31-3.

[59] Dr. Stratford to Lord Harley, 17 June 1714, HMC, *Portland MSS*, VII, 189.

[60] Kreyenberg's dispatch, 12 June 1714, BM, Stowe MSS, 227.

been concealed from me." And here he mentioned the Schism Bill. "I am useless—," he concluded, "Let me be either in or out."[61] "I stand still & let them attaque me," another memorandum ran.

> go out
> I desire rather to *withdraw* than desist. Let them tell
> their scheme. Mine is that the Queen should be easy & safe.[62]

Then, surprisingly, at the moment when Oxford's position was generally thought to be hopeless, he moved to save himself. "I will plague you a little by telling you that the Dragon [Oxford] dy's hard," Arbuthnot wrote to Swift. "He is now kicking & cuffing about him like the divill. & you know parliamentary management is the forte but no hopes of any settlement between the two champions."[63] At the instigation of Oxford and of Shrewsbury the Queen issued a proclamation offering £5,000 for the apprehension of the Pretender should he land in Great Britain, a sum that the House of Commons, over the protests of Bromley and Wyndham, promptly raised to £100,000. This was the proclamation the Queen had agreed to in principle in April, and it was greeted with jubilation by Whigs and Whimsicals.[64] Oxford's timing was shrewd: the session was nearing its close, and his intention was to outmaneuver Bolingbroke by demonstrating to the Hanoverians that he at least was committed to the lawful succession. A few

61 Memorandum in Oxford's hand, 23 May 1714, BM, Portland Loan, 29/10.

62 Memorandum in Oxford's hand, 2 June 1714, *ibid.* The alternate phrasing is Oxford's.

63 Arbuthnot to Swift, 26 June 1714, *Swift Correspondence*, II, 41. On a letter from Lewis which also refers to the "Dragon," Swift notes: "The Dragon Lord Treasurer Oxford so called by the Dean. by Contraryes, and for he was the mildest, wisest and best Minister that ever served a Prince." E. Lewis to Swift, 17 July 1714, *ibid.*, p. 68.

64 *Wentworth Papers*, pp. 393-4; Gatke to Robethon, 25 June/6 July 1714, Macpherson, *Original Papers*, II, 531. L'Hermitage to the States General, 25 June/6 July 1714, BM, Add. MSS, 17,677HHH. *The Lockhart Papers*, I, 471-2.

days after the proclamation had been issued, Peter Wentworth told his brother that "it has been said that Lord T—— has given out that if it had not been for him the Pretender had been here long agoe; and 'tis supposed of late he has been taken into grace and favour of the Whigs, and that he has promised them if they impeach Lord B—— he will not oppose them, and that underhand he has given them some matters to go upon."[65] All this was rumor. But in June, apparently with Oxford's co-operation, both Houses of Parliament began an investigation of matters related to the Asiento contract—by which, as part of the Utrecht settlement, the South Sea Company, under contract from the Queen, was granted the exclusive right to supply slaves to South America for a period of thirty years—and several articles explanatory of the commercial treaty with Spain, which had been widely denounced as injurious to the interests of British merchants. This was, by implication, an attack on Bolingbroke. His friend Arthur Moore was accused of misconduct in the negotiation of the explanatory articles and also of bribery and corruption in attempting to send a private cargo on the first South Sea Company ship licensed for the South American trade. Bolingbroke and Lady Masham, as well as Moore himself, were said to be among those who would profit from this transaction. As Bolingbroke shared the responsibility for the commercial treaty, he stood behind Arthur Moore in both aspects of the accusation. The direction of the attack was not lost upon the Secretary: "Mr. Moore has been this morning with me, and has put into my hands a paper, which he calls, I think not improperly, a charge upon me," he wrote to Oxford early in June.[66] When a number of merchants were admitted to the bar of the House of Lords to present their objections to the treaty, only Bolingbroke defended it: "It was observable that there was not a word said either by Lord Treasurer or any of his Friends in defence of

[65] Peter Wentworth to Strafford, 29 June 1714, *Wentworth Papers*, pp. 394-5.

[66] Bolingbroke to Oxford, 3 June 1714, HMC, *Portland MSS*, V, 454.

the Peace, soe that all readily conclude, that Lord Treasurer endeavours to sacrifice Lord Bolingbroke."[67] Bolingbroke's position became still more precarious when it was rumored that the beneficiaries of the Queen's 22½ percent share of the Asiento contract were Moore, Lady Masham, and himself.[68] But before the investigation could be pursued, and the charges inquired into, the Queen intervened. At the end of June she renounced her share of the Asiento contract, turning it over to the South Sea Company; early in July, to protect Bolingbroke, and to protect her favorite, she prorogued Parliament.[69]

The prorogation was taken as a clear indication that Bolingbroke had prevailed with the Queen. But he was nonetheless infuriated by the attack. "For several weeks before the Session of Parliament rose," he told Strafford, "there were new plots, day after day, concerting against me; and . . . those, in the service of whom I have drudged these fifteen years, were the proposers of new confederacies, the cement of which was to be my ruin." His only crime had been this,

when the Queen's affairs were come by slow, but long observed steps, into the utmost confusion; when the party which was at our feet, had been nursed up and rendered formidable; when the party that only could support us, was under the utmost dissatisfaction, some of them taking part against us, others cool and indifferent spectators; in a word, when every man, who looked on, agreed that we could not carry the business of the Session round, then I presumed, among others, to beg of one man [Lord Oxford], as a friend, that he would alter his conduct, and to represent to the

[67] News Letter, July 1714, *Wentworth Papers*, p. 404.

[68] The nominal assignees, William Lowndes and John Taylor, Secretaries to the Treasury, admitted to being only trustees. Sperling, *The South Sea Company*, pp. 18–19.

[69] *Wentworth Papers*, pp. 396–405; Charles Ford to Swift, 6, 10 July 1714; E. Lewis to Swift, 6 July 1714, *Swift Correspondence*, II, 51–4, 58–9. The South Sea Company established Moore's guilt to its own satisfaction, voting him guilty of a breach of trust. But the inquiry was stopped before Bolingbroke's involvement could be determined.

Queen, as a faithful servant that her government was at the brink of destruction.

He went on to speak of the "deplorable state" of the Queen's affairs, of "some people, who would rather move heaven and earth, than either part with their power, or make a right use of it," and to accuse Oxford of being "in a secret with our enemy." And he concluded: "What the Queen will do to extricate herself from these difficulties and she alone can save herself, I do not know. This I know, that there is no danger, no labour I decline to serve her, except one, which is, that of trusting the same conduct a fifth year, which has deceived herself these four years."[70] From this point on, Bolingbroke pressed for Oxford's dismissal. He wished "to take hold of the present disposition, which there seems to be, to act a clear game with the Tories, and on that foundation to establish the Queen's Government."[71] This was well and good. But the parliamentary inquiry in the final weeks of the session had raised again the question of Bolingbroke's financial integrity, and this could not enhance his reputation with the Queen.[72]

There was speculation as to why Oxford had not pressed his advantage further in the affair of the Asiento and the Spanish treaty. The Hanoverian agent in London reported that the Treasurer had not provided all the assistance he had promised to those who backed the inquiry. He thought Oxford wanted to avoid an open breach with the Queen, and that he feared Bolingbroke's ruin might also be his own.[73] This is probably true. More important, Oxford could not entirely dissociate himself from the Spanish treaty, which was part of

[70] Bolingbroke to Strafford, 14 July 1714, *Bolingbroke Correspondence*, IV, 562–3.

[71] Bolingbroke to the Lord Primate of Ireland, 27 July 1714, *Bolingbroke Correspondence*, IV, 572.

[72] Dickinson points out as well that in this session he had not been able to manage the government's business in Parliament effectively. Here Oxford remained his master. *Bolingbroke*, pp. 124–5.

[73] Bothmer to Robethon, 20, 24 July 1714, N.S., BM, Stowe MSS, 227.

the Utrecht settlement. Tory policy was at issue, and Tory
ministers. Whimsicals could not be counted on to support such
an attack, and without them it could not be carried forward.[74]
Furthermore, there is no indication that Oxford wished to
abandon his Tory following, even to accomplish Bolingbroke's
destruction. He was not now, as he never had been, prepared
to declare for the Whigs.

The day after the prorogation Arbuthnot wrote to Swift:

We are indeed in such a strange Condition as to politicks that no
body can tell now who is for who. it were worth the while to be
here four & twenty hours, only to consider the oddness of the
scene. I am sure it would make yow relish your country life better.
The Dragon holds fast with a dead grype the little Machine [the
staff] if he would have taken but half so much pains to have done
other things, as he has of late to Exert him self against the Esquire
[Bolingbroke], he might have been a dragon instead of a dagon. I
would no more have suffered & done what he has, than I would
have sold my self to the Gallys.[75]

While Oxford's dismissal was daily predicted, he approached
Harcourt and Lord Chief Justice Trevor in an attempt to detach them from Bolingbroke.[76] He begged the Queen to bring
about a reconciliation between him and Lady Masham: "It is
for your Service that you reconcile (L.) M. & O. Tell them
both So. have them ther together. O. will put himself in ye

---

[74] Charles Ford to Swift, 6 July 1714, *Swift Correspondence*, II, 51-2.
Gatke to Robethon, 22 June/3 July 1714, speaks of the indignation of the
October men in the Commons when charges were brought against Arthur
Moore. BM, Stowe MSS, 227. But Bothmer reports that in the Lords, the
Whimsical Earl of Anglesey would apparently have pushed the attack on
Bolingbroke had the Queen not prorogued Parliament. Bothmer to Robethon,
24 July 1714, N.S., *ibid.*

[75] Arbuthnot to Swift, 10 July 1714, *Swift Correspondence*, II, 57-8. A
"dagon" is a statue or idol, a term sometimes used pejoratively.

[76] Auditor Edward Harley to Oxford, 11 July 1714, BM, Portland Loan,
29/143. For a series of letters from Trevor, see *ibid.*, 29/159. For negotiations
with Harcourt, see also F. Lewis to Swift, 17 July 1714, *Swift Correspondence*, II, 67-8.

wrong."[77] But these belated efforts accomplished nothing. The final weeks of the ministry were punctuated by violent outbursts and bitter recriminations on all sides. According to Lewis, Lady Masham

told the Dragon in her own house last thursday morning, these words, you never did the Q. any service, nor are you capable of doing her any, He made no reply, but supped with her and mercurialis [Bolingbroke] that night at her own house, his revenge not the less meditated for that, he tells the words clearly & distinctly to all mankind, those who range under his banner, call her ten thousand bitches & kitchen-wenches. those who hate him do the same.

Lewis added: "From my heart I grieve that she sh'd give such a loose to her passion, for she is suceptible of true friendship, and has many social & domestick virtues."[78] Swift, who in June approved Lady Masham's conduct in withdrawing her support from Oxford, was alarmed by Lewis's report. "What she sd to the Dragon a week ago is of so desperate a Strain," he wrote to Arbuthnot, "that I can not think her in a Temper to be at the Head or the Bottom of a Change; nor do I believe a Change accompanyed with such Passion can ever succeed."[79] Lady Masham was not alone in giving way to intemperate outbursts. "I had intelligence that the Dragon has broke out into a fiery passion with my Lord Ch.——[Harcourt]," Lewis reported on July 24, "sworn a thousand oaths that he w'd be reveng'd, &c. this impotent womanish behaviour vexes me more than his being out."[80] In the calmer intervals, Ford told Swift, "the Dragon and his Antagonist meet every day at the Cabinet: they often eat, and drink, and walk together as if there was no sort

---

[77] Memorandum in Oxford's hand, 4 July 1714, BM, Portland Loan, 29/10. The notes are evidently for an interview with the Queen.

[78] E. Lewis to Swift, 17 July 1714, *Swift Correspondence*, II, 67–8.

[79] Swift to Arbuthnot, 22 July 1714, *ibid.*, p. 175. For Swift's earlier approval of Lady Masham's conduct, see Swift to Arbuthnot, 16 June 1714, *ibid.*, p. 36.

[80] E. Lewis to Swift, 24 July 1714, *ibid.*, p. 80.

of disagreement, and when they part, I hear they give one another such names, as no body but Ministers of State could bear without cutting throats."[81]

At last on July 27 Oxford was dismissed. Lady Masham, informing Swift of the news, wrote that "the Q——n had gott soe far the better of the Dragon as to take her Power out of his hands, he has been the most ungrateful man to her and to all his best friends that ever was born." She had not time to say more because the Queen was not well, "and I think I may lay her illness to the charge of the Treasurer who for three weeks together was teasing and vexing her without intermission."[82] Oxford's friends, not unexpectedly, had a different tale to tell:

The Queen for some time having been persuaded to part with the late Lord Treasurer by some persons who did not think they grew rich fast enough under his administration, and who had, as there is great reason to suspect, some worse designs. Her Majesty was at last prevailed upon by a perpetual teasing to come to a resolution to part with him. On Tuesday in the morning and afternoon, before he delivered up the staff, she expressed a great trouble and concern.[83]

Whichever version one chose to believe, it was the Queen who decided Oxford's fate. Lewis reported that "the Q. has told all the Lords the reasons of her parting with him. viz. that he neglected all business, that he was seldom to be understood, that when he did explain himself, she could not depend upon the truth of what he said; that he never came to her at the time she appointed, that he often came drunk, that lastly to crown all he behav'd himself towards her with ill manner indecency & disrespect."[84] Lewis did not identify his source: while the Queen doubtless complained in strong terms of Oxford's conduct, it is difficult to believe she spoke so harshly. Her final

[81] Charles Ford to Swift, 22 July 1714, *ibid.*, p. 77.
[82] Lady Masham to Swift, 29 July 1714, *ibid.*, p. 87.
[83] [Edward Harley?] to Abigail Harley, 31 July 1714, HMC, *Portland MSS*, V, 480.
[84] Lewis to Swift, 27 July 1714, *Swift Correspondence*, II, 86.

interview with Oxford was long, in marked contrast to her dismissal of Godolphin, whom she refused to see at all.[85] According to Oxford's son, "Her Majesty was pleased to talk with him after his delivery of the staff above two hours," and she told him "that she expected he should come to her again."[86] Several weeks later, after the Queen's death, Lord Berkeley of Stratton wrote: "They say the Queen was very loath to part with the late Treasurer, but was teas'd into it."[87] It seems likely that the Queen was loath to part with Oxford. Her affections ran deep, she dreaded change; and there is no indication that she ever trusted Bolingbroke entirely. But Oxford gave her no alternative: he could no longer attend to business with any regularity, he no longer gave her the support she craved. For some time Swift had thought Oxford should resign; Lewis had "long thought his parts decay'd, & am more of that opinion than ever."[88] Oxford had no more loyal friends than these. He ended by accomplishing his own destruction.

Ironically, no one else could have brought him down. His opponents were not necessarily Bolingbroke's supporters; had he managed to retain the Queen's favor by functioning with any degree of efficiency, it is difficult to see how he could have been dislodged. The old Tory complaints of moderation were in the air: "Most of those call'd Tories were very warm against him, not thinking him enough of their side," Lord Berkeley of Stratton wrote.[89] But the parliamentary session had demon-

---

[85] For Godolphin's dismissal, see Coxe, *Marlborough*, V, 321-3.

[86] A paper written by the second Earl of Oxford, n.d., HMC, *Portland MSS*, V, 481. L'Hermitage says the Treasurer saw the Queen several times on the day of his dismissal, once briefly, and again for three quarters of an hour. L'Hermitage to the States General, 30 July/10 August 1714, BM, Add. MSS, 17,677HHH. See also [Defoe], *The Secret History of the White-Staff*, pp. 53-7.

[87] Lord Berkeley of Stratton to Strafford, 13 August 1714, *Wentworth Papers*, p. 412.

[88] E. Lewis to Swift, 29 July 1714, Swift to Bolingbroke, 7 August 1714, *Swift Correspondence*, II, 89, 109.

[89] Lord Berkeley of Stratton to Strafford, 13 August 1714, *Wentworth Papers*, pp. 412-13.

strated that for the Whimsicals the cause of Hanover was paramount, and on this point they were not inclined to trust Bolingbroke and Harcourt. In the Cabinet, Bolingbroke could count only on Harcourt and Wyndham. Bromley might join him, but only if Oxford's dismissal seemed inevitable. Oxford, for his part, had Dartmouth and Poulett on his side, and while Shrewsbury's position was uncertain, he had not declared for Bolingbroke, and it is unlikely that he would have done so in view of his own moderate principles. Ten days before Oxford's removal, Bolingbroke told Arbuthnot he did not know how he stood with Shrewsbury; and Arbuthnot, reporting this to Swift, commented that "the D S———rry is taken him self to the Dragon, in appearance." In the same letter Arbuthnot wrote that "they have rompu en visiere with the Dragon, & yet dont know how to do wtout him M L M———m has in a Manner bid him defyance without any scheme, or the likeness of it in any form or shape as far as I can see."[90] Lewis agreed. He thought Lady Masham and the Duchess of Somerset meant to increase their power by Oxford's fall. "The man of mercury [Bolingbroke] soothes them in this notion, with great dexterity and reason, for he will be monsr le premier then of course, by virtue of the little seal. his character is to bad to carry the great Ensigns." But Lewis was apprehensive, "for the man, of mercury's bottom is too narrow, his faults of the first magnitude, and we can't find, that there is any scheme in the world how to proceed."[91]

The uncertainty of Bolingbroke's position was underlined by the difficulties he met with in attempting to reorganize the ministry. A week before Oxford's dismissal Ford told Swift he could "guess no reason why matters are delay'd, unless it be to gain over some Lords who stick firm to the Dragon, and others that are averse to the Captain [Bolingbroke]."[92] The Treasury

90 Arbuthnot to Swift, 17 July 1714, *Swift Correspondence*, II, 69.

91 E. Lewis to Swift, 6 July 1714, *ibid.*, pp. 53-4. The "little seal" was the seal of the Secretary of State.

92 Charles Ford to Swift, 20 July 1714, *ibid.*, p. 73.

was to be put into commission, but on the day Oxford gave up the staff Lewis wrote that "the stick is yet in his hand, because they cannot agree who shall be the new Commssrs."[93] Two days later he reported "the new Commission is not yet nam'd, wd not the world have roared ag't the Dragon for such a thing."[94] A long and stormy Council meeting on the evening of Oxford's dismissal brought no agreement: "They that had pressed the removal of the Treasurer could not propose such persons as the Queen would approve to succeed him," a supporter of Oxford's wrote.[95]

The meeting went on past midnight, and the Queen, who had been present throughout, remained to the end. Later that morning she was not well, and it rapidly became apparent that her illness was serious and might prove fatal. On Friday the Privy Council, meeting at Kensington and with the Whig Dukes of Argyll and Somerset present, "resolved unanimously to desire her to put the Treasurer's staff into the Duke of Shrewsbury's hands, which she did, being perfect in her senses."[96] Bolingbroke carried the Council's message to the Queen, that "it would be for the publick service to have the D. of Shrewsbury made Ld Treasurer"; and when she consented, he summoned Shrewsbury to receive the staff.[97] Bolingbroke

---

[93] E. Lewis to Swift, 27 July 1714, *ibid.*, p. 86.

[94] E. Lewis to Swift, 29 July 1714, *ibid.*, p. 89.

[95] [Edward Harley?] to Abigail Harley, 31 July 1714, HMC, *Portland MSS*, V, 480. See also [Defoe], *The Secret History of the White-Staff*, pp. 58–61.

[96] Lord Lansdowne to Oxford, 30 July 1714, HMC, *Portland MSS*, V, 477. See also Bromley to Oxford, 30 July 1714, *ibid.*, pp. 477–8; and L'Hermitage to the States General, 30 July/10 August, 31 July/11 August 1714, BM, Add. MSS, 17,677YYY. Somerset and Argyll had not attended the Council for some time and on this occasion they had not been summoned. But both were Privy Councillors and entitled to attend. Their purpose was to insure the lawful proclamation of the Elector of Hanover, and together with Shrewsbury, they seem to have exercised the dominating influence in the meeting. Trevelyan, *England under Queen Anne*, III, 302–4; Michael, *England Under George I*, I, 52–3.

[97] Charles Ford to Swift, 31 July 1714, *Swift Correspondence*, II, 93–4.

agreed in the Council's choice of Shrewsbury; there was no possibility that the staff would go to him, and he preferred Shrewsbury to the return of Oxford. But Shrewsbury's appointment was generally taken to mean that "the schemes of the new intended Ministry in all appearance are entirely confounded."[98] Two days later the Queen died, and the accession of George I was peacefully proclaimed. "My Dear Mistress's days were numbered even in My imagination & could not exceed such certain Limits," Arbuthnot wrote to Swift, "but of that small number a great deal was cutt off by the last troublesome scene of the contention amongst her Servants. I beleive sleep was never more welcome to a weary traveller than death was to her."[99] With those sentiments there was, for once, no disagreement.

Bolingbroke's hopes for remaining in office were quickly dashed. It was clear there would be no room for him—or for Oxford—in the new political world, and at the end of August he was dismissed. One can only speculate as to what he would have done had the Queen lived. The new Treasury Commission was reported to include Wyndham, Bolingbroke's old friend James Brydges, and two known Jacobites, Sir John Pakington and Henry Campion.[100] Atterbury, another High Tory, was repeatedly mentioned as Dartmouth's replacement for the Privy Seal. These expected appointments suggest that Bolingbroke intended to build the High Tory ministry he had so long urged upon Oxford. "Lord Bolingbroke, and the Chancellor [Harcourt], are to rule the world," an observer reported, "and it is said they will be swingeing Torys, and not a Whig left in place a month hence."[101] But at the same time Bolingbroke realized that he must reach some accommodation

98 [Edward Harley?] to Abigail Harley, 31 July 1714, HMC, *Portland MSS*, V, 480.

99 Arbuthnot to Swift, 12 August 1714, *Swift Correspondence*, II, 121.

100 Charles Ford to Swift, 24 July 1714, *ibid.*, pp. 78–9; News Letter, 24 July 1714, HMC, *Portland MSS*, V, 475.

101 Roger Kenyon to his brother, George Kenyon, 29 July 1714, HMC, *Kenyon MSS*, p. 456.

with the Hanoverian Tories—through the spring he had tried to gain Whimsical support.[102] And in the crisis of the Queen's final illness he went so far as to attempt a rapprochement with the Whigs. Entertaining a number of Whig leaders at dinner— "wt if the Dragon had done so,"[103] Lewis remarked—he declared his loyalty to the Protestant succession. But when his Whig guests named their conditions—including Marlborough's restoration to the command of the army and the Pretender's removal from his current place of residence in Lorraine—and demanded deeds, not words, Bolingbroke was unable to respond.[104]

But whatever Bolingbroke had done, he would not have had an easy time. He had to expect a revival of the inquiry into the Spanish commercial treaty and the Asiento contract when Parliament reconvened. And as long as the succession remained the overriding political issue, it is difficult to see how he could have rallied the Hanoverian Tories, and at the same time kept the confidence of the Queen. Oxford's dismissal was a separate event from Bolingbroke's assumption of power: one did not lead to the other in direct and easy fashion, even while the Queen still lived. Had she survived, his chances of success could have been no better than even. There was, furthermore,

---

[102] See especially Bolingbroke to Anglesey, 25 January 1714, *Bolingbroke Correspondence*, IV, 440–4; and to the Lord Chancellor of Ireland, 20 May 1714, *ibid.*, p. 550.

[103] E. Lewis to Swift, 29 July 1714, *Swift Correspondence*, II, 89.

[104] Lord Mahon [Philip Henry Stanhope, 5th Earl Stanhope], *History of England from the Peace of Utrecht to the Peace of Aix-la-Chapelle* (2nd edn. rev.; London, 1839), I, 128. Michael, *England Under George I*, I, 49–50. There were in fact rumors that he was negotiating with Marlborough, who arrived in England on the day the Queen died. The Auditor declared that "whatever the scheme was it is very plain that the Duke of Marlborough was to be at the head of it," and he said he had heard this from Cadogan, Somerset, and others, who "were engaged in the new plan that was forming by the Lord Bolingbroke." Edward Harley, "Memoirs," HMC, *Portland MSS*, V, 662. See also *The Lockhart Papers*, I, 460–1. On the other hand, in the middle of July Bolingbroke told Strafford he thought Oxford had made overtures to Marlborough. Bolingbroke to Strafford, 14 July 1714, *Bolingbroke Correspondence*, IV, 567.

Lewis's remark that Bolingbroke's character was "to bad to carry the great Ensigns": in the crisis his reputation as a man of pleasure and his lack of solidity counted heavily against him. The Privy Council fixed upon Shrewsbury because he was sure for Hanover, but also because of his character. Enigmatic he might be, mercurial he was not. In the solemn moment of the Queen's death, the Councillors chose to place their trust in a man who in word and action displayed the qualities expected in a minister of state. Thus while Bolingbroke prevailed over Oxford in the personal struggle, there was little to celebrate in his victory. The dying Queen's appointment of Shrewsbury was in some sense Oxford's vindication, for Shrewsbury's moderate policies and temper placed him far closer to Oxford than to Bolingbroke.

Oxford marked his dismissal with a poem which he sent off to Swift, and also to his sister:

> *To serve with love*
> *And shed your Blood*
> *Approved is above*
> *But heer Below*
> *The Example[s] shew*
> *tis fatal to be Good*[105]

And two days after the Queen's death Bolingbroke wrote to Swift: "The Earl of Oxford was remov'd on Tuesday, the Queen dyed on Sunday . . . what a world is this, & how does fortune banter us?"[106]

---

[105] Oxford to Swift, 27 July 1714, *Swift Correspondence*, II, 85–6; Oxford to his sister, Abigail Harley, 29 July 1714, HMC, *Portland MSS*, V, 477.

[106] Bolingbroke to Swift, 3 August 1714, *Swift Correspondence*, II, 101.

Epilogue

NDER threat of impeachment from the new Whig Parliament, Bolingbroke fled to France; Oxford remained to face his accusers. Bolingbroke feared that he would bear the brunt of the Whig attack, but in the "Letter to Sir William Windham" he admitted that he "abhorred Oxford to that degree, that I could not bear to be joined with him in any case. Nothing perhaps contributed so much to determine me as this sentiment. A sense of honor would not have permitted me to distinguish between his case and mine own: and it was worse than death to lie under the necessity of making them the same, and of taking measures in concert with him."[1] Oxford, it will be remembered, told his brother that

common prudence might prompt me to avoid the storm that I see is falling upon me, but having thoroughly considered this matter, and not being conscious to myself of doing any one thing that is contrary to the interest of my country, I am come to an absolute conclusion to resign myself to the Providence of the Almighty, and not either by flight, or any other way to sully the honour of my Royal Mistress, though now in her grave, nor stain my own innocence even for an hour.

He added there are but two ways for a man to die with real honour, the one is by suffering martyrdom for his religion, and the other by dying a martyr for his country. He added further, you are now going to London, and you will be solicited to persuade me to leave the Kingdom; but let not your concern for me influence

[1] Bolingbroke, *Works*, I, 131.

you in this matter, for I am come, by the help of God, to an unalterable resolution of abiding the worst that can befal me.[2]

Inclined to motion rather than rest, without much regard for the consequences, Bolingbroke acted; Oxford resigned himself to Providence and waited out the storm. There could be no more perfect epilogue to these two careers.

Looking back over the association of Bolingbroke and Oxford, one is struck by the fact that on the great issues of the day—the Church, the peace, even the succession—while their attitudes differed at many points, these differences were not irreconcilable. The issue that divided them was the nature of politics itself. Bolingbroke viewed the politics of Anne's reign in terms of party and, after 1708 at least, he was convinced that the struggle for power and office could only be won by an outright commitment to party government. Oxford, believing that party conflict was destructive of the principles of good government, was equally convinced that only a moderate, nonparty administration could save the nation. But Oxford's scheme did not correspond to the reality. The Tory gentlemen in the House of Commons, uninterested in moderation, urged the Tory scheme of government Oxford refused to provide. He had difficulties enough in the first year of his ministry, but when, in 1711, the peace became a party issue, his position was shown to be untenable. From this point on, to the extent that he controlled the ministry, he did so through the concessions he made in the direction of party government as well as through his favor with the Queen.

Bolingbroke's analysis was right, Oxford's was wrong. But in the last year of the reign, when the issue of the succession split the Tory party, Bolingbroke's system ceased to be viable, at least under his leadership. Once the question of the succession took precedence over party loyalty, no ministry could count on favorable parliamentary majorities unless it could reassure the Whigs and Hanoverian Tories of its fidelity to

2 Edward Harley, "Memoirs," HMC, *Portland MSS*, V, 663.

Hanover. And while both Oxford and Bolingbroke were accused of favoring the Pretender, Bolingbroke was the more suspect. Oxford's chances of uniting Whigs and Hanoverian Tories in the interests of securing the Protestant succession were considerable, Bolingbroke's negligible. Thus, ironically, at the moment of his dismissal Oxford's moderate scheme of government had more chance of success than at any time during the course of his ministry. But by July 1714, Oxford was neither intellectually nor emotionally fit to remain at the head of affairs. His manifest inability to exercise the responsibilities of his office gave the Queen no choice but to dismiss him. The peculiar limitations of Oxford's character brought him down in the end. To a lesser extent the same was true of Bolingbroke. Had the Queen thought him fit to head the ministry, it is likely that she would have bestowed some mark of favor upon him when Oxford was dismissed. The Privy Council's choice of Shrewsbury simply confirmed the Queen's mistrust of Bolingbroke. Even had he been able to reassure his colleagues that he was strong for Hanover, and this seems unlikely in the extreme, the man of mercury was, in their view, too impulsive, too erratic to bear the titles of a great officer of state. Oxford, for all his failings, fitted comfortably within an ordinary Englishman's notion of a minister, which is perhaps another way of saying within an ordinary Englishman's notion of himself. Bolingbroke did not: the brilliance of his intellect, the flamboyance of his character ultimately undercut his political ambition.

BIBLIOGRAPHY

Primary Sources

MANUSCRIPTS

British Museum
  Additional MSS: 4163; 5834; 17,677 EEE-HHH; 23,206; 28,055; 32,306; 40,621; 41,843.
  Portland Loan (Loan 29). The Harley Papers.
  Stowe MSS 225–227.   The Hanover Papers.
          248.   Harley's plan of administration, 1710.

Bodleian Library
  Ballard MS 38. Letters of William Bromley and Dr. Arthur Charlett.
  MS Eng. Misc. e. 180. Transcripts of letters of Henry St. John and the Earl of Orrery.

Nottingham University Library
  Portland Collection: Harley MSS (Pw2, Hy).

County Record Offices
  Berkshire Record Office
    Downshire Papers: Trumbull Additional MSS. Letters of Henry St. John and Sir William Trumbull.
  Herefordshire Record Office
    The Harley Papers, C. 64. These are photographic copies of the originals in the possession of Mr. Christopher Harley at Brampton Bryan Hall.
  Hertfordshire Record Office
    Panshanger MSS: Cowper Papers, including Sir David Hamilton's Diary.
  Staffordshire Record Office
    Dartmouth MSS.

Collections in Private Custody
  Blenheim Palace, Woodstock
    Blenheim MSS: Marlborough Papers.
  Longleat House, Wiltshire
    Portland Papers
    Portland Miscellaneous MSS.

PRINTED SOURCES

Addison, Joseph. *The Letters of Joseph Addison.* Edited by Walter Graham. Oxford, 1941.

Arbuthnot, John; Pope, Alexander; Swift, Jonathan; Gay, John; Parnell, Thomas; and Harley, Robert, Earl of Oxford. *Memoirs of the Extraordinary Life, Works, and Discoveries of Martinus Scriblerus.* Edited by Charles Kerby-Miller. New Haven: Published for Wellesley College by the Yale University Press, 1950.

Aufrere, Anthony, ed. *The Lockhart Papers.* London, 1817. 2 vols.

Bolingbroke, Henry St. John, Viscount. *Letters and Correspondence, Public and Private, of the Right Honourable Henry St. John, Lord Visc. Bolingbroke; during the time he was Secretary of State to Queen Anne; with State Papers, Explanatory Notes, and a Translation of the Foreign Letters, etc.* Edited by Gilbert Parke. London, 1798. 4 vols.

———. *The Works of the late Right Honourable Henry St. John, Lord Viscount Bolingbroke.* Published by David Mallet, Esq. London, 1777. 5 vols.

———. *The Works of Lord Bolingbroke. With a Life, prepared expressly for this edition, containing additional information relative to his personal and public character, selected from the best authorities.* Philadelphia: Carey and Hart, 1841. 4 vols.

[Bolingbroke]. *Considerations upon The Secret History of the White Staff Humbly Address'd to the E — of O —.* London, [1714].

Boyer, Abel. *The History of the Life & Reign of Queen Anne.* London, 1722.

――――. *The History of the Reign of Queen Anne, Digested into Annals.* London, 1703–12. 10 vols.

――――. *The Political State of Great Britain.* London, 1711–14.

Buck, Clara, and Davies, Godfrey, eds. "Letters on Godolphin's Dismissal in 1710." *Huntington Library Quarterly*, III (1939–40), 225–42.

Bunbury, Sir Henry, Bart, ed. *The Correspondence of Sir Thomas Hanmer, Bart.* London, 1838.

Burnet, Gilbert. *History of His Own Time.* Oxford, 1833. 6 vols.

Cartwright, Joseph J., ed. *The Wentworth Papers, 1705–1739. Selected from the Private and Family Correspondence of Thomas Wentworth, Lord Raby created in 1711 Earl of Strafford, of Stainborough, County York.* London, 1883.

[Clement, Simon]. *FAULTS on both SIDES.* 2nd edn. London, 1710.

Cobbett, W. *Parliamentary History of England. From the Norman Conquest, in 1066, to the Year 1803.* London, 1806–20. 36 vols.

Davies, Godfrey, and Tinling, Marion, eds. "Correspondence of James Brydges and Robert Harley, Created Earl of Oxford." *Huntington Library Quarterly*, I (1937–8), 457–72.

――――. "Letters of Henry St. John to James Brydges." *Huntington Library Bulletin*, No. 8 (October 1935), 153–70.

――――. "Letters from James Brydges, Created Duke of Chandos, to Henry St. John, Created Viscount Bolingbroke." *Huntington Library Bulletin*, No. 9 (April 1936), 119–66.

[Defoe, Daniel]. *An Account of the Conduct of Robert Earl of Oxford.* London, 1715.

[Defoe, Daniel]. *Eleven Opinions About Mr. H――y; With Observations.* London, 1711.

[Defoe, Daniel]. *The Secret History of the White-Staff.* Parts I and II. London, 1714.

Diary of Mary Countess Cowper, Lady of the Bedchamber to the Princess of Wales. 1714–1720. London, 1864.

Dickinson, H. T., ed. "Letters of Bolingbroke to James Grahme." *Transactions of the Cumberland & Westmorland Antiquarian & Archaeological Society,* LXVIII New Series (1968), 117–31.

Doble, C. E., ed. *Remarks and Collections of Thomas Hearne.* London, 1885–6. 2 vols.

Ellis, Sir Henry, ed. "Lord Coningsby's Account of the State of Political Parties during the Reign of Queen Anne." *Archaeologia,* XXXVIII (1860), 1–18.

Goldsmith, Oliver. *Collected Works of Oliver Goldsmith.* Edited by Arthur Friedman. Oxford, 1966. 5 vols.

Graham, Gerald S., ed. *The Walker Expedition to Quebec, 1711.* The Publications of the Champlain Society, Vol. XXXII. Toronto: The Champlain Society, 1953.

Great Britain. Historical Manuscripts Commission. *Eighth Report. Appendix. Parts I and II.* London, 1881.

———. *Tenth Report. Appendix. Part IV.* London, 1885.

———. *Calendar of the Manuscripts of the Marquis of Bath.* London, 1904–8.

———. *Calendar of the Manuscripts of the Marquess of Ormonde, K.P.* London, 1920.

———. *Calendar of the Stuart Papers belonging to His Majesty the King.* London, 1902.

———. *Report on the Manuscripts of the Duke of Buccleuch and Queensberry, K.G., K.T.* London, 1903.

———. *Report on the Manuscripts of the Earl Cowper, K.G.* London, 1889.

———. *Report on the Manuscripts of the Earl of Dartmouth.* London, 1887.

————. *Report on the Manuscripts of the Marquess of Downshire.* Vol. I: Papers of Sir William Trumbull. London, 1924.

————. *Report on the Manuscripts of Mrs. Frankland-Russell-Astley.* London, 1900.

————. *Report on the Manuscripts of J. Eliot Hodgkin, Esq., F.S.A.* London, 1897.

————. *Report on the Manuscripts of Lord Kenyon.* London, 1894.

————. *Report on the Manuscripts of the Earl of Mar and Kellie.* London, 1904. Supplementary Report, 1930.

————. *Report on the Manuscripts of His Grace the Duke of Portland.* London, 1891–1931.

————. *Report on the Manuscripts of Sir Harry Verney, Bart.* London, 1879.

Hawtrey, F. C., ed. *The Private Diary of William, First Earl Cowper, Lord Chancellor of England.* Eton: From the Press of E. Williams, 1833.

Holmes, Geoffrey, and Speck, W. A., eds. *The Divided Society: Party Conflict in England, 1694–1716.* London: Edward Arnold, 1967.

James, G. P. R., ed. *Letters Illustrative of the Reign of William III. From 1696 to 1708. Addressed to the Duke of Shrewsbury, by James Vernon, Esq.* London, 1841.

Llanover, the Rt. Hon. Lady, ed. *The Autobiography and Correspondence of Mary Granville, Mrs. Delany: with Interesting Reminiscences of King George III and Queen Charlotte.* London, 1861–2. 6 vols.

Luttrell, Narcissus. *A Brief History of State Affairs, from September 1678 to April 1714.* Oxford, 1857. 6 vols.

Macpherson, James, ed. *Original Papers; containing the Secret History of Great Britain, from the Restoration to the Accession of the House of Hannover. To which are prefixed Extracts from the Life of James II. as written by himself. The Whole*

Arranged and published by James Macpherson, Esq. Dublin, 1775. 2 vols.

[Mallet, David]. *Memoirs of the Life and Ministerial Conduct, with Some free Remarks on the Political Writings, of the Late Lord Visc. Bolingbroke.* London, 1752.

Manchester, the Duke of, ed. *Court and Society from Elizabeth to Anne.* London, 1864. 2 vols.

Newman, A. N., ed. "Proceedings in the House of Commons, March–June 1714." *Bulletin of the Institute of Historical Research*, XXXIV (1961), 211–17.

Pittis, William. *The History of the Third Session of the Last Parliament.* London, [1713].

Pope, Alexander. *The Correspondence of Alexander Pope.* Edited by George Sherburn. Oxford: The Clarendon Press, 1956. 5 vols.

Prior, Matthew. *The History of His Own Time. Compiled from the Original Manuscripts of His late Excellency Matthew Prior Esq.; Revised and Signed by Himself, and Copied fair for the Press by Mr. Adrian Drift, His Executor.* Edited and with Preface by J. Bancks. 2nd edn. London, 1740.

Private Correspondence of Sarah, Duchess of Marlborough, Illustrative of the Court and Times of Queen Anne; with Her Sketches and Opinions of Her Contemporaries and the Select Correspondence of Her Husband, John, Duke of Marlborough. 2nd edn. London, 1838. 2 vols.

Rose, Sir G. H., ed. *A Selection from the Papers of the Earls of Marchmont, in the Possession of the Rt. Honble. Sir George Henry Rose. Illustrative of Events from 1685 to 1750.* London, 1831. 3 vols.

Sharp, Thomas. *The Life of John Sharp, D.D., Lord Archbishop of York.* Edited by Thomas Newcome. London, 1825. 2 vols.

Spence, Joseph. *Observations, Anecdotes, and Characters of Books and Men Collected from Conversation.* Edited by James M. Osborn. Oxford: The Clarendon Press, 1966. 2 vols.

Swift, Jonathan. *The Correspondence of Jonathan Swift.* Edited by Harold Williams. Oxford: The Clarendon Press, 1963–5. 5 vols.

———. *The EXAMINER and Other Pieces Written in 1710–11.* Edited by Herbert Davis. Oxford: Basil Blackwell, 1957.

———. *The History of the Four Last Years of the Queen.* Edited by Herbert Davis. With an Introduction by Harold Williams. Oxford: Basil Blackwell, 1964.

———. *Journal to Stella.* Edited by Harold Williams. Oxford: The Clarendon Press, 1963. 3 vols.

———. *The Letters of Jonathan Swift to Charles Ford.* Edited by David Nichol Smith. Oxford: The Clarendon Press, 1935.

———. *Political Tracts, 1711–1713.* Edited by Herbert Davis. Oxford: Basil Blackwell, 1964.

———. *Political Tracts, 1713–1719.* Edited by Herbert Davis and Irvin Ehrenpreis. Oxford: Basil Blackwell, 1964.

Torcy, Jean Baptiste Colbert, Marquis de. *Journal Inédit de Jean-Baptiste Colbert, Marquis de Torcy, Ministre et Secrétaire d'Etat des Affaires Étrangères pendant les Années 1709, 1710 et 1711.* Publié d'après les manuscrits autographes par Frédéric Masson. Paris, 1884.

———. *Mémoires de Monsieur de Torcy.* Londres, 1757.

———. *Memoirs of the Marquis of Torcy, Secretary of State to Lewis XIV. Containing The History of the Negotiations From the Treaty of Ryswic to the Peace of Utrecht.* Translated from the French. London, 1757. 2 vols.

Verney, Margaret Maria Lady, ed. *Verney Letters of the Eighteenth Century from the MSS. at Claydon House.* London: Ernest Benn Ltd., 1930. 2 vols.

Voltaire. *Voltaire's Correspondence.* Edited by Theodore Besterman. Genève: Institut et Musée Voltaire, 1953–65. 107 vols.

Wodrow, the Rev. Robert, Minister of the Gospel at Eastwood. *Analecta: or, Materials for a History of Remarkable Providences, Mostly Relating to Scotch Ministers and Christians.* Printed for the Maitland Club, 1842–3. 4 vols.

Secondary Authorities

BOOKS

Campbell, John Lord. *Lives of the Lord Chancellors and Keepers of the Great Seal of England, from the Earliest Times till the Reign of King George IV.* 5th edn. London, 1868. 10 vols.

Carswell, John. *The South Sea Bubble.* Stanford, Calif.: Stanford University Press, 1960.

Churchill, Winston. *Marlborough: His Life and Times.* New York: Scribner's, 1933–8. 6 vols.

Cooke, George Wingrove. *Memoirs of Lord Bolingbroke.* 2nd edn. London, 1836. 2 vols.

Coxe, William. *Memoirs of John Duke of Marlborough with His Original Correspondence: Collected from the Family Records at Blenheim, and other Authentic Sources,* 2nd edn. London, 1820. 6 vols.

———. *Memoirs of the Life and Administration of Sir Robert Walpole, Earl of Orford.* London, 1798, 3 vols.

Dickinson, H. T. *Bolingbroke.* London: Constable, 1970.

Dickson, P. G. M. *The Financial Revolution in England.* London: Macmillan, 1967.

Douglas, David C. *English Scholars.* London: Jonathan Cape, 1939.

Ehrenpreis, Irvin. *Swift: The Man, His Works, and the Age.* Cambridge, Mass.: Harvard University Press, 1962–7. 2 vols.

Feiling, Keith. *A History of the Tory Party, 1640–1714.* Oxford: The Clarendon Press, 1924.

Foot, Michael. *The Pen and the Sword.* London: MacGibbon and Kee, 1957.

Green, David. *Queen Anne.* New York: Scribner's, 1970.

———. *Sarah Duchess of Marlborough.* New York: Scribner's, 1967.

Hamilton, Elizabeth. *The Backstairs Dragon: A Life of Robert Harley, Earl of Oxford.* London: Hamish Hamilton, 1969.

Harris, George. *The Life of Lord Chancellor Hardwicke; with Selections from His Correspondence, Diaries, Speeches, and Judgments.* London, 1847. 3 vols.

Hassall, Arthur. *Life of Viscount Bolingbroke.* Oxford: B. H. Blackwell, 1915.

Hatton, Ragnhild, and Bromley, J.S., eds. *William III and Louis XIV. Essays, 1680–1720, by and for Mark A. Thomson.* Liverpool University Press, 1968.

Holmes, Geoffrey. *British Politics in the Age of Anne.* London: Macmillan, 1967.

———. *The Trial of Doctor Sacheverell.* London: Eyre Methuen, 1973.

———, ed. *Britain after the Glorious Revolution, 1689–1714.* London: Macmillan, 1969.

Horwitz, Henry. *Revolution Politicks: The Career of Daniel Finch Second Earl of Nottingham, 1647–1730.* Cambridge, 1968.

Klopp, O. *Der Fall des Hauses Stuart und die Succession des Hauses Hannover.* Vienna, 1887. 14 vols.

Kramnick, Isaac. *Bolingbroke and His Circle: The Politics of Nostalgia in the Age of Walpole.* Cambridge, Mass.: Harvard University Press, 1968.

McInnes, Angus. *Robert Harley, Puritan Politician.* London: Victor Gollancz Ltd., 1970.

MacKnight, Thomas. *The Life of Henry St. John, Viscount Bolingbroke.* London, 1863.

Mahon, Lord [Philip Henry Stanhope, 5th Earl Stanhope]. *History of England from the Peace of Utrecht to the Peace of Aix-la-Chapelle.* London, 1839. 3 vols.

Michael, Wolfgang. *England Under George I.* Vol. I: *The Beginnings of the Hanoverian Dynasty.* London: Macmillan, 1936.

Moore, John Robert. *Daniel Defoe: Citizen of the Modern World.* Chicago: University of Chicago Press, 1958.

Petrie, Sir Charles. *Bolingbroke.* London: Collins, 1937.

Plumb, J. H. *The Growth of Political Stability in England: 1675–1725.* London: Macmillan, 1967.

————. *Sir Robert Walpole.* London: The Cresset Press, 1956–60. 2 vols.

Quintana, Ricardo. *The Mind and Art of Jonathan Swift.* London and New York: Oxford University Press, 1953.

Salomon, Felix. *Geschichte des letzten Ministeriums Königin Annas von England.* Gotha, 1894.

Sichel, Walter. *Bolingbroke and His Times.* New York: Longmans, Green, 1902. 2 vols.

Speck, W. A. *Tory & Whig: The Struggle in the Constituencies, 1701–1715.* London: Macmillan, 1970.

Sperling, J. G. *The South Sea Company, An Historical Essay and Bibliographical Finding List.* Boston, Mass.: Baker Library, Harvard Graduate School of Business Administration, 1962.

Sutherland, James. *Defoe.* Philadelphia: Lippincott, 1938.

Trevelyan, G. M. *England under Queen Anne.* London: Longmans, Green, 1934. 3 vols.

Walcott, Robert, Jr. *English Politics in the Early Eighteenth Century*. Cambridge, Mass.: Harvard University Press, 1956.

ARTICLES

Ansell, Patricia M. "Harley's Parliamentary Management." *Bulletin of the Institute of Historical Research*, XXXIV, no. 89 (May 1961), 92–7.

Bennett, G. V. "Robert Harley, the Godolphin ministry, and the bishoprics crisis of 1707." *English Historical Review*, LXXXII (1967), 726–47.

Davies, Godfrey. "The Seamy Side of Marlborough's War." *Huntington Library Quarterly*, XV (1951–2), 21–44.

Dickinson, H. T. "The Attempt to Assassinate Harley, 1711." *History Today*, XV, no. 11 (November 1965), 788–95.

———. "Henry St. John: A Reappraisal of the Young Bolingbroke." *Journal of British Studies*, VII (1968), 33–55.

———. "Henry St. John, Wootton Bassett, and the General Election of 1708." *Wiltshire Archaeological and Natural History Magazine*, LXIV (1969), 107–11.

———. "The October Club." *Huntington Library Quarterly*, XXXIII (1969–70), 155–73.

Fieldhouse, H. N. "Bolingbroke's Share in the Jacobite Intrigue of 1710–14." *English Historical Review*, LII (1937), 44–59.

Holmes, G. S. "The Attack on 'The Influence of The Crown' 1702–16." *Bulletin of the Institute of Historical Research*, XXXVIII, no. 98 (November 1965), 47–68.

———. "The Commons' Division on 'No Peace without Spain,' 7 December 1711." *Bulletin of the Institute of Historical Research*, XXXIII (1960), 223–34.

———. "The Hamilton Affair of 1711–1712: A Crisis in Anglo-Scottish Relations." *English Historical Review*, LXXVII (1962), 257–82.

———, and Speck, W. A. "The Fall of Harley in 1708 Reconsidered." *English Historical Review*, LXXX (October 1965), 673–98..

McInnes, Angus. "The Appoint nent of Harley in 1704." *Historical Journal*, XI (1968), 255–71.

———. "The Political Ideas of Robert Harley." *History*, I (October 1965), 309–22.

Michael, W. "Who is John Bull?" *Contemporary Review*, CXLIV (July–December 1933), 314–19.

Morgan, W. T. "Queen Anne's Canadian Expedition of 1711." *Queen's Quarterly*, XXXV (August 1927–October 1928), 460–89.

Snyder, H. L. "The Defeat of the Occasional Conformity Bill and the Tack: A Study in the Techniques of Parliamentary Management in the Reign of Queen Anne." *Bulletin of the Institute of Historical Research*, XLI, no. 104 (November 1968), 172–92.

———. "Godolphin and Harley: A Study of Their Partnership in Politics." *Huntington Library Quarterly*, XXX (1966–7), 241–71.

Speck, W. A. "The Choice of a Speaker in 1705." *Bulletin of the Institute of Historical Research*, XXXVII, no. 95, (May 1964), 20–46.

Sperling, J. G. "The Division of 25 May 1711, on an Amendment to the South Sea Bill: A Note on the Reality of Parties in the Age of Anne." *Historical Journal*, IV (1961), 191–202.

Trevelyan, G. M. "The 'Jersey' Period of the Negotiations Leading to the Peace of Utrecht." *English Historical Review*, XLIX (1934), 100–5.

UNPUBLISHED WORKS

Hill, B. W. "The Career of Robert Harley, Earl of Oxford, from 1702–1714." Ph.D. thesis, Cambridge University, 1961.

MacLachlan, A. D. "The Great Peace: Negotiations for the Treaty of Utrecht, 1710–1713." Ph.D. thesis, Cambridge University, 1965.

INDEX

War of Spanish Succession (*cont.*)
unpopularity of, 161, 171, 175;
Harley's views on, 98, 161, 187–8;
profits of moneyed interests resented, 113, 161; recruitment for,
161; secret order of suspension of
offensive action, 238–9; Tory
vacillation on, 8, 113, 114, 117–18,
161; Treaty of Grand Alliance,
220; Whig support for, 8, 118;
Whig support essential, 122, 125,
129; *see also* peace negotiations;
Treaty of Utrecht
Wentworth, Peter, 184, 192, 195, 206,
211, 215, 229, 230, 233, 237, 251–2,
280
West Indies, 200, 230
Wharton, Thomas, Marquis of, 12,
231
Whigs, 7–8, 9, 12, 103, 157, 267, 271–
2; Bolingbroke's attack on, with
Schism Bill, 277–8; B.'s late attempt
at rapprochement with, 290;
charge Tory government with
conspiracy with France, 86,
221, 261–2; charge Tories with
conspiracy with Pretender, 221,
261–3, 272; coalition with Court
Tories, 120; divisions among
(1708–10), 130–1, 140 and *n.*, 161;
fear dissolution of 1710 Parliament, 173, 175–83; in Godolphin-
Marlborough ministry, 105–6, 118,
122–7, 131, 133–4, 138, 147, 159–60;
in Godolphin Cabinet, refusal to
serve under Harley (1708), 136,
174; and Greg treason affair, 133;
in Harley ministry, 109, 175–82,
184, 185, 190, 224–5, 248–9; H.'s
origins with, 5, 98, 109; impeachment of their lords in 1701, 98–9,
112; and impeachment of Dr.
Sacheverell, 163 and *n.*, 164;
moderates, and Harley, 130, 131,
140–1, 170, 175–82; moneyed interest of, 8, 112–13, 171–2, 189;

offer of cooperation to Harley, in
1711, 216, 217; "Old," 98; parliamentary majority in early 1710,
163, 167; in power in 1715, and impeachment of H., 5; 1705 election
gains of, 122, 123; in 1713 campaign, 261–2; their support sought
by Harley during last months of
ministry, 272, 276–7, 279–80;
wooed by *FAULTS on both
SIDES*, 108–10
—Junto leadership, 98, 104, 109,
111, 131, 133, 140, 147, 161; Godolphin-Marlborough "capitulation"
to, 47, 159–60; feared by Harley,
104, 123, 141, 147; gains entrance
into Godolphin ministry, 123;
Harley's goal of separating dissident Whigs from, 125, 130–1,
140–1; patronage demands for support of Court, 125, 128, 129–31; and
Queen Anne, 126, 151–3
—political positions of, 8; opposition to Preliminary Articles of
Peace, 221–2, 228, 230–4; against
proceeding peace negotiations,
239; against provisions of peace
treaty, 247–8, 250–1, 253; support
for Hanoverian succession, 8, 261–
3, 272, 274, 293–4; support for
toleration of dissent, 8; support for
war with France, 8, 118, 122, 125,
129
Whimsicals, 251, 264, 268, 276, 283,
290; *see also* Hanoverian Tories
William III, King of England, 7, 12,
15 *n.*, 98, 112, 272 *n.*; and question
of Spanish succession, 99
Winchcomb, Sir Henry, 58
Works of Lord Bolingbroke, The,
59 *n.*
Wren, Sir Christopher, 163 *n.*
Wyndham, Sir William, 55 *n.*, 66 *n.*,
90, 94, 245, 277, 279, 287, 289;
Chancellor of the Exchequer, 255;
Secretary-at-War, 255

A NOTE ABOUT THE AUTHOR

Sheila Biddle was born in Philadelphia. She took both her
M.A. and Ph.D. in history at Columbia University. After
teaching at Vassar College, she became Assistant Professor
of History at Columbia in 1970.

A NOTE ON THE TYPE

This book was set on the Linotype in Janson, a recutting made direct from type cast from matrices long thought to have been made by the Dutchman Anton Janson, who was a practicing type founder in Leipzig during the years 1668–87. However, it has been conclusively demonstrated that these types are actually the work of Nicholas Kis (1650–1702), a Hungarian, who most probably learned his trade from the master Dutch type founder Dirk Voskens. The type is an excellent example of the influential and sturdy Dutch types that prevailed in England up to the time William Caslon developed his own incomparable designs from them.

Composed, printed and bound by
American Book–Stratford Press, Inc.
New York, New York
Typography and binding design by
Virginia Tan